Imported America: Jamestown 1607

Discovery to Servitude
A Documented History

Kelli Rea

This book contains information obtained from authentic and highly regarded sources. Reprinted materials and excerpts have been used from several primary and secondary sources throughout this book the full citation of materials is given. The Author and Publisher gratefully acknowledge the materials reprinted from the original authors. It was our wish to compile many ancient sources together for our readers in one book, documents otherwise hard to obtain. Many of these works are more than 200 years old and has been modernized, such as spelling and grammar. In certain instances, capitalization and punctuation has been modernized for the convenience of the reader.

Printed in the United States of America
First Printing, 2017
ISBN 10-946292-29-2
ISBN 13:978-1-946292-29-2

www.cavalierspublishing.net

To the immigrant servants whose suffering and sacrifice made this land possible, and to whom I am grateful to be an American.

IMPORTED AMERICA ~
JAMESTOWN 1607

DISCOVERY TO SERVITUDE
A DOCUMENTED HISTORY

KELLI REA

Contents

Introduction

Jamestown is the birth city of the America we know today. Before Jamestown really got on its feet, Virginia went through many changes. It was a process of trial and errors, slowly learning and changing, and finally finding solid footing. Before we really explore how America took its first steps, before Paul Revere made his famous ride shouting: 'The British are Coming' and America moved out of the house of the Mother Country, there are many stories and milestones. Some have been told, some have escaped notice.

To be able to fully understand how and *why* Virginia walked the path it walked, you must understand the circumstances of the times. Queen Elizabeth I believed thought that trying to discover and colonize the New World was a waste of time and money. King James really took no part in colonizing, he had nothing to lose by giving a charter. No money out of the Crowns pocket yet a possibility of gain. Unfortunately, by revoking Virginia Companies Charter, he made some very powerful enemies. Those enemies ultimately went to war with his son, King Charles. This ended in the King's execution, and the demise of a monarchy in England for several years. It would be fair to say that the Birth of Virginia killed the King of its Mother County. Let us start from the very beginning, from our discovery, and our first colonies.

The actual true and complete story of the discovery of America has been lost in history, lost on Americans. We have been given selected information, so far from the complete story. Without diving into ancient historical accounts, what we learn in school does not even hit the waterline of the iceberg. This is America's History. I think it deserves more than just tidbits, main character lists and timelines.

We all know about Columbus, even if you're not a history buff or slept through that class, there is Columbus Day to remind you. Most of us know about Jamestown and John Smith. If you do not, I am certain you have heard the story of Pocahontas. Of course, many of us know about 'The Mayflower'. Just in case you missed that one, there is something called 'Thanksgiving' to remind you of that story.

The English claim to the New World, from Newfoundland to Florida was based on a patent that was granted to John and Sabastian Cabot. Have you heard of them? Probably not. That patent was granted by King Henry VII., in 1497, before Columbus or Amerigo Vespucci had discovered what is now America. That patent is the oldest American State Paper in England. The Cabot's are believed to be the first explorers to declared this land in the name of King Henry VII, yes even before Queen Elizabeth, American soil flew the English flag.

It was so difficult to make the decisions of what and what not to include in this book. One example was the extent of discoveries, from plants, animals to the 'naturals', what the English first called the Indians. I did include many accounts of that. It was very important to realize that when the Virginia Company of London was making its decision to colonize, or extract riches from the land, it was these early reports that influenced both King James and potential investors.

America would have not been colonized if it had not been considered a good investment, for both England and the stock holders of the company. Virginia was an investment, I cannot express that enough. In the early years when Virginia needed labor, it became more of a penal colony. There are many statements, documents and personal accounts that talk about how the 'streets of England were swept of scum and vagrants to be shipped to Virginia.'

Part One

1497

First Discoveries of the New World

Records of Cabot's Journey's

John Cabot was married to a Venetian woman, who followed him to England, and we find it recorded that on the 27th of August, 1497, she was living at Bristol, England, with her children Lewis, Sebastian and Sanctus. At that time, they were apparently all of age, Sebastian having attained at least the age of twenty-three. Sebastian was born in 1474. According to ancient historians, Sebastian Cabot's native place was England, this statement carries little weight, as it seems he was actually born in Venice, Italy. His father was naturalized a Venetian in 1476, after being a constant residence of fifteen years in Venice, Sebastian must have then been not less than two years old. Many authors say that he was a Venetian, specially Ramusio, Andrea Navajero, Contarini, Oviedo, Peter Martyr , etc.

We are inclined to believe that John Cabot removed from Venice to England in 1490, and previous to that he visited Portugal and Spain to obtain royal aid to undertake transatlantic discoveries. He also visited Mecca, where he met caravans bringing spices from afar. He believed in the sphericity of the earth, and inferred from their replies that these spices came originally from the West. He resolved himself to finding a shorter route to Cathay.

In the year 1496, Cabot obtained letters-patent from Henry VII for a voyage of discovery westward. He left Bristol in the beginning of May, 1497, on a small ship called the Matthew, manned by eighteen men. When the vessel had reached the west coast of Ireland, it sailed towards the north, then to the west for seven hundred leagues, and reached the mainland. He then sailed along the coast three hundred leagues. Returning to Bristol, Cabot saw two islands to starboard. This is the summary of his first voyage.

'On or about May 20, 1497, John Cabot set sail from Bristol on a ship called *The Matthew*. A vessel of fifty tons carrying a crew of eighteen men. It was the equivalent of a fair-sized modern yacht.

Going around the south end of Ireland, he last sighted land at Dursey Head. His plan, route, was a favorite one with westbound mariners in that age. He was to follow a parallel of latitude straight west. Dursey Head is in latitude 51° 33'.

At 5am on June 24th, Cabot came in sight of land again. He had made the Atlantic crossing in thirty-one days. The exact spot where he first saw the coast of North America has been much disputed, and the dispute has been made foggy by local patriotism, various places trying to be "firsts." Samuel Eliot Morison, whose account is one of the best, concludes that what Cabot saw was Cape Dégrat on the northeast tip of Newfoundland (latitude 51° 37', only 4' off Dursey Head latitude).

If this is true, he had performed a real feat of navigation, having travelled almost straight west from the Irish Coast. Furthermore, he was only five miles from where it is believed Leif Erikson had landed in 1001. Turning south, Cabot entered Griquet Harbor, where he made his only landing. Here he formally took possession of the country in the name of Henry VII. Continuing his southward course, he skirted the whole east side of the island and rounded its southern tip into Placentia Bay. From Placentia, he turned about, retraced his course to Cape Dégrat, and on July 20 left for home. After a fast passage of fifteen days, he made landfall at Ushant on the coast of Brittany, headed north, and on August 6 was in Bristol. Cabot had not found the way to Japan or China, and he had brought back neither gold nor spices, but he had found a coast teeming with codfish—a most important fact.

Cabot wasted no time in Bristol, but hurried to London to make his report to Henry. The King gave him £10, and on the thirteenth of the following December, settled on the explorer a pension of £20 per year.

Peter Martyr d' Anghiera's relation is a little different; but of Cape Breton, not a word:

> "Cabot directed his course so far toward the north pole, that even in the month of July he found monstrous heaps of ice swimming on the sea, and in continual day light. Yet saw he the land in that tract, free from ice. Thus, seeing such heaps of ice before him, he was enforced to turn his sails and follow the west, so coasting by the shore, that he was thereby brought so

far into the south by reason of the land bending so
much southward that it was there almost equal in latitude
with the sea called Fretum Herculeum, having the north
pole elevate in manner in the same degree. He sailed like
wise in this tract so form towards the west, that he had
the Island of Cuba on his left hand in manner in the same
degree of longitude. "

On February 3, 1498, Henry issued new letters patent giving Cabot authority to impress six ships for a second voyage to the new world. Cabot was now to explore more thoroughly the coast he had touched, and when he had reached the source of the spice trade, to set up a trading factory with the intent of funneling that desired commodity to English ports. Cabot succeeded in obtaining five ships with which he sailed from Bristol at the beginning of May, 1498. One ship turned back, but Cabot and the other four disappear from the pages of history. To this day, no one knows what happened to any of them.

The Cabot story does not end with the disappearance of John. Much more is known about his son Sebastian. Sebastian may, as a boy of fifteen, have accompanied his father on the first voyage. He said that he did, but his statement is not particularly good evidence. He also claimed to have made in 1508 a voyage to discover the fabled Northwest Passage, but as he was a "genial and cheerful liar," we do not know that this is true. He certainly knew how to feather his own nest. He set up as an expert adviser to would-be explorers and was paid by the kings of both England and Spain for his advice. He died in England about 1557. Eventually, John's name was practically forgotten, and historians took Sebastian as the first discoverer of America.'

*Cabot's Voyages, 1497-1498. Discovering U.S. History, Gale, 2003.

Queen Elizabeth gives permission to discover 1578

Queen Elizabeth I, has sat on the throne of England for twenty years. The New World has been occupied in the South, which is Florida, by the Spanish. Canada is occupied by the French. England has yet to establish any occupation in the New World. We know that there were private voyages by the Cabot's, unfortunately there are few historical documents that legitimately back that up, and what happened to John we may never know. Perhaps he did occupy and try to establish relations with the natives. Perhaps we can add the Cabot explorers to the first 'lost colony".

Despite countless requests from wannabe explorers of the time, Queen Elizabeth had shown no interest in the discovery or resources of the New World. Why would she have when her ships and sailors, and she had the best of both, were busy plundering the rich treasure-fleets of Spain.

Yet, actual colonizing had been done in the New World, just not by the almighty and powerful England. Drake and Hawkins had been busy burning the Spanish settlements in the South, the North remained somewhat unnoticed and ignored. Honestly, perhaps it was thought that the French were not worth plundering, after all, there was no gold to be had there. Queen Elizabeth, who could and probably should have led the expedition on colonizing and expanding her countries land, did nothing. The French and the Spanish beat the most able country to it, which in retrospect, probably irritated those able English explorers who were biting at the bit to do so, yet held back by their Queen.

The Savage cruelties of Alva, and the massacre of St. Bartholomew, had kindled religious animosity into a fierce flame. The Prince of Orange was about to fall under the assassin's knife. Plots were thickening about the exquisite and dangerous Mary Stuart, plots which would lead her and some of England's most powerful to the scaffold. The Renaissance and the reformation had broken the shackles of intellect, and widened the horizon of thought, and great discoveries had opened new fields of human energy. Men were giving up speculations about the heavenly world, which had absorbed the intellectual activities of the middle ages. Men were now turning to the practical conquest of a world beyond the seas. England, and its Protestants, were gathering their forces for the last great struggle with Spain and the Latin Church, for supremacy in the old world, and mastery in the new.

Finally, Elizabeth graciously gave her permission to those sought-after requests of discoverers, specifically to Sir Humphry Gilbert. I need to clarify, her permission, and nothing more. Elizabeth's permission was given not because Queen Elizabeth expected riches to come from this unknown land, nor because she had ideas of colonizing this new land and expanding an overpopulated Europe. Elizabeth had dreams of succeeding where Columbus failed, Elizabeth sought infamy, she wanted to be the one to find a short passage to China. To be the first to discover what everyone had failed and to triumph for herself and her country for this discovery.

Queen Elizabeth *reluctantly* granted Gilbert a royal charter in 1578 for six years. (See the letter of Patent- Document 1) After four years of preparation and fitting his fleet, Gilbert was almost ready to set off on his adventure with five ships. Despite the Queen, who had tried in vain to turn him from his purpose. Sir Humphrey Gilbert truly believed this was his destiny and nothing and no-one, not even the Queen of England could dissuade him from that purpose.

"Through the efforts of a few public-spirited men, who had their country's good more at heart than gain, yet desired glory with honor, there came such a change that, from being most backward. Englishmen suddenly grew most forward in setting forth both discovery and colonization. Must it be told that these ardent champions of their country's glory were left to raise their own colonists, and to fit out their own ships, precisely as titled buccaneers had been doing? Elizabeth gave gracious permission, and no more. But that was enough. Perhaps national pride had been humbled seeing Spain and France so much more active in the New World. Perhaps jealousy may have had something to with bringing about change, or possibly the time had just grown ripe for it. In any case, it was thought a shrewd thing to have let the Spaniards and French beat the bush for other men to catch the birds. That was England's Way of looking at it." -The Making of Virginia

Sir Humphrey Gilbert

"What manner of man was this who could thus brave the displeasure of his royal mistress? Of gentle blood, yet nobler far by nature; neither corsair nor adventurer, yet of lofty courage; he was, perhaps, a little of a dreamer- an enthusiast. In him greatness of soul was strikingly combined. Take for instance, this plea of his for the dreaded Arctic voyage: "He is not worthy to live at all that, for fear or danger of death shuneth his country's service, and his own honor, seeing death is inevitable and the same of virtual immortal."

-Sir Humphry Gilbert's Creed

Gilbert's first dream had been of a Northwest Passage. It has been speculated that colonizing the New World was just an aid to make that dream possible. Gilbert had planned to plant himself on the mainland adjoining Newfoundland, 'where the nearness of that island, a rendezvous for fishing fleets, promised some support'. This island was then called Norombega.

Gilbert had one misfortune that many history books have failed to mention. Before his successful trip to the New World, there was one trip that failed….

"Sir Humphry Gilbert, with the assistance of many other gentlemen, prepared to put to Sea with a noble Fleet. At the moment of departure, upon a disagreement and dissention, he was deserted by his associates, and left with only a few of his firm and faithful friends. With these, however, he ventured to sea, but having been exposed to some misfortunes, and lost a large ship of his fleet, he was obliged to return without effecting anything.

These expensive and unsuccessful preparations had so impaired his fortune, that it was 1583, before he made any further attempt. But then having sold his estate, and being joined by several gentlemen of fortune, he again set sail with two ships and three small barks. Coming near Newfoundland, he was refused entrance by the fishing vessels within, to the number of thirty-six sail, of all nations. He was therefore prepared to make his way good by force of arms: but first sent his boat to inform them that he had a commission from the Queen, to take possession of those lands for the Crown of England. Queen Elizabeth's name was reverenced through all Europe and her power and authority at Sea, in particular, much honored and revered. They therefor readily submitted, and even made a contribution of provisions to supple the wants of the small fleet"

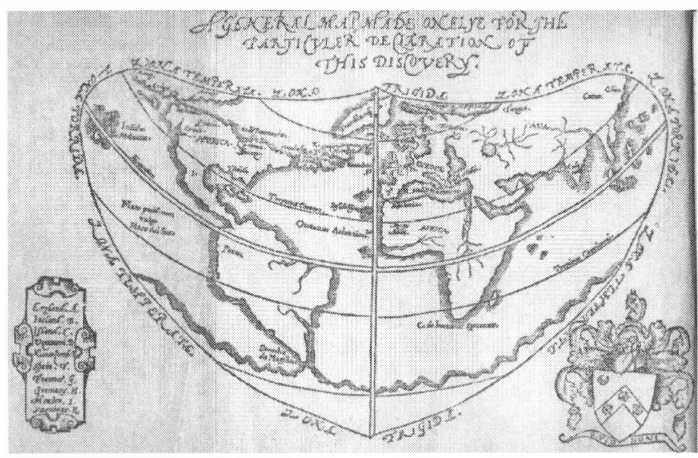

Sir Humphrey Gilberts Map

Only four of the five ships safely reached Newfoundland. Gilbert went ashore, attended by his Captains, Masters, Gentlemen, and Soldiers, he summoned all to be present at his taking a formal and solemn possession of the Country. He then had his Commission to be read.

By virtue of his commission, he took possession of the Harbor of St. Johns and the territory two hundred leagues every direction, and invested her Majesty with the Title and Dignity thereof. And having a twig and turf of the soil delivered to him, he entered possession also for himself, his heirs, or assigns forever. He further signified to those present and through them to all men, that, from thence forward, they should look upon those territories as appertaining to the Queen of England, and upon himself, as authorized by his Majesty. To possess and enjoy them, with power to ordain laws, under which all people coming thither for the future, either to inhabit or to trade, should submit themselves and be governed. To exercise his power and jurisdiction, he enacted three laws immediately to take place and be of force.

Gilbert set out on several excursions to search the country, and the possible discovery of a silver mine, *with which Sir Humphrey was much gulled and delighted,* they set sail in order to discover the main Coast. Experiencing some tempestuous weather, danger and fatigue they decided to return to England. However, Gilbert wanted to explore the Coast, and to run up creeks and harbors in search of a Northern Passage. "*He boarded a small bark of ten tons, and could not afterwards be persuaded to leave her in their return homewards, till her lights were suddenly extinguished in the night at which time she was supposed to sink, and was never after seen or heard of.*"

Queen Elizabeth has been famously quoted saying "*a man of no good hap by sea*" of Sir Humphreys death. I believe it much more likely that the Queen may have said this *after* his first failed trip to the New World rather than after his untimely death. After all, he had not failed, he gave his Queen a New Land.

Gilbert had not died in vain, his purpose lived on. His half-brother Sir Walter Raleigh, whom the Queen had forbid to go on this journey, picked up where Gilbert had left off, almost as though colonizing the New World was an inheritance that he must accept. On Lady Day, March 25, 1584, Queen Elizabeth issued to Raleigh a patent of discovery. *See the complete patent in Documents

'Though so different in mind, character, and purpose, these two men seem to have bound up together, in a sense, and their work should so stand in history.'

Sir Walter Raleigh

Raleigh was rich, powerful and in high favor with Elizabeth. She had given him much, and he knew she could unmake him just as easily if he dared to disobey her. Elizabeth ruled with an iron rod. Not of noble birth, he was a nobleman, one of England's most noble. He was vain as well as proud, he was one of the most distinguished and intellectuals of his time. Having won the Queen's favor by laying down his new velvet cloak at her feet. Of course, Elizabeth noticed this handsome man richly jeweled. I do believe that Walter Raleigh must have been witty and entertaining to be around as well. From some of the stories that have been recorded by authors of the time, his personality seems to have been infectious.

In his closet, Raleigh became a poet, historian, philosopher. At time, he was involved in all the drama at court, at other times he was seeking seclusion in his study. He could 'toil terribly," as his writings show to this day. We wonder, and wonder again, at the inconsistencies of his character, yet through all we see a strong desire to be the benefactor of his race, and that is something we can and do admire in spite of all his failings. Americans will forever honor the name Raleigh. He was the type of man who could make the world move on, what some would call an 'old soul.' He knew every rope on a ship; he knew exactly how to provide for a voyage. He could call to his aid men of the most qualified to his need.

Raleigh and Queen Elizabeth

One day, while visiting with the Queen and smoking his pipe of Tobacco, Raleigh made a wager with the Queen that he could exactly tell the weight of smoke in every pipe of tobacco he burned. The Queen at once laid a wager of twenty angels that he could not. Raleigh first carefully weighed a pipeful of tobacco, and, after he finished smoking it, then as carefully weighed the ashes.

"Your Majesty cannot deny," He said, "that the difference hath gone up in smoke."

Men have called Raleigh selfish, ungrateful, untruthful, but never incapable. He was full of grand ideas and always at his best when setting forth to execute them. Needless to say, I love Raleigh just as much as the most of England in his day. Raleigh hated Spain. His greatest aim in life up to this point was to destroy and humiliate them. At the early age of seventeen he left the University of oxford to join a band of a hundred gentleman volunteers. He went to the aid of Admiral de Coligny and the Huguenots in Florida. "A gallant company, nobly mounted, and bearing the motto on their standard, let valor decide the contest."

France was then aflame with the reports of the massacre of the Huguenots in Florida, and the idea germinated in Raleigh's mind that a mortal blow might be dealt to the enemy beyond the seas. From the service of de Coligny he passed to that of William the Silent, and all the while was growing in him the conviction which he expressed later in life: That the possession of the New World would decide the question of the supremacy of Spain or England.

'For whatsoever Prince shall possess it, shall be greatest, and if the King of Spain enjoy it, he will become irresistible. I trust in God that he which is Lorde of Lords, will put it into her heart which is Lady of Ladies to Possess it."

Part Two

Landing in Roanoke 1584

Raleigh did his homework. He set his plan and then he set it in motion. On April 27, 1584, Captains Barlow and Amadas set sail out of the Thames on two ships. Raleigh had mapped out the Southern route that had been taken by Columbus. On May 10th, they sighted the Canaries, the West Indies on June 10th, and on July 2nd they were off the Florida Coast. Avoiding the Spaniards, they set sail North and soon saw the Carolina Coast, 'girt with foam'. They anchored near the inlet of the North Carolina coast, near Roanoke.

"Keeping good watch, and bearing but slack sail, the fourth of the same month (America's fated day!) we arrived upon the coast, which we supposed to be a continent, and we sailed along the same 120 miles before we could find any entrance, or river issuing into the Sea. The first that appeared unto us we entered, and cast anchor about three harquebus-shot within the haven's mouth: and after thanks given to God for our safe arrival thither, we manned our boats, and went to view the land next adjoining, and to take possession of the same, in right of the Queens most excellent Majestic."

The explorers had coasted northward two days along the Banks, and entering at New Inlet or Trinity Harbor. They anchored not far from Roanoke Island. "We viewed the land about us, being whereas we first landed, very sandy and low towards the water side, but so full of grapes, as the very beating and surge of the sea overflowed them, of which we found such plenty, both on the sand and on the green soil on the hills as well on every little shrub, as also climbing towards the tops of high Cedars. I think that in all the world the like abundance is not to be found."

This is evidently the luxuriant North Carolina Scuppernog grape, whose strong aromatic perfume might well be perceived from some distance from shore. They began exploring. Every now and then firing off their muskets, like frolicsome schoolboys, just to see the great flocks of cranes rise and scream in the air. Like charmed men they wandered up and down, until the low sun warned them this it was time to go back to the ship.'

'It was not until the third day did they see any humans. On that day three savages cautiously approached them in a canoe. After some coaxing one even ventured on board. When they gave him meat to eat, and a shirt and hat to cover his nakedness, he was so delighted that he brought them a boatload of fish to his delightedness.' At which time one is quoted as saying, 'Surely, here are peace and plenty.'

On the fourth day: "There came unto us several canoes came, and in one of them the King's brother, his name being Granganameo, with forty or fifty men. Very handsome and goodly people, and in their behavior as mannerly and civil as any in Europe....

"The soil is the most plentiful, sweet, fruitful, and wholesome of all the World. There were above fourteen several sweet-smelling timber trees, and the most part of their underwoods are Bayes and such like. We came to an Island which they call Roanoke, distant from the harbor by which we entered seven leagues: and at the north end thereof was a village of nine houses. Built of cedar, and fortified roundabout with sharp trees to keep out their enemies, and the entrance into it made like a turn pike very artificially. The wife of the King's brother, Granganameo came running out to meet us very cheerfully and friendly.

When we were come into the utter room, having five rooms in her house, she caused us to sit down by a great fire. She took off our clothes and washed them and dried them. Some of the woman plucked off our stockings and washed them, some washed our feet in warm water, she herself making great haste to dress some meat for us to eat. We were entertained with all love and kindness, and with as much bounty as they could possibly devise. We found the people most gentle, loving and faithful, void of all guile and treason, and such as live after the manner of the golden age."

The English went to meet them armed and watchful, though the chief of the tribe often stroked his head and breast in sign of friendship. Although they could only converse in signs, distrust soon worn off. These simple savages, who stood little above brutes of the white men, soon showed themselves by no means wanting in true hospitality.

The King of this tribe, whose name was Wingina, at that time lay at his chief town, ill from the wounds which he received in a recent battle.

The Natives were a proper, well-proportioned people, very civil in their behavior, and highly respectful to Granganameo. For none of them sat down or spoke a word in his presence, except four. Of whom the English also bestowed presents. But Granganameo took them all from them, and made signs, that everything belonged to him. After some small traffic, he went away; but returning in two days, he ate and drank very merrily with them. Not long after, he brought his wife and children on board. They were of mean stature, but well favored, and very bashful and modest. His wife had a white coral about her forehead, and bracelets of pearl in her ears, hanging down to her middle, of the bigness of large peas. As to the rest, they were decked with red copper, and such ornaments, as are at present in fashion and esteem among the Indians.

After this there came down, from all parts, great numbers of people, with leather, coral, and several kinds of dyes. But when Granganameo was present, none durst trade but himself, and those, who wore red copper on their heads as he did. He would have engaged a bag of pearl for a Suit of Armor, but the English refused, as not regarding it, the they might thereby the better learn, where it grew.

He was very just to his promise, for they often trusted him, and he never failed to come within his day to keep his word. He commonly sent the English every day, a Brace of Bucks, Conies, Hares, and fish. Sometimes Melons, Walnuts, Cucumbers, Peas, and several kinds of roots. The English, to try the strength and goodness of the soil, put some of their peas into the ground, which were were found in ten days' time, fourteen inches high.

The chief wore on his forehead a broad plate, whether of copper or gold the English could not tell, for the prince refused to be touched. This led the explorers to think there might be gold in the country, and think of little else. Elizabeth's last orders had been, '*find out if there be gold in the country*." Gold, yellow, glittering, precious gold could lure men to the ends of the earth, it was this quest that eventually would bring Raleigh's proud head to the block and lure settlers to the untamed west and California.

The relationships between the Indians and the Englishmen only improved. From their accounts, the explorers had only praise for the New World. However, they had only seen it at its best. They landed in a cozy temperature that July, the natives they thought friendly people, the woods and waters were alive with game and fish. However, they had not really found what could be called a safe harbor, nor had they spent the time to test the accuracy of their first impressions. They had seen fruit and bounty and the possibilities of gold and riches on the shores of the New World.

White's 1585 Painting of 'Secotan' Indian Village

This exploration remained on the shores of the New World for only two months, and returned to England around mid-September. They had brought back with them two natives, Wanchese and Manteo. Their arrival brought with them much excitement in England. The whole of the Atlantic coast was now regarded as under the dominion of France England and Spain; now known as Canada, Virginia and Florida. The reports that they brought back to England were encouraging. Raleigh was now even more determined to colonize this vast New World, and believed it was rich with possibility. His fame rose higher than ever before as he had now given his Queen a new Country. Elizabeth, some historical documents say, gave it the name of 'Virginia', after herself, the 'eternal maiden queen' or because the land seemed to retain virgin purity and plenty of the first creation. Other documents say that Raleigh named the new land after his 'virgin' Queen. Elizabeth was by all accounts pleased and excited. She knighted Sir Walter Raleigh, and once again he was one her most favorites.

1585 Raleigh's First Colonization attempt:

In April, seven ships, with one hundred and eighty colonists were ready for the voyage to their new home Virginia. Raleigh had chosen Sir Richard Greenville, a valiant sea captain, and gave him command over the fleet. Ralph Lane, a soldier of fortune, was given command over the Colony. Raleigh spared neither himself nor his purse in this venture. Captain Amadas, was also going back to Virginia, along with Manto the Indian.

Others were specifically hand chosen for this journey, John White, an artist was to go. Thomas Hariot, a capable mathematician was sent to survey and study the country. Raleigh wanted maps and drawings of this New Land, he wanted a full account. The fleet was of good strength to resist the Spaniards if they attacked it. Every detail had been thoroughly thought out by Raleigh himself. Raleigh had dedicated every moment of his time to this journey, that in just seven short months since the return of Barlow, his new Colony was ready to sail away.

Greenville left Plymouth Port on the ninth of April. They arrived off the coast of the West Indies in May, and on June 20, 1585 sighted the Florida coast, and narrowly escaping a shipwreck at Cape Fear. The fleet cast anchor at Roanoke in a mere eighty days.

An exploring party was immediately dispatched to the mainland and travelled as far south as to the Indian Village where they were met with friendly greetings. Unfortunately, this visit did not go well. According to reports, a silver cup was stolen from the explorers during this visit. The explorers were angry, and sought revenge. They set fire to the Village as they returned to the ship. This single incident could very well have led to their ultimate downfall.

Raleigh had instructed them to take whatever means possible to ensure good faith and relationships with these people. Weather his Captains thought they were wiser than Raleigh, or a rouge colonist had acted out, we will never know. It does not take a wise man to study the past and realize that this was the first act that would end this venture in a tragic way. The Indians became leery, and they certainly did not forget, or forgive this new group of white men.

The Northeast corner of Roanoke Island was chosen for the new colony. This sight was situated with passages leading east and west and was thought to be easily defended from an attack. As they began to settle, Grenville took sail back to England, and Lane took charge of the Roanoke Colony of Virginia.

In all fairness, these settlers were like the exploration group before them. They were gold seekers, after that precious yellow glittery nugget of fortune and wealth. Lane, along with the new colonists, they had set out hunting for the gold before they had even begun to find adequate shelter or means to live. After building a meager fort, the exploring party set out North. There they encountered a tribal that called themselves the *Chesapeakes*. Another exploring party went up the Albemarle Sound, encountering many Indians, yet no gold or silver.

Sir Richard Grenville returned to England that summer. On his way home, he had taken another Spanish prize of three hundred tons, richly laden, and with her arrived at Plymouth on the 18th of September. He had left behind him 108 persons, as a colony, to keep possession of, and inhabit the country. Of these he constituted Mr. Ralph Lane as Governor, a military man of note, who was afterwards knighted and a great writer of his time. It is largely of Mr. Lane's writing that I use to write this part of the history of America.

Life in the New World, Ralph Lane

The farthest discovery, and most documented, was Secotan. An Indian village that was approximately 240 miles ('80 leagues') to the south of the Roanoke fort. To the North they went 130 miles to the Chesapeake's, a Nation of Indians seated on a small river of whom they say the word Chesapeake signifies in the Indian language, 'The Mother of Waters', implying that it was the parent and grand reservoir of all the great rivers within it. This is of course an assumption, considering the unstableness and vast mutability of the Indian tongues, and that nobody at present can pretend to understand their language at that time.

These discoveries went up Albemarle Sound and Chowan River, one hundred and thirty miles, to a nation of Indians called the Chaiuonocks, (Chowan, Chowanoke) who inhabited an area above the fork of that river. This would be the Meherrin and Nottoway Rivers in Virginia.

The King of the Chaiuonocks, whose name was Menatonon, was lame, but the most sensible and understanding Indian they had met with. He amused Mr. Lane and his company with a story of a copper mine, and of a pearl fishery. From the description given it was located somewhere near the coast, and with a 'strange' relation of the 'head of the river Moratuc, now called Roanoke. This river was described as springing out of a rock, so like the Sea, that in high winds, the surge beats over into the spring. The colonists, thinking that this could be the passage they sought, or perhaps the bay of Mexico or the South Sea, were determined to locate this place. They formed many schemes and underwent a very fatiguing hazardous voyage up that river. So eager were they, and resolutely bent on this golden discovery, they could not be persuaded to return. Not as long as they had one pint of corn, a man left.

Lane rowed up the Roanoke River in search of 'the great passage.' As he advanced the Indians abandoned their towns, hid their corn, and fled before him, thus showing they could practice that kind of warfare as well as civilized nations. In three days' travel Lane did not see an Indian or find a grain of corn. After toiling on against the current a hundred and sixty miles. Only two days' food remained. Sensible, at last, that he had come on a fool's errand, Lane left it to his men to say whether they would go on or not. One and all chose to persevere, even if they should have to kill and eat their dogs. For two more days, they tugged at the oar, as night began to close in on them, they heard a blast of a horn that was instantly followed by a flight of arrows which brought them to a standstill. The assailants fled, but the explorers having already 'come to their dogs porridge,' as they say, now thought best to make haste back to Roanoke as empty handed as they came.

The death of Granganameo had caused a great alteration in the affairs of the Colony. While he had lived, he had been their champion and was able to restrain the Kings perfidy and malice towards the colonists. However, on his death, Wingina became a secret and bitter enemy of the English. The English learned of his hatred and false friendship towards them, they learned that he had also given secret intelligence to the Indians that they had encountered on their journey up river. Warning them of their coming and had craftily instigated bitterness into the Indians against the English, and into the English of the Indians. Wingina began to openly blaspheme the God of the English and endeavored, by all devices he could hurt and annoy them.

Wingina under the pretense of solemnizing his father's funeral, had laid a scheme of drawing together sixteen or eighteen hundred Indians in the hopes of cutting off the English at once. His plan had been discovered by Lane by his prisoner Skico, the Kings son. The

English then went out and seized all the canoes upon Roanoke, thinking that the Indians would be at their mercy with no means of escape. There was a small skirmish, in which five or six Indians were slain, the rest escaped and fled into the woods. After this there was little trust on either side. Not long after, the English entrapped Wingina and killed him along with eight of his chief men. ~

This account was given by Mr. Hariot

In this time of danger and distress, help came in the most unlooked for way. The Indians were attacked by a deadly sickness, which exceedingly terrified them. They believed that the whites had sent it upon them in revenge for withholding food. All Indians were firm believers in the power of an Evil as well as a Good Spirit, to whom their soothsayer, or medicine man, offered up prayers- to one to spare them from the sickness, famine, or trouble: to the other of thanksgiving for heath, plenty, or success in war. This medicine man was consulted in all matters of importance, as the ancients consulted their oracles. The Indians resolved to rid themselves of the white man. They set a plan in motion, how the Englishmen learned of this plot is a mystery, war was imminent.

Wingina was to give the signal by striking the first blow. Lane spoiled this plan by falling upon the Island Indians himself, and scattering them before they could put their plan into motion. He then crossed over to the main, where a still larger force of Indians was assembled. Chasing them off with his musket, many were killed. By Lane's brave acts, and luck, the Colonists were saved from destruction. Though still in dire straits. One certainty, every Indian was declared the enemy and vice versa. The Colonists would have to rely upon themselves, and even they knew those were not great odds of survival. They described their situation as like that of a horse starving in the stable with the grass growing outside, as the proverb has it.

For some time, the Island Indians had shown themselves as bad neighbors, and though they refrained from open enmity, they were shrewd enough to see that without their help the wasteful whites would soon come to want. In other words, it would be easier to starve them out than drive them off. So indeed, it fell out, as victuals soon ran so low in the settlement that Lane had to scatter his men abroad to live as they could, though he knew they would be more easily cut off.

Captain Stafford, with twenty other men, had been sent to

Croatan on the South part of Cape Lookout to fish for themselves, and to see if they could spy any sail passing by the coast. He also dispatched eleven other men to Hatteras, and others to the Main so that they could live *upon roots and oysters*. Only seven days after Wingina's death, Captain Stafford sent Mr. Lane word that he descried twenty-three sail of ships, and the next day, he came with a letter from Sir Francis Drake.

While encamped on a neighboring Island one of these foraging parties saw a great fleet crowding all sail for this shore. Thinking they were Spaniards coming to attack the Settlement, the watchers hastened to give alarm there. It proved, however, to be no Spaniard, but Sir Francis Drake.

Sir Francis Drake was then returning from an expedition against the Spaniards in the West Indies, where he had taken Cartagena and he had burnt the cities of St. Anthony and St. Helena on the Coast of Florida, Drake had done much damage to his enemies. He had orders from the Queen to visit the Colony of Virginia in his return, and to afford them such assistance and encouragement, as was proper. He therefor, offered to supply their wants, and to do anything in else in his power towards their relief. He appointed them a ship of seventy tons, with a hundred men and four months' provisions.

On June 10, 1586 Sir Francis Drake anchored off the coast with a fleet of twenty-three sail, and furnished Lane with a 'very proper barke of seventy ton, and took present order for bringing of victual aboard her for 100 men for four months.' On the 13th, there arose a great storm which drove her to sea with many of the chief Colonists on board, and she did not return.

These men were never seen from again. Losing hope after this disaster. And knowing that that they would not survive through the winter without any relief from home. The Colonists unaware that Grenville was on his way with provisions from England, the Colonists abandoned Roanoke and boarded Drakes ship. They arrived in Portsmouth on the 27th of July.

AN EXTRACT OF MASTER RALPH LANE'S LETTER TO M. RICHARD HAKLUYT ESQUIRE, AND ANOTHER GENTLEMAN OF THE MIDDLE TEMPLE, FROM VIRGINIA.

IN the meanwhile you shall understand, that since Sir Richard Grenville departure from us, as also before, we have discovered the main to be the goodliest soil under the cope of heaven, so abounding with sweet trees, that bring such sundry rich and pleasant gummes, grapes of such greatness, yet wild, as France, Spain nor Italy have no greater, so many sorts of Apothecary drugs, such several kinds of flax, & one kind like silk, the same gathered of a grass, as common there, as grass is here. And now within these few days we have found here Maiz or Guinie wheat, whose ear yielded corn for bread for many, and the cane maketh very good and perfect sugar, also Terra Samia, otherwise Terra sigillata. Besides that, it is the goodliest and most pleasing Territory of the world: for the continent is of a huge and unknown greatness, and very well peopled and towned, though savagely, and the climate so wholesome, that we had not one sick since we touched the land here. To conclude, if Virginia had but horses and kine(cow) in some reasonable proportion, I dare assure myself being inhabited with English, no realm in Christendom were comparable to it. For this already we find, that what commodities so ever Spain, France, Italy, or the East parts doe yield unto us, in wines of all sorts, in oils, in flax, in rosens, pitch, frankincense, currans, sugars, and such like, these parts are abound with the growth of them all, but being Savages that possess the land, they know no use of the same. And sundry other rich commodities, that no parts of the world, be they the West or East Indies, have, here we find great abundance of. The people naturally are most courteous and very desirous to have clothes, but especially of course cloth rather than silk, course canvas they also like well of, but copper carries the price of all, so it be made red. Thus good M. Hakluyt and I have joined you both in one letter of remembrance, as two that I love dearly well, and commending me most heartily to you both, I commit you to the tuition of the Almighty.

From the new Fort in Virginia, this third of September, 1585.

Your most assured friend,

Ralph Lane

The Colony at Roanoke
Ralph Lane
1586

The first English Colony of Roanoke, originally consisting of 108 Englishmen, was founded in 1585, 22 years before Jamestown and 37 years before the Pilgrims landed in Massachusetts, under the ultimate authority of Sir Walter Raleigh. In 1584 Raleigh, had been granted a patent by Queen Elizabeth I to colonize America.

This Colony was run by Ralph Lane after Sir Richard Grenville, who had transported the colonists to Virginia, returned to Britain for supplies. These colonists were ill-prepared and not particularly clever, because, although they depended upon the local Indians for food, they also antagonized the Indians by such tactics as kidnapping them and holding them hostage in exchange for information. Unfortunately for the colonists, who were desperately in need of supplies, Grenville's return was delayed. As a result, when Sir Francis Drake put in at Roanoke after destroying the Spanish colony of St. Augustine, the entire colony returned with Drake to England.

Interestingly, when Drake picked up these colonists, he left behind 15 of his own men, who were never heard from again. This foreshadowed one of the great mysteries of North America. Roanoke's so-called "Lost Colony" of 90 men, 17 women and 9 children, founded in 1587 and discovered to be missing in 1590. No sign except for the word "Croatan" carved on a post. Although both the English and the Spanish searched for clues to the colony's disappearance for many years, the mystery has yet to be solved.

The first Roanoke colony, before this great mystery, has also left us with many mysteries. The first Colonists lasted a total of ten months. This account, a fascinating description of American before European settlement, is taken from Ralph Lane's report on the adventure to Sir Walter Raleigh.

"To the Northwest the farthest place of our discovery was to Chawanook distant from Roanoke about 130 miles. Our passage thither lies through a broad sound, but all fresh water, and the channel of a great depth, navigable for good shipping, but out of the channel full of shoals...

Chawanook itself is the greatest province and Seigneurie lying upon that river, and that the town itself is able to put 700 fighting men into the field, besides the force of the province itself.

The King of the said province is Menatonon, a man impotent in his limbs, but otherwise for a savage, a very grave and wise man, and of a very singular good discourse in matters concerning the state, not only of his own country, and the disposition of his own men, but also of his neighbors round about him as well far as near, and of the commodities that each country yields.

When I had him prisoner with me, for two days that we were together, he gave me more understanding and light of the country than I had received by all the searches and savages that before I or any of my company had had conference with: it was in March last past 1586. Among other things he told me, that going three days' journey in a canoe up his river of Chawanook, and then descending to the land, you are within four days' journey to pass over land Northeast to a certain king's country, whose province lies upon the Sea, but his place of greatest strength is an island situated, as he described unto me, in a bay, the water round about the island very deep.

Out of this bay he signified unto me, that this King had so great quantity of pearls, and does so ordinarily take the same, as that not only his own skins that he wears, and the better sort of his gentlemen and followers are full set with the said pearls, but also his beds, and houses are garnished with them, and that he has such quantity of them, that it is a wonder to see...

The king of Chawanook promised to give me guides to go overland into that king's country whenever I would: but he advised me to take good store of men with me, and good store of victual, for he said, that king would be loath to suffer any strangers to enter into his country, and especially to meddle with the fishing for any pearls there, and that he was able to make a great many of men in to the field, which he said would fight very well.

And for that not only Menatonon, but also the savages of Moratoc themselves do report strange things of the head of that river, it is thirty days, as some of them say, and some say forty days' voyage to the head thereof, which head they say springs out of a main rock in that abundance, that forthwith it makes a most violent stream: and further, that this huge rock stands so near unto a Sea, that many times in storms (the wind coming outwardly from the sea) the waves thereof are beaten into the said fresh stream, so that the fresh water for a certain space, grows salt and brackish: I took a resolution with myself, having dismissed Menatonon upon a ransom agreed for, and sent his son into the pinnace to Roanoke, to enter presently so far into that river with two double wherries, and forty persons one or other, as I could have victual to carry us, until we could meet with more either of the Moraroks, or of the Mangoaks, which is another kind of savages, dwelling more to the westward of the said river: but the hope of recovering more victual from the savages made me and my company as narrowly to escape starving in that discovery before our return, as ever men did, that missed the same.

And that which made me most desirous to have some doings with the Mangoaks either in friendship or otherwise to have had one or two of them prisoners, was, for that it is a thing most notorious to all the country, that there is a province to the which the said Mangoaks have resource and traffic up that river of Moratoc, which has a marvelous and most strange mineral. This mine is so notorious among them, as not only to the savages dwelling up the said river, and also to the savages of Chawanook, and all them to the westward, but also to all them of the main: the country's name is of fame, and is called Chaunis Temoatan.

The mineral they say is Wassador, which is copper, but they call by the name of Wassador every metal whatsoever: they say it is of the color of our copper, but our copper is better than theirs: and the reason is for that it is redder and harder, whereas that of Chaunis Temoatan is very soft, and pale: they say that they take the said metal out of a river that falls very swift from high rocks and hills, and they take it in shallow water: the manner is this.

They take a great bowl by their description as great as one of our targets, and wrap a skin over the hollow part thereof, leaving one part open to receive in the mineral: that done, they watch the coming down of the current, and the change of the color of the water, and then suddenly chop down the said bowl with the skin, and receive into the same as much or as will come in, which is ever as much as their bowl will hold, which presently they cast into a fire, and forthwith it melts, and does yield in five parts at the first melting, two parts of metal for three parts of ore.

Of this metal the Mangoaks have so great store, by report of all the savages adjoining, that they beautify their houses with great plates of the same: and this to be true, I received by report of all the country, and particularly by young Skiko, the King of Chawanooks son of my prisoner, who also himself had been prisoner with the Mangoaks, and set down all the particulars to me before mentioned: but he had not been at Chaunis Temoatan himself: for he said it was twenty days' journey overland from the Mangoaks, to the said mineral country, and that they passed through certain other territories between them and the Mangoaks, before they came to the said country.

Upon report of the premises, which I was very inquisitive in all places where I came to take very particular information of by all the savages that dwelt towards these parts, and especially of Menatonon himself, who in everything did very particularly inform me, and promised me guides of his own men, who should pass over with me, even to the said country of Chaunis Temoatan, for overland from Chawanook to the Mangoaks is but one day's journey from sun rising to sun setting, whereas by water it is seven days with the soonest: These things, I say, made me very desirous by all means possible to recover the Mangoaks, and to get some of that their copper for an assay, and therefore I willingly yielded to their resolution: But it fell out very contrary to all expectation, and likelihood: for after two days' travel, and our whole victual spent, lying on shore all night, we could never see man, only fires we might perceive made along the shore where we were to pass, and up into the country, until the very last day.

In the evening whereof, about three of the clock we heard certain savages call as we thought, Manteo, who was also at that time with me in the boat, whereof we all being very glad, hoping of some friendly conference with them, and making him to answer them, they presently began a song, as we thought, in token of our welcome to them: but Manteo presently betook him to his piece, and told me that they meant to fight with us: which word was not so soon spoken by him, and the light horseman ready to put to shore, but there lighted a volley of their arrows among them in the boat, but did no hurt to any man.

Choosing a convenient ground in safety to lodge in for the night, making a strong corps of guard, and putting out good sentinels, I determined the next morning before the rising of the sun to be going back again, if possibly we might recover the mouth of the river, into the broad sound, which at my first motion I found my whole company ready to assent unto: for they were now come to their dog's porridge, that they had bespoken for themselves if that befell them which did, and I before did mistrust we should hardly escape.

The end was, we came the next day by night to the river's mouth within four or five miles of the same, having rowed in one day down the current, much as in four days we had done against the same: we lodged upon an island, where we had nothing in the world to eat but pottage of sassafras leaves, the like whereof for a meat was never used before as I think. The broad sound we had to pass the next day all fresh and fasting: that day the wind blew so strongly and the billow so great, that there was no possibility of passage without sinking of our boats. This was upon Easter eve, which was fasted very truly. Upon Easter day in the morning the wind coming very calm, we entered the sound, and by four of the clock we were at Chipanum, whence all the savages that we had left there were left, but their wares did yield us some fish, as God was pleased not utterly to suffer us to be lost: for some of our company of the light horsemen were far spent. The next morning, we arrived at our home Roanoke.

This fell out the first of June 1586, and the eight of the same came advertisement to me from captain Stafford, lying at my lord Admiral's Island, that he had discovered a great fleet of three and twenty sails: but whether they were friends or foes, he could not yet discern. He advised me to stand upon as good guard as I could.

*Drake was on his way home from raiding and pillaging in the West Indies, and had just burned St. Augustine Florida.

The ninth of the said month he himself came unto me, having that night before, and that same day traveled by land twenty miles: and I must truly report of him from the first to the last; he was the gentleman that never spared labor or peril either by land or water, fair weather or foul, to perform any service committed unto him.

He brought me a letter from the General Sir Francis Drake, with a most bountiful and honorable offer for the supply of our necessities to the performance of the action we were entered into; and that not only of victuals, munition, and clothing, but also of barks, pinnaces, and boats; they also by him to be victualed, manned and furnished to my contentation.

The tenth day he arrived in the road of our bad harbor: and coming there to an anchor, the eleventh day I came to him, whom I found in deeds most honorably to perform that which in writing and message he had most courteously offered, he having beforehand propounded the matter to all the captains of his fleet, and got their liking and consent thereto.

With such thanks unto him and his captains for his care both of us and of our action, not as the matter deserved, but as I could both for my company and myself, I (being beforehand prepared what I would desire) craved at his hands that it would please him to take with him into England a number of weak and unfit men for any good action, which I would deliver to him; and in place of them to supply me of his company with oar-men, artificers, and others.

That he would leave us so much shipping and victual, as about August then next following would carry me and all my company into England, when we had discovered somewhat, that for lack of needful provision in time left with us as yet remained undone.

That it would please him withal to leave some sufficient Masters not only to carry us into England, when time should be, but also to search the coast for some better harbor, if there were any, and especially to help us to some small boats and oar-men.

While these things were in hand, the provision above-mentioned being brought, and in bringing aboard, my said masters being also gone aboard, my said barks having accepted of their charge, and my own officers, with others in like sort of my company with them (all which was dispatched by the said general the 12th of the said month) the 13th of the same there arose such an unwonted storm, and continued four days...

This storm having continued from the 13th to the 16th of the month, and therefore my bark put away as abovementioned, the general coming ashore made a new offer unto me; which was a ship of 170 tons, called the bark Bonner, with a sufficient master and guide to remain with me the time appointed, and victualed sufficiently to carry me and my company into England, with all provisions as before: but he told me that he would not for anything undertake to have her brought into our harbor, and therefore he was to leave her in the road, and to leave the care of the rest unto myself, and advised me to consider with my company of our case, and to deliver presently unto him in writing what I would require him to do for us; which being within his power, he did assure me as well for his captains as for himself, should be most willingly performed.

Hereupon calling such captains and gentlemen of my company as then were at hand, who were all as privy as myself to the general's offer; their whole request was to me, that considering the case that we stood in, the weakness of our company, the small number of the same, the carrying away of our first appointed bark, with those two special masters, with our principal provisions in the same, by the very hand of God as it seemed, stretched out to take us from thence; considering also, that his second offer, though most honorable of his part, yet of ours not to be taken, insomuch as there was no possibility for her with any safety to be brought into the harbor: seeing furthermore, our hope for supply with Sir Richard Grenville, so undoubtedly promised us before Easter, not yet come, neither then likely to come this year, considering the doings in England for Flanders, and also for America, that therefore I would resolve myself with my company to go into England in that fleet, and accordingly to make request to the general in all our names, that he would be pleased to give us present passage with him...From whence the general in the name of the Almighty, weighing his anchors (having bestowed us among his fleet) for the relief of whom he had in that storm sustained more peril of wreck than in all his former most honorable actions against the Spaniards, with praises unto God for all, set sail the nineteenth of June 1596, and arrived in Portsmouth the seven and twentieth of July the same year"

~ Ralph Lane

Immediately after these men left Roanoke Island with Admiral Drake, the ship captained by Grenville that Sir Walter Raleigh provided sending provisions arrived.

The *First Forgotten* Lost Colony of Roanoke

July 1585-June 1586

Everyone has heard about the legendary, mysterious lost colony of Roanoke. Recently made famous by the television show American Horror Story and countless mysterious tales. This is not about *that* colony. There was another that disappeared in Roanoke *before* them. Perhaps, their disappearance should have made them leery, at the very least. As superstitious as the people in the 16th century were, I am actually very surprised it did not. Perhaps they did not know the whole story behind these men's disappearance. Perhaps they did know, but rather than start from scratch they had wanted to use the fort already built in Roanoke, or perhaps they had orders to search and find the lost men and had no choice. We will never know exactly why they chose this ill-fated spot. Hindsight, it was a decision that led to their disappearance and possible demise.

For some reason this lost colony, although documented from several sources, has been left out of our history books and stories. If by chance a book did include them, it was a brief sentence that did not lead the reader to believe that the event was significant at all.

The first thing that I need to clarify is that while many sources state that 'fifteen' men were left in the colony, Stith, a writer and explorer of the time wrote that 'fifty' men had been left. Other accounts do not give a number but state, 'some men'. In the following pages, you will see that inconsistency, however I entered their accounts as written.

After reading many accounts, and given the timelines provided from original recorders of the time, we are given insight to what may have taken place. These can only be theories, however if you take ALL the accounts into evidence even though they do at times, contradict each other, you can within reason come up with a most probable theory. I am providing you every account written in that time, so that you may form your own opinion of what may have happened.

Do you remember the ship with 'many' men that Sir Francis Drake was going to provide the colonists? That ship was complete with four months of provisions for a total of 100 men. That ship had disappeared in a storm with several 'chief colonists' on board and was never seen from again.

So, during this time frame, we have an unknown number of men who disappeared on a ship, loaded with provisions, that was never heard from or about again. A number of men from 15-50 according to written accounts, that were left by Grenville, to maintain possession of Roanoke for England. These men were also never heard from again, however according to one document, the 'bones of one man', was found by the new colonists that landed and took possession of the fort.

"Immediately after departing of our English colony out of this paradise of the world, the ship sent at the charges of Sir Walter Raleigh, freighted with all manner of things in most plentiful manner, arrived at Hatorask; who after some time spent in seeking our Colony up in the country, and not finding them, returned with all the aforesaid provisions into England. About fourteen days after the departure of the aforesaid ship, Sir Richard Grenville. General of Virginia arrived there: who not hearing any news of the Colony, and finding the places which they inhabited desolate, was unwilling to lose the possession of the country was determined to leave some men behind to retain it. Whereupon landed fifteen men in the Isle of Roanoke, furnished plentifully with all manner of provisions for two years.

Hardly had they left the coast when a supply ship hove in sight of Hatteras. After making a vain search for the colony, she sailed home again. Only a fortnight later Grenville himself arrived with three ships. Finding Roanoke deserted, he left a few men to hold it till relief should reach them. So perished this colony, when help was almost within its grasp. If Lane could have held out just a little longer, perhaps Raleigh's efforts might not have gone for naught. It seemed fated that one colony should rise on the ruins of its predecessor."

About a fortnight after the departure of this ship, Sir Richard Grenville arrived with three ships more, well provided; but he neither found that ship, according to his explanation, nor could hear any news of the colony, which he himself seated and left there the year before. Therefore, after travelling in vain up and down to seek them, finding their habitation abandoned, and being unwilling to lose the possession of the Country, he landed fifty men on the Island of Roanoke, plentifully furnished with provisions for two years, and so returned to England."

What happened to these men, to the Colony, or the men that were aboard Drakes ship that disappeared we will never know. What we do know, is that they were neither seen nor heard of again. They had transportation and provisions had they survived. Roanoke Island was not a safe place for the white man, that is well documented. From the stolen cup to Lane's final battle on the Island relations between them were hostile. It would not be farfetched to assume that these colonists, who wanted to maintain possession of these lands for their Queen relocated.

In several accounts given in the following pages, mentions of the disappearance of these men that were left to secure Roanoke is often given during the second landing at Roanoke August 1587.

Recent geological digs have found many clues that could back up this theory, although most of them are looking for the legendary lost colony. Who knows, perhaps these men, came to the rescue of the next colonists of Roanoke that also disappeared. Several archeologists have found 'Spanish relics' in recent digs around and near the Roanoke fort. It would be reasonable to also assume that perhaps the ship that Drake had provided, after looting the Spanish, the very one that was swept away during the storm that began June 13, 1586 with "chief colonists' aboard found its way back to Roanoke after the departure of Drake. They would have had to arrive after Grenville left the men on the Island, since his account states that there was no sign of inhabitants.

I think that with these details, it is much more probable these archeological findings are from Drakes ship rather than the Spanish, which there is absolutely no ancient documents stating they were ever living or settled in the vicinity of Roanoke. Unfortunately, since both the men left at Roanoke and the men aboard the ship were never seen again, we can only guess as to what happened.

National Geographic News Article
America's Lost Colony: Can New Dig Solve Mystery?
Willie Drye: March 2, 2004

More than four centuries ago, English colonists hoped to carve out a new life—and substantial profits—in the wild and strange land of North America. One group of colonists gave up and returned to England. A second colony, in what is now North Carolina, vanished in the 1580s and became immortalized in history as the "Lost Colony."

Today the prosperous little town of Manteo, North Carolina, surrounds the Fort Raleigh National Historic Site, a national park protecting the place where the English tried to establish their first American colony—before Plymouth, before even Jamestown.

Archaeologists know that the colonists spent some time at this spot on the north end of Roanoke Island, but they don't know much more about those unlucky settlers.

That might change soon, however. A group of archaeologists and historians met in Chapel Hill, North Carolina, earlier this month to launch the First Colony Foundation to raise money for new archaeological excavations in the Fort Raleigh park. They plan to start digging into one of the United States' most enduring historical puzzles early this summer.

Even as the excavation looms, not everyone is eager for the answer to the Lost Colony mystery. North Carolina attorney Phil Evans, who helped start the First Colony Foundation, said, "I've always said I'd be just as happy if it was never solved. I like it being a mystery."

First Settlement

The story of the first English colony in North America has been fascinating historians and curiosity seekers for a very long time. The saga began on a summer day 420 years ago, when co-captain Arthur Barlowe and a few dozen other Englishmen stood at the railing of their ship and peered anxiously across the water at a strange new world.

They had no idea what to expect, but the odor wafting to them from the small islands off the coast of what is now North Carolina filled Barlowe with wild hopes. The vegetation was at its summer peak, and the aroma was like that of "some delicate garden" full of fragrant flowers, he wrote later.

Barlowe was part of an expedition sent by Sir Walter Raleigh, an English courtier, to find a place for a colony. Roanoke Island, protected from the Atlantic Ocean by the slender sand dunes that came to be known as the Outer Banks, seemed a likely spot.

The soil, Barlowe said, was "the most plentiful, sweet, wholesome and fruitful of all the world." And the Native Americans living on the island were, in Barlowe's opinion, "gentle, loving and faithful, void of all guile and treason."

Based on Barlowe's report and backed by Queen Elizabeth, Raleigh sent an all-male colony of more than a hundred settlers to Roanoke Island in July 1585. For a while things went well.

Among the colonists were a brilliant scientist named Thomas Hariot and artist John White. Hariot set up the New World's first science laboratory, while White made detailed maps and drawings of the Indians and his new surroundings.

Problems soon befell the Englishmen, however. The Indians, angered by the harsh tactics of the colony commander, Sir Ralph Lane, became hostile. Supply ships from England didn't arrive, and food became scarce. So, when Sir Francis Drake, on his way home from the West Indies, arrived at Roanoke Island in the summer of 1586, the discouraged colonists opted to return to England with Drake.

When the supply ships arrived shortly after Drake's departure, the crews found only a deserted settlement. Sir Richard Grenville, commander of the supply fleet, left behind 15 men to hold the island and sailed back to England.

Later, at an abbey in Ireland, Hariot started writing a book about the wonderful new land on the other side of the world. But on Roanoke Island, the tiny English garrison left by Greenville was in serious trouble.

The Indians had decided they'd had enough of the foreigners and attacked the settlement. The outnumbered Englishmen scrambled into their boat and fled.

They were never seen again.

Second Attempt

A second colony of about 115 English settlers—including women and children—landed on Roanoke Island in August 1587. They found only the charred ruins of the village. It was an ominous welcome. But the colonists decided to rebuild and make a new start.

John White, the artist who had returned as governor of the second colony, went back to England to gather more supplies. He intended to return to Roanoke Island right away, but war between England and Spain delayed him.

When White finally reached Roanoke Island in August 1590, he discovered that something had gone terribly wrong on the sweet-smelling island of fruitful soil. The colony was gone.

The only clue left was the cryptic word "Croatoan" carved on a tree. The word could have been a reference to a tribe of friendly Indians who lived south of Roanoke Island.

Some scholars think Indians may have killed the colonists; others think the English settlers moved farther inland and married into Native American tribes. A third theory says the colonists were killed by Spanish troops who came up from Florida. No one knows for certain what happened to the colonists.

The site of the settlement began gradually disappearing beneath the vegetation and shifting sands of Roanoke Island.

In 1607 England sent more colonists to the New World. This time they landed up the coast from Roanoke Island and founded a settlement called Jamestown in what is now Virginia. This colony managed to hold on through difficult times, and England had its permanent presence in North America. The Lost Colony of 1587 became a historical curiosity.

Recent Clues

Souvenir seekers have been digging on Roanoke Island at least since 1653, when trader John Farrar and three friends from Virginia landed on the island and left with artifacts from the English colonies.

Union soldiers stationed on Roanoke Island during the Civil War dug for artifacts, and in 1895, Philadelphia journalist Talcott Williams, who was also an amateur archaeologist, did some excavations in the area now enclosed by the national park boundaries.

Professional archaeologists have done several excavations since the late 1940s. They found artifacts undoubtedly left by the colonists, including remains from Hariot's science laboratory. But they didn't find the site of the colonists' village.

The members of the First Colony Foundation hope to learn more about Hariot's laboratory and the location of the village. Their curiosity has been piqued by several clues.

In 1982 Evans—who was then a student working at the Fort Raleigh National Historic Site—discovered the remains of an old well thought to be from the 16th century. Evans found the remnants in Roanoke Sound, an indication of serious erosion on the northern end of the island.

In 2000 National Park Service archaeologists using ground-penetrating radar discovered rectangular-shaped objects buried beneath several feet of sand. (Park Service staff did not excavate the objects, but suspect they could be related to Hariot's work.) In 2002 a swimmer stepped on a 16th-century ax head in shallow water just off the northern end of Roanoke Island.

Finding the well and the ax head offshore has prompted some members of the First Colony Foundation to wonder if the site of the colonists' village eroded away and now is submerged. Underwater archaeologist Gordon Watts says that at least 600 feet (180 meters) and perhaps as much as a quarter-mile (0.4 kilometer) of the island has gone underwater since the 16th century.

"That's one fact that you cannot ignore," Watts said. "If you're doing a comprehensive search for the 1585-1587 settlement, you can't ignore the possibility that the site is now underwater."

Like any classic mystery, however, there's polite disagreement among some of the experts about where the village might have been. Acclaimed archaeologist Ivor Noël-Hume, who led an excavation in the Fort Raleigh National Historic Park in the 1990s, thinks it's highly unlikely the village site is now underwater.

"That's only a personal view, I do assure you," Noël-Hume said. "I wouldn't want to discourage further excavations. But I think you're going to find the remains of the settlement on a piece of land."

Noël-Hume says he'd like to see an excavation done in an area of sand dunes near the beach on the northern end. That could be "very informative," he says.

Virginia archaeologist Nick Luccketti, who also has worked at Fort Raleigh, says he has a reason to believe that maybe the village site hasn't been lost to erosion. "I've talked to collectors who have walked the beach on the north end for 30 years, and they don't have any 16th-century European artifacts in their collections," Luccketti said.

Despite their disagreements about where the colonial village may have been, the experts concur that the English effort to plant colonies on Roanoke Island was a milestone in U.S. history.

"It earned its place in American history when Thomas Hariot worked in the science center and sent back a report that said America is worthy of commercial investment," Noël-Hume said.

Luccketti thinks lessons learned at Roanoke Island helped ensure the survival of the Jamestown colony 20 years later. Hariot told the Jamestown colonists about the Native Americans' extreme fondness for copper ornaments, and so the colonists brought copper with them. When the Jamestown colonists were on the verge of starving, they traded copper to the Indians for food, and that saved the Jamestown colony from extinction, Luccketti says.

Still, Evans thinks the mystery of the Lost Colony also is important because it lures people into the story of Roanoke Island.

"As long as the Lost Colony is unexplained, it stays fascinating for a lot of people," Evans said. "It's their entry into the story. They go in trying to figure out what happened to the colonists, and then they learn history. I don't want to take away the mystery. That's what makes it different and exciting."

Second Colony of Roanoke

August 1587

Men commonly lay the blame of their failures upon everything but themselves. Yet that was not the case with Hariot or Lane. They praised Virginia just as highly as ever. The fault, then, was not with the country. Most men would have given up the whole idea at once after its failure. The difficulties seem only to have strengthened Raleigh's purpose to succeed. Keep in mind, one important details that our later history books seem to have forgotten, Roanoke in their minds was still occupied!

Raleigh was busy planning and fitting ships for an even larger expedition over which he appointed John White as Governor. Raleigh once again was obsessed, planning out every small detail and focusing on even the tiniest detail. He named twelve men who were to be White's advisers. They became a cooperation, like that of a city. He furthermore advised White to investigate a situation in the Chesapeake Bay, as the Carolina Coast was condemned by all sea captains who had been there, on the account of its shallow waters and unsafe harbors.

Instead of sending out only men, as before, of the one hundred and fifty settlers, seventeen of them were women. Raleigh thought that the men had grew disconnected and homesick without the other sex. The men who had gone before had never thought of Roanoke as a home, but more of a temporary station. With their wives present, it was thought that they would think of the new colony as a home. The colonists were also allowed to share in the government of their colony.

This colony was to be the beginning toward planting the seed of the commonwealth; whereas Lane had merely commanded a sort of military post.

"Reaching Hatteras on the second of July, White immediately went on shore to look for the men Grenville had left. When he came to the fort no living thing was to be seen. Some few houses were still standing, but weeds grew rank and tall about them, and both they and the fort were fast going to decay. As the newcomers searched here and there, they came across the bones of a man bleaching among the grass. The sad story was easily read in these perishing relics. The forlorn hope had either been all slain or driven off the island. And nothing was ever heard of them."

Roanoke, such a doomed spot that these colonists decided to pick up and plant their hope. A spot where so many of theirs had miserably perished. Against Raleigh's orders, White was persuaded, for whatever reason, to resettle the ill-fated island. The Colonists soon had reason to regret this decision, within a few days one of their chief men was found by the shore riddled with arrows. What the white man before them had sown, these colonists were now reaping. It was they who begged for peace.

A few men were chosen to try to make peace and offer treaty with the Croatan Indians. This was effected through their old friend and ally, Manteo, who on many occasions had served them well and faithfully.

The next year, three ships were sent under the command of Mr. John White, and twelve assistants, as a council. To these Sir Walter Raleigh gave charter, and incorporated them by the name of the governor and assistants of the City of Raleigh in Virginia with express directions to seat at Chesapeake: which however useful and important, they never the less disobeyed and neglected.

They went immediately to Roanoke to look for the fifty men left there by Sir Richard Grenville. They found nothing but the bones of a man, and where the plantation had been. The houses were undestroyed, but overgrown with weeds and the fort defaced. They refitted the houses. Mr. George Howe, a member of the council, straggling abroad, was slain by the Indians.

Soon after, Captain Strafford, with twenty men and Manteo, who I believe had been again in England this voyage, went to Croatan to enquire if they could hear any news of the colony. There they understood that the fifty, left the year before, had been suddenly set upon by three hundred Indians of Secotan, Aquascogoc and Dassamonpeake; that after a small squirmish, in which one Englishman was slain, they retired' – Drake, The Making of Virginia

Another Lost Colony at Roanoke

History has preserved no stranger, more mysterious story than the next experiment of Sir Walter Raleigh. To insure the permanence of his second colony, he decided to send families women and children, to the fruitful Islands of Roanoke, to make a permanent home, and found "The City of Raleigh." A fleet of transport ships carried eighty-nine men, seventeen women, and eleven little children, with every appliance for comfort, and ample provision of implements of husbandry. The colony arrived in August, after a five months ' voyage, and were dismayed to find the island strewn with human bones.

They had "expected sundry decent dwelling houses," they found the ruins of the houses and forts their predecessors had erected. The men who had been left behind by the first governor had been murdered by the loving, gentle, and faithful people.

There was nothing to do but make the best of it. But the charm was broken. The colonists were alarmed and disheartened. The Indians were not friends — that became evident at once.

Realizing their danger, weakness, and utter dependence upon England, the heartsick immigrants looked with dismay upon the departure of the ships, and they implored their Governor to return and represent their true condition to Elizabeth, "The Godmother of Virginia" and to the powerful Raleigh, her servant.

On the 18th of August, according to the ancient author's report, "Elinore, the Governor's daughter, and wife to Ananias Dare, was delivered of a daughter in Roanoke, which being the first Christian there borne, was named Virginia. 'The Governor was loth to leave his colony, his daughter, and grandchild, but they thought none would so truly procure their supplies as he, which though he did what he could to excuse it, yet their importunity would not cease till he undertook it; and had it under all their hands how unwilling he was but that necessity and reason did doubly constrain him."

Of course, the Governor promised to hasten his return. The story is a strange one, of feeble effort, cupidity, and indifference.

The Governor did not reach England until November. Raleigh at once fitted out two small vessels which sailed the following April, but the crew, [1] "being more intent on a gainful voyage than the relief of a colony, ran in chase of prizes, were themselves overcome and rifled." In this maimed, ransacked, and ragged condition, they returned to England, and, the writer adds, "their patron was greatly displeased." After this, for a whole year no relief was sent. Raleigh had now spent forty thousand pounds on his colonies with no return, and he turned them over to Sir Thomas Smith.

When White sailed again with three ships, history was repeated. He "buccaneered among the Spaniards, until three years elapsed before he actually arrived at Roanoke."

Nothing was to be seen of the settlers there. The Governor seems to have taken things with admirable coolness. His own account is an amazing bit of narrative, when we remember the one hundred and fifteen men, women, and little children, his own Elinore, and infant grandchild Virginia Dare. He tells first of his troublesome voyage. The sea was rough and his "provisions were much wet, the boat when they attempted to land tossed up and down, and some of his sailors were drowned, so it was late when he arrived.

The Governor was romantic. He and his company sang old familiar English songs, but no chorus came in response from the silent shore. "Seeing a fire through the woods we then sounded a trumpet, but no answer could we hear. The next morning, we went to it; but could see nothing but the grass and some rotten trees burning. We went up and down the hills and at last found three faire Romane Letters carved: C. R. 0., which presently we knew to signify the place where I should find them, according to a secret note between them and me: which was to write the name of the place they would be upon some tree, door, or post: and if they had been in any distress, to signify it by making a cross above it. But we found no sign of distress, then we went to a place where there were sundry houses, and on one of the chief posts, carved in fayre capital Letters, C. R. O. A. T. A. N., without any sign of distress."

Lead and iron and shot were scattered about overgrown with weeds, and some "chests were found which had been hidden and digged up again, which when I saw I knew three to be my own, but books, pictures, and all things else were spoyled. Though it much grieved me, yet it did comfort me to know they were at Croatan."

But the Governor never went in search of them at the Indian village indicated. He weighed anchor to that end, but cables broke. Considering they had but one anchor and their " provision near spent," they determined to go to Trinidad or some other island "to refresh ourselves and seek for purchase that winter, and the next spring come again to seek our countrymen." But they met in the meantime with "many of the Queen's ships and divers others," and "left seeking our colony, that was never any of them found nor seen to this day 1622."

This this was the conclusion of this plantation after so much time, labor, and charge consumed. Whereby we see, continues the Governor, who was poetic as well as romantic:

"Not all at once nor all alike, nor ever hath it been, That God doth offer and confer his blessings upon men."

A most philosophic Governor, truly. Even to this day we feel more emotion at the possible fate of these hapless Englishmen. Had they perished from famine? Had they fallen before the Indian tomahawk? Had the women and children been spared and given to the chiefs according to savage custom? Alas for Virginia Dare, three years they had looked for succor, and been basely forsaken by their countrymen. They were not forgotten altogether. Part of the errand of every ship thereafter, and part of every order sent out to the colony, was to "seek for Raleigh's men."

But they had disappeared utterly, as silently and surely as the morning dew before the sun. Twenty years later friendly Indians told a story of doubtful value to William Strachey and others, but the secret is still a secret, and this disappearance of more than a hundred human beings is one of the strangest events in our history.[2]

Part Three

Jamestown

1603

When Lord Bacon was informed that his great Queen Elizabeth had died just before daybreak, he exclaimed, "A fine morning before sun-rising the rising of King James the First. Far more appropriate would have been the words, "The sun has set before the night."

James the First shambles across the pages of history as a grotesque figure, tottering on weak legs which seem incapable of supporting his padded dirk-proof doublet, with pockets further distended by the unread petitions "siffli cations" as he termed them of his unhappy subjects.

Only three years before the Virginia colonists set forth upon their momentous enterprise, Sir Charles Percy and Thomas Somerset had posted down to Scotland to hail James Stuart King of England. As King James of Scotland had led rather a hard life, and although his mother's beautiful head had but lately fallen under an English axe, and although he had vowed eternal vengeance upon her murderers, he accepted the crown with childish eagerness.

His first request was peremptory, he must have money forthwith for his journey to London, and the crown jewels of England must be immediately forwarded for the use of his homely wife. The Council ventured to ignore the latter. They thought he would hurry to London to attend the funeral of Elizabeth, seeing she had herself named him as her successor. 'Give not my crown to a rascal!' she had said with her dying breath; "My cousin of Scotland is a king!" It was not to be supposed, however, that he would hasten his movements to honour "the defunct Queen," as he called her (seeing she had cut off his mother's head), so he dawdled on the way, hunting, feasting, and discovering the charms of "Theobald's" in Hertfordshire, where he afterwards spent so much of his royal time.

All the way, in season and out of season, he would indulge in the often-repeated words, "I am the King," as if to reassure himself of the fact and recall his powers and privileges. Casting about for opportunities to use them, his eye fell upon a petty thief, a cut-purse who had stolen some trifling coin from a courtier, had confessed his guilt, and begged for mercy.

James had the man hanged without legal trial, and when some cringing follower suggested that this procedure was irregular, had exclaimed, "God's wounds! I make what likes me law and

gospel." (His oath, and each one of England's sovereigns had his own favorite profanity, and was a little milder than Elizabeth's "God's death" and stronger than previous kings' "God's blood," "God's eyes," etc.) " God's wounds," stammered King James, "I make what likes me law and gospel!"

He also made what liked him knights and lords. Shutting his eyes, which could never endure the sight of a naked blade, for good reason, he laid the knight-conferring sword on shoulders which might well tingle under the accolade, seeing how narrowly eyes escaped being put out, and ears cut off. He bestowed this distinction upon nearly every person he met during his journey.

By the time he set foot in his palace of Whitehall, he had knighted two hundred individuals, without respect to distinction of merit or station. Before he had been three months a king, he had bestowed the hitherto highly esteemed honour of knighthood upon seven hundred. It seemed to be a relief to his feelings, immediately after a tedious oration or ceremony, to create twenty or more knights.

Nor was he chary even of the honour of the English peerage, which Elizabeth had held at so high a value. He presently added sixty-two names to the list of peers. By that same token those of us who hunger for noble descent are very shy of the strawberry leaves that grew in James the Firsts time, and diligently seek for those that nourished under the smiles of earlier potentates.

This was the grotesque figure before which England's great noblemen kneeled down and did their homage; Lord Bacon, Cecil, the Earl of Northumberland, Lord Grey, and hosts of others.

To Northumberland, Lord Bacon had written:

"Your Lordship shall find a prince the furthest from vain-glory that may be, and rather like a prince of the ancient form than of the latter time. His speech is swift and cursory, and in the full dialect of his nation, in speech of business short, in speech of discourse large."

Other persons, however, were less indulgent than Bacon. They marked his "legs too weak to carry his body, his tongue too large for his mouth, his goggle eyes, rolling and yet vacant, his apparel neglected and dirty, his unmanly fears and ridiculous precautions," and expressed their consequent astonishment and disgust. As time went on, these personal defects paled in importance compared with the low tastes and principles he developed. It matters not that he was learned in the Latin tongue, and an obstinate supporter, in word at least, of the Protestant faith.

All history of poor human nature proves that taste, beauty, learning may coexist with diabolical wickedness. It is hard to believe it, although we see it every day. It was abundantly proven in King James's reign.

Of course, we may imagine the society led by such a court. Never was there more injustice, outrageous favoritism, disregard of the rights of birth and property, more vice in high places, more extravagance, drunkenness, and debauchery. (Until we come to the Merry Court of Charles II)

It was unsafe to walk in the streets of London after nightfall. A portion of the city was set apart as a refuge for murderers and lawbreakers, whence the law had no power to drag them. Life was held cheap in King James's time. Heads fell on the block as a matter of course. Great ladies drove in their coaches to see Mrs. Turner executed. "Saw three men hanged and so to breakfast," said Samuel Pepys a little later.

The common people were wretchedly poor. They slept on straw and lived on barley. Only the servants of the rich could eat rye bread.

Vagrants and beggars swarmed over the kingdom. In a pamphlet entitled "Grievous Groans of the Poor," the writer complains that: *"The country is pitifully pestered with those who beg, filch, and steal for their maintenance, and travel the highway of hell until the law bring them to fearful hanging."*

What to do with these swarming "rogues," in case they could not be hanged, was a tough question with Lord Coke, conveniently answered later by imposing them upon the starving colonists. [3]

The picturesque beggar was not a very costly luxury. A curious pamphlet entitled, *Stanley's Remedy*, or *The Way to Reform Wandering Beggars, Thieves, Highway Robbers, and Pickpockets*, was published in 1646. The pamphlet estimated the cost of the diet and maintenance of every thievish, idle, drunken person in the kingdom was about three pence a day at least.

Of course, it was unsafe for "true men" to travel about this time, except in numbers and well-armed, and whoever was about to take a journey had to wait until a tolerably strong caravan had mustered for the same route. Among the chief places of danger was Gadshill in Kent, where Falstaff achieved the glory of killing the already dead Percy.

Thieves are always more interesting in a story than noblemen, but the Virginia colony was more intimate with the latter than the former, at least until the King graciously reinforced their numbers with a cargo of outlaws. The company that undertook the support the colony was a London Company, and the adventurers were mainly citizens of London.

Those who held the title of *gentlemen* may reasonably be supposed to have known something of the luxuries they were now exchanging for the hardships of colonial life.

The Virginia Company

Bartholomew Gosnold, Richard Hakluyt, Robert Hunt, John Smith, and others succeeded in obtaining a royal charter from the King. King James them busied himself in drawing up the instrument for the government of the new colony. [4] "Everything began and ended with the King." A council of thirteen in London, appointed by himself, was to govern, controlling a subordinate council in Virginia. Trial by jury was allowed to criminals. The Christian religion was to be preached to the Indians. In other respects, the colony would have no rights other than those which King James the First chose to allow it.

There were to be two colonies, one hundred miles to intervene between the boundaries of the two.

The boundaries of the southern colony were enlarged and exactly defined in 1609. It was to embrace the territory two hundred miles north and two hundred miles south of the mouth of James River, and "to reach up into the land from sea to sea."

This vast territory was coolly claimed by the King of England, without the slightest regard to the present sojourners on the soil. Had they been wandering tribes never remaining long in one place, had the area of country been a debatable land, the claim might have been reasonable, but it soon appeared that the kingdom of Powhatan had descended to him from generation to generation, or been acquired by conquest. The land was accurately measured and " staked out," and was owned by his captains, who knew and respected their boundaries.

All these things combined, we can better understand the disasters and sufferings which ensued upon the landing of our adventurers.

The most momentous hour in the history of this country was when three small ships "fell down the Thames from London," freighted with one hundred and five Englishmen on their way to plant England's first colony.

"This was the event," said a great American, "which decided our own fate, which guided our destiny before we were born, and settled the conditions in which we should pass that portion of our existence which God allows to men on earth."

The story of the company which was organized in London for this expedition, of the charter granted by James the First, of the means adopted and to insure its success, and the mistakes we can now so easily perceive, all this has been told in many histories. It is a long story, and also one involving side issues not within the scope of many historical writings. It is sufficient to say that the emigrants were subjected to the ordinances of a commercial corporation of which they could not be members, and to the dominion of a domestic council in the appointing of which they had no voice. One which was under the control of a superior council in England which had no sympathy with their rights, and finally to the arbitrary legislation of the sovereign.

[5]Of the names of the three little ships which fell down the Thames, we can be quite sure of two, the Discovery and the Goodspeed. The other, the Flagship, is quoted sometimes as Sarah Constant, or as Susan Constant. They were small ships, one only a "pinnasse", and were under the command of Christopher Newport.

Newport was an "experienced navigator," but his career in Virginia abundantly illustrated the fact that England's great hero was not the only admiral who could do some very foolish things on land. However, he brought our colony safely, and through many sea perils to Virginia.

We happen to know something of his men, and everything of his cargo. Of the latter, we have a careful list. Each man had one suit of "apparel, three pair of Irish stockings, four pair of shoes," and canvas to make a bed. Of arms and tools, he had no stint, also iron utensils for cooking and wooden spoons and platters.

The ration for each man was twelve bushels of cereal (oatmeal or peas), one gallon of aqua vitse, two gallons of vinegar, one of oil. These were the provisions given for a whole year. Some of the grain was to be carefully "kept for sowing." For meat, the immigrant must rely on his gun, and the rivers would yield him food.

The admiral was provided with a goodly cargo of small mirrors, bells, and glass beads with which to purchase the friendship of "the naturells," and also substantial articles of food. The tiny ships afforded small space for furniture, bedding, or other household articles.

The officers of the colony, Governor, Council, etc., were not yet known, and could therefore claim no privileges. The eccentric King had ordered their names to be placed in a sealed box, to be opened when they landed. Some private packages were, however, allowed. The clergyman, Master Robert Hunt, carried 'a goodly number of books.' Master Wingfield had also, as he tells us, '*sorted many books in my house to be sent up to me in a trunk at my going to Virginia with several fruits, conserves and preserves, which I did set at Master Croft's house at Ratcliff. I understand that my trunk was there broken up, much lost, my sweetmeats eaten at his table, some of my books seen in his hands, and whether amongst them my Bible was there embezzled I know not.*'

Books and Bibles could be bought or borrowed, but very little sugar was imported into England at that time, and sweetmeats were a rare and costly luxury. The Englishman had no marmalade for his breakfast until the Queen of Scots introduced it.

There were, as stated, one hundred and five men who went forth to subdue the wilderness. These men were to make the reign of James the First memorable as the commencement of the English colonies in America.

"Colonies," says Hume, "established on the noblest footing that has been known in any age or nation." They were destined for more than this, more than the historian's fancy could have foreseen in its wildest flight into the regions of romance.

Most of the company at this time were 'gentlemen', *-unuse to labour, who probably had never handled an axe or suffered a physical privation. There were forty-eight gentlemen and twelve labourers, a halfpenny-worth of bread to an intolerable deal of sack, one surgeon, one blacksmith, two bricklayers (for a country where there were no bricks), a drummer, and some boys. They were going to a wilderness in which not a house was standing and there were only four carpenters.*

In the next supply jewelers and perfumers were sent out to help subdue the American wilderness. Their recognized guide and leader, during the voyage, was their captain, Christopher Newport (having left to return to England and then once again return to Virginia.)

To his care was committed the sealed box of instructions which was to remain unopened until the adventurers reached Virginia. The *box*, they knew, contained the names of their future rulers, and they felt great solicitude on this subject.

Every prominent man was scanned and measured, and strong party feeling grew up immediately among them on the first voyage. It was not possible, they well knew, that any choice of their own would decide the matter. Of the two " experienced navigators" whose services had already been acknowledged by the King, were Gosnold and Newport, one only would be eligible. Captain Newport was to take the ships back to England, but Gosnold might be their Governor.

One who was preeminently conspicuous was Captain John Smith, who had commenced life as a poor orphan, and was already famous at twenty-seven. It was possible he might be their ruler despite his years. He was old in experience, in suffering, and in those elements which lie at the foundation of greatness.

Among them was the son of the great Earl of Northumberland, George Percy, of the same age as John Smith, but in striking contrast to him in every respect, fresh from the cloisters of the Middle Temple, quiet, thoughtful and of the ancient powerful family of Percy, he took his place modestly with the rest.

Wingfield was on board, also Master Crofts, and Gabriel Archer, Thomas Studley, John Martin, and Anas Todkill, all to be heard from again in the colony of which they were to become the historians. These and others were gentlemen and all possible rulers.

A certain John Lay also appears among the labourers, he was destined to win the first English maiden who set foot on the soil of Jamestown, and would become the father of the first child born in the established colony of Virginia. -Virginia Dare if you recall bears the title of being the first English born on American soil.

Without doubt, Smith, Gosnold, Newton, and some others were possessed with the prevailing spirit of adventure, the incentive of rivalry, and a high ambition for the glory and honour of England. George Percy, to whom England had been a stern mother indeed, not so Robert Hunt, whose heart burned with the spirit of the Christian missionary, and (if need be) of the Christian martyr as well, was not so the spendthrift "gentlemen" who sought the "pearl and gold" promised by the poet, nor the boy who frankly confessed that he had run away "being in displeasure of my friends."

The company seems to have been gathered at haphazardly, and not at all with regard to its fitness, but simply by accepting the few who were willing to brave the dangers of life among the savages.

Of the Indian, they had learned enough to fear him. He had early dropped his "gentle and loving" mask, and revealed himself in his true colors. "An Englishman was his natural enemy to be slain wherever seen, shot to death with arrows if distant, and clubbed by wooden swords if nearer at hand, ambushed and trapped, deceived and betrayed, whenever circumstances forbade open warfare."

Knowing all of this, the failed attempts colonizing Roanoke, there was no military preparation for this expedition. Its authors affected to be inspired solely by zeal for the conversion of the Indian to Christianity, and their messengers were men of peace. Whatever their station, whatever their motives, these were the men ever to be held by us in grateful remembrance.

They made many mistakes, of which we learn from their own confessions and criticisms of each other; but the sacrifices and sufferings awaiting them were beyond all precedent. They "broke the way with tears which many followed with a song."

Voyage to the New World

The sailing of the ships awakened so little interest in England that the event is hardly noticed in history. All of England was shaken to its foundation by the discovery of the Gunpowder Plot, and the punishment of the conspirators. That three little vessels were to depart, as many had departed before, to seek a footing in America, was, by comparison with the troubles at home, of small consequence.

The voyage of the Virginia colonists began, as it ended, in a storm. One of their number, Thomas Studley, tells the story in quaint language.[6] "*By unprosperous winds we were kept six weekes in the sight of England; all of which time, Maister Hunt our Preacher was so weak and sicke that few expected his recoverie. Yet although he were but 10 or 12 miles from his habitation (the time we were in the Downes), and notwithstanding the stormie weather, nor the scandalous imputations (of some few little better than Atheists, of the greatest ranke amongst us) suggested against him; all this could never force from him so much as a seeming desire to leave the businesse so many discontents did then arise ; had he not, with the water of patience, and his godly exhortations (but chiefly by his true devoted examples) quenched those flames of envie and dissension."*

By "the Atheist of greatest rank," he no doubt referred to George Percy, the Roman Catholic. However, in the light of his subsequent career, it is impossible to believe him guilty of "scandalous imputations" or "disastrous designs." We can imagine young Percy wrapped in his cloak and pacing the deck of the ship, his face perhaps turned northward where lay his forefathers' estates, crowned by Alnwick Castle, the princely home for many generations of the Percy's, Earls of Northumberland, "for virtue and honour second to not any in the country."

From Alnwick Castle had gone forth more than one Harry Hotspur to risk all and lose all in the border wars, and later in the intestine wars of England. An Earl of Northumberland had taken arms in defense of the unhappy Queen of Scots and paid for his devotion on the scaffold. His brother Henry, Earl of Northumberland, father of George Percy, had been committed to the Tower, accused of conspiring to liberate Queen Mary, and had destroyed himself "to balk Elizabeth of the forfeiture of his lands." Decision between conflicting parties had often been forced upon these noble earls, and been met openly, bravely, and loyally, whether or not the cause had prospered.

Upon the accession of James to the throne, the fortunes of the family had seemed to revive. George Percy's brother had been assigned the honour of announcing to him the death of Elizabeth. The present Earl of Northumberland (the eldest brother of George Percy) had rapidly risen in the King's favor. Then the discovery of the fatal Gunpowder Plot, the treason of fanatic Catholics, had revealed a Percy among its most active ringleaders. Although a distant relative of the Earl, he was still a Percy, and all who bore the name suffered from unjust suspicion. The Earl of Northumberland was now a prisoner in the Tower, accused of no crime except a desire to be a leader of the detested Roman Catholics.

George Percy could hope for no honour, no career, no home in England. Nor could he expect to find a career, home, or honour in the wilderness, but there he could at least hide his breaking heart. That he was a brave, honorable gentleman we know from the testimony of those who labored with him for the good of the colony.

Without doubt he held himself aloof from his fellows on the voyage. He was on the deck on the night of the 12th of February, and perhaps turning his longing eyes toward his northern home, when he saw a blazing star, which flashed out of the sky for a moment and was as suddenly hidden in darkness, fit emblem of the fallen fortunes of his house. He simply records the fact in his calm "Discourse of the Plantation" He writes, 'Presently there came a storm. The baleful flames of envy and dissension were not altogether quenched by good Master Hunt's waters of patience. They broke out again and again during the long voyage of five months.'

John Smith appears to have angered his fellow travelers in some way, and he was held in confinement during part of the voyage. It is even stated that when they arrived at the island of Mevis, gallows were erected for him, but 'He could not be prevailed upon to use it.' He was, by far, the ablest man among the first colonists. In the twenty-nine years of his life he had adventures enough for all the historical novels of a century. Perhaps he boasted of them too much, and thus excited *envy and dissension.*

He could tell of selling his books and satchel when he was a boy to get money to run away from home; of startling events all along until he fought the Turks in Transylvania; of cutting off the heads, in combat, of three of them *to delight the Ladies who did long to see some court-like pastime,* of inventing wonderful fire-signals which were triumphantly successful in war; of beating out the brains of a Bashaw's head, of imprisonment and peril, in which lovely ladies comforted him. What wonder that all this, and more, told in a masterful way, should have aroused suspicion that he intended to seize the government of the colony, aided and abetted by conspirators already at hand in all three of the ships.

Evidently the voyage was not a dull one. It was diversified also by frequent storms, no light matter in the little rolling vessels. The path of the ships was not the one we now travel in six days. The mariner in the sixteenth century and the early days of the next knew but one path across the ocean. They turned their prows southward, "watered" at the Bahamas, and then sought the Gulf Stream to help them northward again. Captain Newport's destination was Roanoke Island, of course, part of his duty was to search for Raleigh's lost colony.

Three days "out of his reckoning" his passengers, like Columbus's crew, grew discontented and discouraged, and wished to return homeward.

The Landing of America

As they sighted the shores of Virginia, a tempest blew them within the capes of Chesapeake Bay. Upon one of these isles, they erected a cross, naming the cape "Henry," in honour of the Prince of Wales. The opposite point was named after the King's second son, the Duke of York, afterward Charles the First.

Attempting to land here, they were met with a flight of arrows, a stern Virginia welcome, and two men in their party was wounded. The new nation was born in a storm, its baptism was of blood, and the furies relentlessly hovered over its cradle.

When the sealed box was finally opened, the appointed council was found to be Bartholomew Gosnold, Edward Maria Wingfield, Christopher Newport, John Ratcliffe, John Martin, George Kendall, and their prisoner John Smith. Captain Smith had been charged during the voyage with fostering a mutiny, and was under arrest when they landed. His innocence was made manifest, or, at any rate, his accusers failed to convict him, and on the loth June he was permitted to take his seat in the council.

This council was to elect their own President for one year. Later they elected Wingfield. [7] He and the Council were invested with the government; affairs of moment were to be examined by a jury, but determined by the Council. The first presidential election in the United States of America was held April 26, 1607.

LANDING AT JAMESTOWN IN 1607.

Instructions to the Colony

1607

AS we doubt not but you will have special care to observe the ordinances set down by the King's Majesty and delivered unto you under the Privy Seal; so for your better directions upon your first landing we have thought good to recommend to your care these instructions and articles following. The land, making choice of such a one as runs farthest into the land, and if you happen to discover diverse portable rivers, and among them any one that has two main branches, if the difference be not great, make choice of that which bends most toward the North-west for that way you shall soon find the other sea. When you have made choice of the river on which you mean to settle, be not hasty in landing your victuals and munitions; but first let Captain Newport discover how far that river may be found navigable, that you [may] make election of the strongest, most wholesome and fertile place; for if you make many removes, besides the loss of time, you shall greatly spoil your victuals and your casks, and with great pain transport it in small boats. But if you choose your place so far up as a bark of fifty tons will float, then you may lay all your provisions ashore with ease, and the better receive the trade of all the countries about you in the land; and such a place you may perchance find a hundred miles from the river's mouth, and the further up the better. For if you sit down near the entrance, except it be in some island that is strong by nature, an enemy that may approach you on even ground, may easily pull you out: and if he be driven to seek you a hundred miles [in] the land with boats, you shall from both sides of the river where it is narrowest, so beat them with your muskets as they shall never be able to prevail against you. And to the end that you be not surprised as they were in Florida by Melindus, and the Spaniard in the same place by the French, you shall do well to make this double provision. First, erect a little store at the mouth of the river that might lodge some ten men; with whom you shall leave a light boat, that when any fleet shall be in sight, they may come with speed to give you warning. Secondly, you must in no case suffer any of the native people of the country to inhabit between you and the sea coast; for you cannot carry yourselves so towards them, but they will grow discontented with your habitation, and be ready to guide and assist any nation that shall come to invade you: and if you neglect this, you neglect your safety. your six score men into three parts: whereof one party of them you may appoint to fortify and build, of which your first work must be your storehouse for victuals; the other[s] you may employ in preparing your ground and sowing your corn and roots; the other ten of these forty you must leave as sentinel at the haven's mouth. The other forty you may employ for two months in discovery of the river above you, and on the country about you; which charge Captain Newport and Captain Gosnold may undertake of these forty discoverers. When they do spy any high lands or hills, Captain Gosnold may take twenty of the company to cross over the lands, and carrying a half dozen pickaxes to try if they can find any minerals. The other twenty may go on by river, and pitch up boughs upon the bank's side, by which the other boats shall follow them by the same turnings. You may also take with them a wherry [light rowboat], such as is used here in the [River] Thames; by which you may send back to the President for supply of munition or any other want, that you may not be driven to return for every small defect. that out of the same lake you shall find some spring which run[s] the contrary way towards the East India Sea; for the great and famous rivers of Volga, Tan[a]is and Dwina have three heads near joined; and yet the one falls into the Caspian Sea, the other into the Euxine Sea, and the third into the Paelonian Sea. [they] have any: and this you must do before they perceive you mean to plant among them; for not being sure how your own seed corn will prosper the first year, to avoid the danger of famine, use and endeavor to store yourselves of the country corn. Your discoverers that pass over land with hired guides must look well to them that they slip not from them: and for more assurance, let them take a compass with them, and write down how far they go upon every point of the compass; for that country having no way nor path, if that your guides run from you in the great woods or desert, you shall hardly ever find a passage back. And how weary so ever your soldiers be, let them never trust the country people with the carriage of their weapons; for if they run from you with your shot, which they only fear, they will easily kill them all with their arrows. And whensoever any of yours shoots before them, be sure they may be chosen out of your best marksmen; for if they see your learners miss what they aim at, they will think the weapon not so terrible, and thereby will be bold to assault you. When you have discovered as far up the river as you mean to plant yourselves, and landed your victuals and munitions; to the end that every man may know his charge, you shall do well to divide You must observe if you can, whether the river on which you plant does spring out of mountains or out of lakes. If it be out of any lake, the passage to the other sea will be more easy, and [it] is like enough, In all your passages you must have great care not to offend the naturals [Indians], if you can eschew it; and employ some few of your company to trade with them for corn and all other lasting victuals if they have any. of yours, they will make many adventures upon you. If the country be populous, you shall do well also, not to let them see or know if your sick men, if you have any; which may also encourage them to make many enterprises. You must take special care that you choose a seat for habitation that shall not be over burdened with woods near your town: for all the men you have, shall not be able to clean twenty acres a year, besides that it may serve for a cover for your enemies round about. for some part of that coast where the lands are low, have their people bleary eyed, and with swollen bellies and legs: but if the naturals be strong and clean made, it is a true sign of a wholesome soil. You must take order to draw up the pinnace that is left with you, under the fort: and [to] take her sail and anchors ashore, all but a small anchor to ride by; least some ill-disposed persons slip away with her. You must take care that your mariners that go for wages, do not mar your trade; for those that mind not to inhabit, for a little gain will debase the estimation of the exchange, and hinder the trade for ever after: and therefore you shall not admit or suffer any person whatsoever, other than such as shall be appointed by the President and Council there, to buy any merchandises or other things whatsoever. It was necessary that all your carpenters and other such like workmen about building do first build your storehouse and those other rooms of public and necessary use before any house be set up for any private person: and though the workmen may belong to any private persons yet let them all work together first for the company and then for private men. And seeing order is at the same price with confusion, it shall be advisably done to set your houses even and by a line, that your streets may have a good breadth, and be carried square about your market place, and every street's end opening into it; that from there, with a few field pieces, you may command every street throughout; which market place you may also fortify if you think it needful. several kinds, and so of all other things else to advertise particularly; and to suffer no man to return but by passport from the President and Council, nor to write any letter of anything that may discourage others. the way to prosper and achieve good success is to make yourselves all of one mind of the good of your country and your own, and to serve and fear God the Giver of all Goodness, for every plantation which our Heavenly Father has not planted shall be rooted out.

The First Days....

Seventeen days were spent in quest of a place of settlement, sailing up and down the river, on the banks of which the Indians were clustered like swarming bees. Sundry adventures of small moment introduced them rather favorably to the Indians, who seemed, Percy thought, "as goodly men" as any he had "ever seen of savages, their prince bearing himself in a proud, modest fashion with great majesty." What they thought of the English had already been expressed in an unequivocal manner. They, however, offered no further violence.

According to instructions in their locked box, the colonists were admonished not to settle too near the bay because of the Spaniards, nor away from the highway — the river — because of the Indians. At last they found a peninsula which impressed them favorably. It was on the north side of the river Powhatan, as James River was called by the savages, and fifty-eight above the Virginia capes. [8] The peninsula, now an island, was small, only two and three-fourths miles long and one-fourth of a mile wide. It was connected with the mainland by a little isthmus, apparent only at low tide; and this was the spot selected for the settlement which was named, in honour of the King, Jamestown.

They could hardly have made a worse selection. The situation was extremely unhealthful, being low and exposed to the malaria of extensive marshes covered with water at high tide. The settlers landed, probably in the evening because of the tide, on the 13th of May, 1607. [9] This was the first permanent settlement effected by the English in North America, after a lapse of one hundred and ten years from the discovery of the continent by the Cabots, and twenty-two years after the attempt to colonize it under Sir Walter Raleigh

Upon landing, the Council took the oath of office; Edward Maria Wingfield, as we have seen, was elected President, and Thomas Studley, Cape-Merchant or Treasurer. Smith was excluded from the Council upon some false pretenses. Dean Swift says, *"When a great genius appears in the world, the dunces are all in confederacy against him."*

One reason for the selection of the low peninsula was the fact that the water was deep enough near the banks of the river for the ships to be moored close to the land and tethered to the trees, thus facilitating the transportation of the cargo. These trees presented a novel appearance to the Englishmen. The Indians had stripped them of their lower branches as high as a man could reach, for they had no axes to aid them in collecting fuel. All the tangled undergrowth had been cleared away and burned. A horseman could safely ride through them.

The grove was like a great cathedral with many columns, its floor tiled with moss and sprinkled with flowers. We may be sure that good Master Hunt gathered his flock around him without delay, and standing in their midst under the trees uttered, for the first time in the western world, the solemn invocation:

"The Lord is in His Holy Temple; Let all the earth keep silence before Him."

The new land had been claimed for an earthly potentate; he now claimed it for the King of kings. Immediately "all hands fell to work." Every article, every utensil, was removed from the ships, which were to be no longer the homes of the colonists. The stores were brought on land and covered with old sails, a hasty barricade was thrown up for defense against the savages, tents were set up, but we are told that the soft May air was so delicious, the men elected to lie upon the warm earth; and there, having set their watch to "ward all the night," with nothing but the whispering leaves between them and the stars, they slept the sweet sleep of weariness of body and contentment of soul.

When the colonists looked around them on the first day in their new home, they beheld a scene which will never again in the history of this world be spread before the eyes of man. Before them lay a vast land just as God made it. No furrow had followed the plough or wheel of civilization. The earth had been pressed by nothing sterner than the fight hoof of the reindeer or the moccasin foot of the Indian. No seed had ever drifted hither on the winds, or been brought by a bird wanderer from a distant country. The land was bounded by vast, untraveled seas. The earth had been stirred in cultivation only by the hands of women and children, unaided by any implement of steel or iron. In the forests and fields the great mystery of birth and death and birth again had silently gone on unmarked for countless ages. There was literally no known past, no record of a yesterday which might explain the problems of today.

Of course, the English colonist would be keenly curious as to the fauna and flora of the new land. There were "such faire meadows and goodly tall trees," says Percy,[10] "with such fresh-waters running through the woods, as I was almost ravished at the first sight thereof. My self and three or four more walking into the Woods, by chance we espied a path-way like to an Irish pace. We were desirous to know whither it would bring us. Wee traced along some four miles, all the way as we went having the pleasantest Suckles, the ground all bespred and flowing over with faire flowers of sundry colors and kinds as though it had been any Garden or Orchard in England."

"There be many Strawberries" continues Percy, "and other fruits unknowne. We saw the woods full of cedar and cypress Trees with other trees (out of) which issues our sweet gummes like to Balsam, and so we kept on our way in this Paradise.

There were no sheep, oxen, goats, or horses, no chickens or other domestic poultry. There were wild turkeys, none domesticated. The deer was king, but never used as a beast of burden. Bears, rabbits or hares, squirrels, the otter and the beaver; birds without number, (their king the eagle) these were indigenous to the new land, planted there when God made it, their flesh the food of man, their skins his garment.

And there, too, was man as God made him. To this day nothing is known of the origin of the North American Indian, from where he came, or his early history. Yet, there he was, having evolved little for himself. His one discovery had been fire. He had used what he found, but manufactured little except bows and arrows, rude mats and baskets woven of grass, earthen pipes and pots, and uncouth garments fashioned without scissors or knives, and sewed with the sinews of the deer. He had no textile fabric of any kind. When necessary to defend himself against the cold, he had killed a deer or raccoon and slipped his shivering limbs within the skin, or fashioned a mantle of the warm feathers of the turkey.

The pious men who emigrated to Virginia within the first twenty years of its settlement firmly believed that Satan had here established his kingdom; that the priests were his ministers, inspired by him to threaten the people unless they held to the ancient customs of their fathers. It was remembered that in all ages of the world this arch-enemy of mankind had demanded human sacrifice from his followers, from the times of the ancient Carthaginians, Persians, and Britons. Now, in Florida, he claimed the firstborn male child, and in Mexico prisoners taken in war. The priests of Powhatan failed not to instruct the Werowances that if the prescribed number of children were withheld, Okeus, who was sure to prevail in the end, would then be appeased only by a hecatomb of children. Nor would any sacrifice avert his wrath if a nation despising the ancient religion of their forefathers was permitted to inhabit.

Historians of the Indians have asserted that the tribes under King

Philip and those subject to Powhatan were of a higher class than many other of the North American Indians, more restrained by social and tribal laws, more cleanly in their habits, more intelligent in every way. They are an intensely interesting and mysterious people, and romantic writers love to invest them with virtues which the Powhatans, at least, did not possess. John Smith and Strachey argue that, "They are inconstant in everything but what peace constrained them to keep. Crafty, timorous, quick of apprehension, and very ingenious, some bold, most cautious, all savage, easily moved to anger, and so malicious they seldom forget an injury."

The persistent enmity of Powhatan to the English was planted long before their arrival in 1607. Strachey and Purchas, men of high character and great learning, consider it absolutely certain that he ordered the massacre of both of the Roanoke colonies. He was said, in 1610, to be more than eighty years old. He had been a daring, ambitious ruler in his youth, perpetually on the war-path, enlarging his dominions by conquest, like Alexander, only quiet when there were no more worlds to conquer. He "awaits his opportunity, inflamed by his bloody priests," says Strachey, "to offer us a taste of the same cup which he made our poor countrymen drink of at Roanoke. He has established a line of sentinels, extending from Jamestown to any house where he holds his court, and news of any movement by the English ships quickly passes from one to another and reaches him wherever he happened to be. He is persuaded that the English are come to dethrone him and take away his land."

"The Indians, like all barbarous people, danced to some kind of metrical sound, either from a cane on which they piped as on a " recorder," or drums stretched over hollow bowls or gourds, or rattles contrived from shells. These accompanied the voice in " frightful howlings." They had also " amorous ditties," and scornful songs inspired by their hatred of the English. The historian Strachey gives a copy, in the Indian language, of one of these, of four stanzas, not rhyming but metrical, in which they not only exult over the men they had killed in spite of our guns, but they tell how Newport had never deceived them for all his presents of copper and the crown for Powhatan ; and how they had continued to kill and take prisoners, "Symon" and others, for all their bright swords and tomahawks, ending each verse with the chorus or cry, "Whe, whe ! yah, ha, ha ! Tewittawa Tewittawa!"

The Indians were considered heathen, the relations poor despite any lessons that could have been learned from Roanoke. Here is a great article that explains the hardship as well as the relationship with the

Powhatons.

The Colonists came to the New World unaware of the hardships of labor they faced here. Most of these were classified as gentlemen. Out of the first 295 settlers, according to The Virginia Company records; 104 of them were Gentleman. This gave the Colony a population of gentlemen that was six times greater than that in England. "*Gentleman*" in the early 1600s, by definition, had no manual skills, and neither did the majority of their servants.

According to Smith, Coke, 2 Inst. 729 and 734 (Travels and Works,Vol i, Vol ii)

Most of the Colony's laborers "*were for the most part footmen, and such as they that were adventurers brought to attend them, or such as they could perswade to goe with them, that never did know what a dayes worke was.*"

England expected them to live off the land, while that may sound easy enough for us today ~imagine 104 wise-men offering advise while a few did the work. Simply put, there were too many bosses, you must agree that would have be a fair description of the havoc in Jamestown at the time. Smith wrote that he could never get any real work from more than 30 out of the 200, and later stated that *of all the people sent to Virginia, 100 good laborers would have done more than a 1000 of those who went.*

Jamestown needed laborors, free labor was the right price. This is when England did something no other nation had ever done, they sold their own.

King James through request, sent hundreds of Irish boys and girls to Virginia, "*those vagrants and orphans*". The Virginia Company then appealed to the mayor of London to rid the city of its "*swarme of unnecessary inmates*" by sending to Virginia '*any who were destitute and lying in the streets.*" Unfortunately, this act sent another supply of men, and women, who were not prepared to tackle the work of settling in the wilderness. Many did not survive the voyage and nearly half died within the first few months after arrival.

The Colony now had a growing population, yet still unskilled, and was they were now even more desperate for food. While the Company sent supplies, those supplies only sufficed for a month. The Settlers were struggling to take care of themselves, starving even. They did according to records, grow corn, 'that Indian Corn", yet very little was grown, although doing so would have required only a fraction of the brief working time specified in the labor Laws of Jamestown that had been established in 1609, a work program under Gates and De la Warr.

(The Laws of Virginia, Virginia Company Records)

Colonial Pride and Problems

Perhaps it was pride? The settlers of Jamestown shunned the simple planting of corn that sustained the Indians. Why would they want to be like those heathens they asked themselves? Yet history shows us that although they were starving, they refused to plant the heathens corn. Now we come to a problem that has historians, and yes even us authors, at a disagreement where we find ourselves at odds with each other to this very day. The Indian and Colonist relations have been, to say the least, a controversial debate for hundreds of years and hundreds more no doubt.

The Indians presented a challenge that the settlers were unprepared and reluctant to face. They challenged their self-esteem, the very image of themselves, their conviction that they were superior over foreigners like the barbarous Irish and the Indians. If you were a Colonist, you knew that your technology was superior to the Indians'. You knew that you were civilized, and they were mere savages. It was evident in their firearms, their clothing, housing, government, and their religion.

The Indians were supposed to be overcome with admiration and join them in extracting the riches from the land. Their technology proved insufficient to extract anything from the land. The Indians laughed at their superior methods and lived from the land more abundantly than they did. They even furnished the colonists with food that they could not supply for themselves. To now be condescended by the heathen savages was intolerable.

When their own people started to desert, to live with them, it was too much. They knew that if it came to that, the entire enterprise of Virginia would be over. What now? Pride, arrogance, the colony in jeopardy they declared war. They killed the savages, tortured them, burned their villages and cornfields. Now having proven superiority, in spite of your own people who succumbed to their way of life, they still struggled in this strange land, starving, and having now lost the kindness given by those barbarous people.

England looked down on them, the Irish hated them, they had nothing left. They struggled, maintaining a civilized way of life, they had their pride, but they still did not have corn to fill their bellies. The Colonists had conquered and claimed the New World, named it Virginia, call their city Jamestown after their beloved King. Yet these 'gentleman' were not laborers of the earth, they knew they were incapable of surviving, they beg for servants from their King. In desperation, they enslave their own kind. The Irish, the Scottish and yes, the poor English.

Poverty was a crime, the vagrants, the spinsters, the orphans that riddled England the King was more than happy to send to Virginia. The Irish, he sent in the hundreds. Laws were enacted and petty offenders where swiftly swept away across the Atlantic. The Colony was now saved, and would under slave labor flourish for many years.

The White Slave Boy and the Indian Baby
A story written about 1610 and passed through time...

Henry Spelman, an English boy who was sold to an Indian chief, lived as a servant for many years among the savages. He relates an incident of domestic life in the household of the king of Paspetanzy, who "went to visitt another king, and one of his wives after his departure would goe visitt her father, and she willed me to goe with hir and take hir child and carye him thither in my armes, being a long days journey from the place where we dwelt, which I refusing she strook me 3 or 4 blows." This it appears was too much for the free-born Briton. " I gott to hir and puld hir downe, giving hir some blows agayne which the other King's wives perseyvinge they fell on me and beat me so as I thought they had lamed me." It appears the lady's filial intentions were not carried out, the heavy child being quite too much for her strength. All awaited the return of the king, and the indignant Henry boldly told his side of the story. There had been quarrels and fights before in the king's household, and he knew how to deal with them. The remedy was at hand. Taking up a "paring iron" he struck his wife and felled her to the ground, whereupon Henry, by no means sure upon whom the instrument of domestic discipline would fall next, fled to a neighbour's house and hid. His position was a perilous one, his fate uncertain. The Indian baby settled the question. Henry had been an affectionate nurse and perhaps bedfellow to the little pappoose, who now lifted up his voice in loud lamentations, howling for his white friend until midnight. The king was weary and longed for sleep. Search was made for Henry, and at midnight the child was sent to him, as he says "to still; for none could quiet him so well as myself."

The king, having had a good night's rest, was up early next morning to interview Henry, and to assure him that no evil intent was cherished against him, that his "Queene" was all right, that everybody loved him, and none should hurt him, his Majesty content, as we all can understand, to eat a good bit of humble-pie rather than lose a good nurse ! "I was loth to goe with him," says Henry, "and at my cumminge the Queene looked but discontentedly at me, but I had the Kinge's promise and cared ye less for others frownes."

There is something very pathetic in the boy's narrative. He was the son of an eminent scholar, Sir Henry Spelman, but, impatient of restraint, had run away from a comfortable English home, and here he was in the great wilderness, soothing the hunger of his heart in the companionship of a savage baby.

The Virginia Company of London: The Great Exploitation

The Virginia Company of London, created by letters patent from King James, April 10, 1606, was organized as a joint stock company on the general plan of such commercial corporations, and particularly on that of the East India Company. The two Companies had the same Governor. The distinction between them lay in the fact that the avowed object of the Virginia Company was to establish a colony of which trade was to be a result, while the India Company aimed at trade alone, and the colonization which resulted was merely incidental. [11]

Though the Virginia Company was composed of two separate divisions, the London Company and the Plymouth Company, the former, which alone effected a permanent colonization, is of interest to us. The charter members of this Company were largely merchants of London, and after its organization was perfected two classes of membership were distinguished: first, "Adventurers," who remained in England and subscribed money towards a capital stock; and, land and second, "Planters," who went in person as colonists, and were expected by their industry or trade to greatly enlarge the stock and its profits.

Shares of adventure were granted for each subscription of a certain sum to the stock, and also for each "adventure of the person," entitling the holder to participate proportionately to his shares in all divisions of profits. Both those resulting from the industry of the colonists, and those resulting from trade, were to receive a land grant of some nature for each share.

A community of property, and of trade was to be established in the colony for five years after the first landing of the colonists, and at the end of that time a division of profits and of land was promised. [12]

This so-called communal system was provided for in his Majesty's instructions issued a short time after the granting of the patent to the Company. They were to "trade together all in one stock or dividable, but in two or three stocks at most and bring not only all the fruits of their labors there, but also all such other goods and commodities which shall be brought out of England or any other place into several magazines or store-houses, every person of the said several colonies was to be furnished with all necessaries out of those several magazines or store-houses for and during the term of five years. An officer called the treasurer or cape merchant was to administer this magazine in connection with the President and council, and give an accounting for all goods taken into and withdrawn from this joint stock. [13]

Ancient Planters of 1607 received in later years, grants of lands for their personal adventure, and also for subscriptions to stock. Captain Gabriel Archer's brother inherited one grant of land from him, and Anthony Gosnold, in 1621, received a share for personal adventure sixteen years before at his own charge.

The position of an early planter was thus theoretically that of a member of the company, who was to receive in lieu of his service for a term of years his maintenance during that time, or his transportation and maintenance, at the Company's charge.

For the adventure of his person, as well as for every subscription of £12, he received a bill of adventure which entitled him to the proportion that would fall to a single share in a division of land and profits. As a member, he stood on an equal footing with all other members and stockholders. Practically, however, as we shall see, he was, at least during the first twelve years of the Company's government, little better than a slave that was manipulated in the interest of the Company, held in servitude beyond a stipulated term, and defrauded of his just share in the proceeds of the undertaking.[14]

The administration of Sir Thomas Smith, the first Treasurer of the Company, even when we allow for the exaggerated statements of the planters, was undoubtedly hurtful to the welfare of the infant colony. His policy was one of immediate gain. The success of the East India Company, of which he was the first Govenor, as a trading corporation, probably led to his desire to conduct the Virginia Company on much the same principles.

The welfare of the colonists was neglected, and the project of true colonization seems to have been lost sight of in the desire to exploit the riches of an unknown country and to discover the long sought-for passage to the South Seas. Though some 80,000 had been spent in twelve years, the Company, when turned over to Sir Edwin Sandys in 1619, was in debt 8000 or 9000, and there had survived but a bare fourth of near two thousand colonists that had been sent over. [15]

Restrictions had been put upon the planting of corn, and the colonists were wholly dependent on the poor supplies from England or the doubtful generosity of the Indians. This policy had reduced the colony in 1609 to but fifty persons, and discontent with the aristocratical form of the Company's government and its bad administration led to a petition for a new charter. This charter constituted the London Company of Virginia a separate corporation from the Plymouth, defined the boundaries of its territory, and vested it with powers that gave it a more independent and republican character.[16]

To obtain fresh settlers the Company now issued broadsides and pamphlets, with specious promises, which, however honest its purpose, were certainly never fulfilled. There is evidence, however, in these advertisements to indicate that the Company consciously imposed on prospective settlers. One broadside solicits "workmen of whatever craft they may be men as well as women, who have any occupation, who wish to go in this voyage for colonizing the country with people they will receive for this voyage five hundred reales [17]for each one houses to live in, vegetable gardens and orchards and also food and clothing at the expense of the Company and besides this they will have a share of all the products and profits that may result from their labor, each in proportion, and they will also secure a share in the division of the land for themselves and their heirs forevermore."[18]

A letter to the Lord Mayor, Aldermen and Companies of London offers similar terms and a definite grant of " one hundred acres for every man's person that hath a trade or a body able to endure days' labor, as much for his child that are of years to do service to the colony with further particular reward according to their particular merits and industry." The full policy of the Company appears in a pamphlet issued by it about the same time; the object was to raise both men and money. Shares were set at twelve pounds ten shillings, and every "ordinary" man, woman and child above ten years that went to the colony to remain was allowed for his person, a single share as if he had subscribed the required sum of money.

Every "extraordinaire" man, such as divines, governors, ministers of state and justice, knights, gentlemen, physicians, or such as were, of worth for special services, were rated and registered by the Council according to the value of their persons. The Company, based on their 'value,' then agreed to bear all the charges of settling them and maintaining the plantation as well as furnishing all supplies in a joint stock for seven years.

There was to be no private trading, and "as we supply" they said, "from hence to the Planters at our own charge, and all necessaries for food and apparel, and for fortifying and building of houses in a joint stock, so they are also to return from thence the increase and fruits of their labors for the use and advancement of the same joint stock till the end of seven years; at which time we purpose, God willing, to make a division by Commissioners appointed of all the lands granted unto us by his Majestic to every one of the colonists according to each man's several adventure agreeing with our Register book which we doubt not will be for every share of twelve pounds, ten shillings, five hundred acres at least."

A large increase of the stock is anticipated from the success of the colony, "which stock is also as the land to be divided equally at the seven years end or sooner, or so often as the Company shall think fit for the greatness of it to make a dividend."

It was hoped that this would free them from further disbursements and would be an encouragement to the planters, as their share in the profits would thus be larger from a smaller number of shares owned by adventurers coming into the dividend. In order to secure promptness in the payment of subscriptions, every man was to be registered according to the time his money or person began to adventure. The division of lands was to be just, and to insure this it was to lie in scattered lots both good and bad, while the commissioners were to be chosen equally by adventurers and planters.

Regardless of these professions, when the seven years had passed the Company proposed to allow only fifty acres of land to a share in a division of land about to be made, and alleged in excuse that they were not in possession of more, and that it was not as yet freed from the encumber of woods and trees nor thoroughly surveyed, yet they hoped future opportunity will afford to divide the rest which we doubt not will bring at least two hundred acres to every single share.

The division was in fact to be made not in performance of their obligations, but as a measure to raise further money for the expenses of the Company. No adventurer was to be permitted to share in the division unless he made a further subscription of £12. (or more if he chose) to the Company's treasury. If he failed to do this he was to wait for some future division for his share, which would lie in some remote place and not along James river and "about the new townes erected," as the lands of the present division did. The Company even went to the extent of admitting new adventurers, on a payment of the subscription, to equal shares in the division, in utter disregard of the rights of the old adventurers and of the planters in Virginia.

Captain Argall was sent with commissioners and surveyors in 1616 to affect this division, and was granted in his own right a large plantation in the colony. It does not appear that the Virginia planters, except large shareholders like Captain John Martin and Lord Delaware, and possibly the men who had obtained their freedom in 1617 for building Charles City, ever participated in the division at all.[19]

No general private ownership of land in severalty seems to have existed in Virginia until the arrival of Yeardley as Governor in 1619. The body of the colonists were forcibly kept out of their rights, and if they had estates, had no assurance of their titles before that time. Certain corporate rights to land, however, belonged as early as 1617 to such corporations as Bermuda's Hundreds, and a few "particular plantations" that had been established by the common action of a number of adventurers or planters who had banded together in societies, sometimes with exceptional grants of jurisdiction that made them practically independent towns. Though the grants themselves in some cases dated as early as 1616, the establishment of these independent proprietaries was comparatively slow, and they increased in number very little before 1616.[20]

This year seems to have marked a change in the policy of the Company toward land grants, and in general to the disadvantage of the colonist. When an actual division of land was made to shareholders in 1619 only those who had subscribed or had come to the colony before the departure of Dale in 1616 were considered to hold "Great Shares," or "Shares of Old Adventure," which entitled them to a grant of 100 acres, while the holders of shares issued since that time could claim but 50 acres a share.[21]

Though a few exceptional grants were possibly made to individuals by governors before Yeardley, they had no assurance of their titles, and we can regard no earlier date than 1619 as that of the full and general establishment of the rights of private property in land in Virginia. [22]

Lotteries were also used as a means of obtaining ready money, and in one to be drawn in 1614, every man who adventured 10 shillings in the lottery could have either his prize or a Bill of Adventure to Virginia, with his part in all lands and profits arising from it. Adventurers who had not paid up their subscriptions were permitted, on the payment to the treasurer, in money, of double the sum for which they had subscribed, both to be free of the Company and to share in the lottery for the whole amount paid in. If not satisfied with their drawings, they could have Bills of Adventure instead.

The Company even declares that if the colonists in Virginia were *now but a little while supplied with more hands and materials, we should the sooner resolve upon a division of the country by lot, and so lessen the general charge by leaving each several tribe or family to husband his own.*

Whatever difficulties faaced a new plantation, the company may have had to overcome, these were undoubtedly enhanced by the troubled administration of Sir Thomas Smith and his officers. The accounts were left in such a disorderly state when the government was turned over to Sandys that Smith's integrity was open to grave doubts. Though his accounts were carefully examined and he was given an opportunity to clear up the discrepancy, it was never satisfactorily explained. [23]

The first of the societies, plantations, were known as 'Hundreds'. Those of any importance was Smith's Hundred, so called from Sir Thomas Smith, one of the subscribers to its fund, and it seems to have been established subsequently to April, 1618.

In 1620 it became Southampton Hundred. Another was Martin's Hundred. Other plantations were established either by some ancient adventurer or planter, associating others with him, as Argall's, Martin's and Lord Delaware's plantations, or by new adventurers joining themselves under some one person, an example of which is seen in Christopher Lawne's plantation. The failure of the Company itself as a successful colonizing agent, and it's very weak financial condition was the sole occasion of this private enterprise.

No dividend, except of lands, was ever declared in favor of the colonists, nor is there any record of a division of profits amongst the adventurers generally. The division of land that was made fell far short of the promises of the Company under which the shares were taken.

The Ancient Planters, by the Company's orders, in 1619 were to have the 100 acres as a first division, and a future increase of this was promised only to those who had gone at their own charge. Their rights to be favored above those who went after the greatest hardships were over were apparently recognized by the instructions, but they themselves in their first assembly seem to have felt sufficient doubt as to its possible construction to petition the Company that "they have the second, third and more divisions as well as any other planter," and shares also for their male children and issue. The latter request was not granted, but they appear to have been put on equal footing with other planters in subsequent land grants, which depended on a peopling of the tract first granted. I can find no evidence of a second or third division ever having been made.[24]

This communal system continued without a break until the year 1613, when a variation was introduced in the conditions of service of a number of the colonists and in their relation to the land. A sort of qualified property right was given them by the introduction of a tenancy-at-will on small tracts of land belonging to the Company, either at a fixed rent or on certain conditions of service to the colony.[25]

This change was brought about by the intolerable conditions of servitude and the right which the few remaining colonists of 1607 probably had to demand a release under a five-year contract now expired. The Bermuda planters petitioned Governor Gates for permission to plant corn for a subsistence, as the Company had been derelict in furnishing supplies. This petition was denied unless they accepted a tenant ship-at-will, paying a yearly rent of three barrels of corn and giving a month's service to the colony. [26]

The condition of the rest of the colonists was less fortunate, they were either retained in their servitude or granted, as tenants, small farms on condition of giving eleven months of the year to the benefit of the common store, from which they received but two barrels of corn.

By 1616 further modifications had taken place, chiefly in favor of the farmer class, who had become a source of profit to the Company and now numbered nearly a third of the colonists. The time of their service was reduced to thirty-one days, rendered at their convenience, and they were allowed to rent laborers from the colony as their servants. They paid a small rent for their farms and were responsible for their own maintenance and that of their servants.

These laborers were men transported at the Company's charge, and could be disposed of by the Governor for the best interests of the colony, as their maintenance would otherwise devolve upon the Company. Governor Dale placed a number of these on a tract of land called the "common garden," and applied the proceeds of their labor to the maintenance of their overseers and the public officers of the colony.

The skilled laborers and artificers, such as carpenters and smiths, constituted another class and worked at their trades for the colony, while they had land and time allotted them to till ground for their maintenance.[27] The freedom thus given to officers, farmers and skilled laborers was only conditional, depending on a responsibility for their own maintenance, while full control continued to be exercised over those who depended on the Company for support. This system continued without any important change until 1619.

Some distinction of classes existed in the colony from the earliest days. Society was influenced by its personnel, and doubtless also by the fact that many of the colonists, unable to pay their transportation, were either sent upon the common charge of the Company or of adventurers in England. Many of the gentlemen among the first immigrants took with them valets and servants on stipulated wages.

The Company itself, besides its seamen and soldiers, had servants in its employ on wages.[28] This class, however, was small and exceptional, and the bulk of the colonists went as members of the Company, either at their own charge or at the charge of the Company or of some private person. The hardships of the early years left little opportunity for the growth of an aristocratic sentiment, though we find the distinctions of class frequently recognized and the offices absorbed by a limited number of gentlemen. Beyond this, little practical distinction existed. All were colony servants alike and suffered much the same exactions.

Up to 1613 they were worked as hirelings of the Company, receiving but a miserable support in lieu of their services. A portion of them, we have seen, then became tenants on the Company's land on hard conditions of tenure.

Others, through the influence of Dale, were induced to serve the colony in the "building of Charles City and Hundred "three years longer, on the promise of absolute freedom from the "general and common servitude" so much abhorred.[29]

They were allowed but a month in the year and a day in the week to provide for themselves, and were afterwards deprived of half of this time, so that they were forced, as they say, " out of our daily tasks to redeem time wherein to labor for our sustenance thereby miserably to purchase our freedom."[30] The favored Bermuda planters were finally given a charter of incorporation and enjoyed better terms, but were bound to the performance of certain duties for a limited time before they could have their freedom.[31]

When Lord Delaware came in 1610 with fresh supplies he thoroughly organized the colony as a labor force under commanders and overseers. [32]Dale afterwards applied a rigorous military system adopted from the Low Countries, and enforced it with great severity in carrying out his plans for establishing new plantations. The colonists were marched to their daily work in squads and companies under officers, and the severest penalties were prescribed for a breach of discipline or neglect of duty. A persistent neglect of labor was to be punished by galley service from one to three years. Penal servitude was also instituted; for petty offences, they worked as slaves in irons for a term of years."

The planters affirm that there were *"continual whippings and extraordinary punishments,"* such as hanging, shooting, breaking on the wheel, and even burning alive. The system at least proved salutary. Towns were built and palisaded, and the colony was reduced to thorough order. [33]

Crime and Punishment *in Early Jamestown*
Excerpts from the Virginia Court Records

June 4, 1640

Hugh Gwyn petitioned the court in Jamestown that three of his servants had run away to Maryland. A letter was written to the Governor of Maryland requesting the return of the servants to Virginia.

"do order that a letter be written unto the said Governor to the intent the said servants may be returned hither to receive such exemplary punishment as the nature of the offense shall justly deserve and then be returned to their said master."

July 9, 1640~ Mr. Gwen's servants were then returned to Jamestown from Maryland. There the servant stood before the court to receive the punishment for running away. This was a serious offense. If they were not working, they were not farming tobacco. Tobacco was at that time the only type of currency used among the Colonists.

"Three servants formerly run away from said Gwyn, the court doth therefor order that the said three servants shall receive the punishment of whipping and to have thirty stripes apiece. One called Viaor, a Dutchman, the other a Scotsman called James Gregory, shall first serve out their times with their master according to their Indentures, and one whole year apiece after the time their service is expired to compensate for the loss by their absence. And after the said service to their master to serve the colony for three whole years.

"Christopher Miller, A Dutchman, should receive the punishment of whipping and to have thirty stripes, and to be burnt on the cheek with the letter R, *(this represented a 'runaway') and to work with shackle on his leg for one whole year, and longer if his master should see cause and after his full time of service is expired with his said master, to serve the colony for seven whole years." ~Virginia Court Records Christopher Miller died a slave.*

1609 Company, Colony, Chaos, and a Spanish Spy

When the Council met, it was seriously discussed whether so unpromising a venture should not be abandoned. But there was the country, so fruitful and delightful; and here at court was Zuniga, the Spanish ambassador, urging its abandonment. Here, too, was Captain Newport, refusing to relinquish the enterprise and stoutly adhering to his first opinion, that gold would finally reward their search.

The fate of the colony hung upon a slender thread, but finally the president of the Council informed Cecil that they had decided to send Newport out again with one hundred settlers and 'all necessaries to relieve them that be there' hoping to arrive the next January, and taking out with his ship a "nymble Pinnace" in which to return quickly and make report.

The advice of the King could not be had. He was away at Theobald's for the August shooting, and woe to that man who should interrupt him! Zuniga's ears were wide open to the news from Virginia, and he wrote to the King of Spain: "It is very desirable that your Majesty make an end of the few who are now in Virginia, as that would be digging up the Root so it could put out no more. It will be serving God and your Majesty to drive these villains out from there, hanging them in time which is short enough for the purpose."

Philip III wrote regularly to his minister, agreeing with him, but doing nothing. The Spanish Council of State advised the King instantly to make ready a fleet "and forthwith proceed to drive out all who are in Virginia' and this, they argued, "will suffice to prevent them from again coming to the place."

After the resolution of the London Council, Zuniga again urges Philip: "I hear that three or four ships will return to Virginia. Will your Majesty give orders that measures be taken in time, because now it will be very easy, and very difficult afterwards when they have taken root. If they are punished in the beginning the result will be that no more will go there."

But Philip was disposed to take his own time, overruled by that Providence which brought us safely through so many perils. He had his own private schemes. A princess of England was growing up, and he meant to ask her hand in marriage.

Finally, he agreed that the colonists were to be driven out, but the thing must be done secretly. Zuniga continued to be his faithful spy, reporting every step taken by the London Council. It was Zuniga, we remember, who was sent to London a few years afterwards to ask for the Princess Elizabeth.

Before we return to the little colony, happily unconscious of its many enemies, we must be allowed one more of the letters incident upon Newport's return. All of them are extremely interesting as illustrative of the time, but we must not pause too long in our history, a history so rich in events that it is difficult to choose the most important.

The letter is dated August 18, 1607, and informs John Chamberlain that —

"Captaine Newport is come from our late adventures to Virginia, having left them in an Island in the midst of a great river 120 miles into the land. They write much commendation of the aire and the soile and the commodities of it: but silver and golde have they none, and they cannot yet be at peace with the inhabitants of the country. They have fortified themselves and built a small towne which they call 'James towne and so they date their letters; but the towne methinks hath no gracefull name, and besides the Spaniards, who think it no small matter of moment how they stile their new populations, will tell us, I doubt, it comes too neere 'Villiaco.'

Master Porie tells me of a name given by a Dutchman who wrote to him in Latin from the new towne in Virginia, Jacobopolis and Aster Warner hath a letter from Master George Percy who names their town, Jamesfort, which we like best of all the rest because it comes neere to 'Chemes-ford.' Yours most assuredly, Dudley Carleton."

The "small towne" was a bit of prophetic imagination. Up to the hour of Newport's sailing the colonists had been employed, with infinite labor and toil, in felling trees and hewing them into clapboards for freighting the two returning ships, the Goodspeed and Susan (or Sarah) Constant. The Discovery, a little pinnace of twenty tons, was left behind for the use of the colony, in case of flight from the savages.

It is wonderful, in view of ensuing events, that the colonists did not at once reembark in the pinnace and seek some healthier spot for the proposed town. The famous river in Christendom, seems to have held them with a strange fascination.

Distress, Death and Desperation in Jamestown

There was absolutely no dwelling of any kind erected during the summer. [34]Some of the settlers slept in holes in the ground, roofed with rails. A rough palisade had been made of boards, and rude cabins covered with sail cloth sheltered the ammunition and stores. The first church was a log between two trees to serve as a lectern, and a rotten sail was stretched overhead in case of rain; for in all weathers, rain or shine, the good Master Hunt ministered to his flock, morning and evening, leading them in supplication for protection to Almighty God; and from an unhewn log as an altar, administered to them the holy emblems of the Christian faith.

Before the men could begin to build comfortable quarters, they were smitten with illness, which continued until September. More than half of their number perished. The story is told so well by George Percy-

"Our men were destroyed with cruel diseases, as swellings, flixes, burning fevers, and by warres; and some departed suddenly; but for the most part they died of meere famine! There were never Englishmen left in a foreigne Country in such miserie as wee were in this new discovered Virginia. Wee watched every three nights, lying on the bare, cold ground, what weather soever came; and warded all the next day, which brought our men to bee most feeble wretches. Our food was but a small can of barlie sodden in water to five men a day. Our drinke, cold water taken out of the River, which was at a flood verie salt; at a low tide, full of slime and filth; which was the destruction of many of our men.

Thus, we lived for the space of five months in this miserable distress, not having five able men to man our Bulwarkes upon any occasion. If it had not pleased God to put a terror in the Savages hearts, we had all perished by those wild and cruel Pagans, being in that weak estate as we were; our men night and day groaning in every corner of the Fort most pitiful to hear. If there were any conscience in men, it would make their hearts to bleed to hear the pitiful murmurings and outcries of our sick men without relief every night and day for the space of six weeks; some departing out of the World, many times three or four in a night; in the morning, their bodies trailed out of their cabins like dogs to be buried. In this sort, did I see the mortalities of several of our people."

Among those who perished was our friend, Thomas Studley, the "Cape Merchant," and another was Elizabeth's brave mariner, Bartholomew Gosnold, the projector of the enterprise, and one of the Council. How strange that he should, after his many voyages, have so eagerly insisted upon this colonization of Virginia, to find there his own grave, far away from the England whose honour he loved so ardently!

His unhappy comrades did what they could, smitten with fever and weakened by starvation, they bore him to his humble grave, reverently and decently, "having all ordinance of the fort shot off, with many vollies of small shot."

Thus, old Virginia received her first-born into her bosom! She lovingly holds him there still. We can imagine these scenes, softened by the faithful, untiring care of Thomas Walton, the surgeon, and the priestly offices and consolations of good Master Hunt. It seems unthinkable that England should have so starved her colony. In Elizabeth's reign the narrow, selfish charter and the meagre outfit would have been impossible. All things were possible to James that could in any way contribute to his own self-aggrandizement. Bitter as was the lot of the unhappy adventurers, they were too manly to complain. "When some affirm," says a historian of the time, [35] "that it was ill done of the Council to send forth men so badly provided, this uncontradictable reason will show them plainly they are ill-advised to nourish such ill conceits first, the fault of going was our own, what could be thought fitting or necessary we had; but what we should find or want or where we should be, we were all ignorant, and supposing to make our passage in two months, with victual to live, and the advantage of the spring to work; we were at sea five months where we both spent our victual and lost the time and opportunity to plant by the unskillful presumption of our ignorant transporters that understood not at all what they undertook.

Such actions have ever since the world's beginning been subject to such accidents and everything of worth is found full of difficulties; but nothing so difficult as to establish a commonwealth so far remote from men and means and where men's minds are so untoward as neither to do well themselves nor suffer others."

The closing sentence was a very mild commentary indeed upon the state of things at Jamestown. The miniature republic for such it rapidly grew to be in nearly everything except in name, held within its borders just the elements that distinguish the great republic of today: some noble spirits with high aims and fervent patriotism; some sordid soul's intent alone on gain; some unprincipled, desperate characters; others simply useless, idle, and ignoble.

Of the latter class, the President, Wingfield, was notably conspicuous. It was evident, from the first, that he was utterly unfit for his position. One of the earliest efforts of the convalescents was to get rid of him.

The store held in common, of "oil, vinegar, sack and aqua vitse, " being nearly all spent, the Council ordered that the sack should be reserved for the Communion table, and all the rest sealed up against greater extremities if there could be greater. John Smith accused Wingfield of using the reserved stores for his own benefit and that of his friends. Wingfield soon appeared in his true character, and added cowardice to incapacity. He made an effort to seize the pinnace and escape to England, thus leaving the colony to the mercy of the savages. This baseness roused the indignation even of the emaciated survivors, and they deposed him and appointed Captain Ratcliffe in his place.

Wingfield's defense, addressed to his government, now preserved among the manuscripts of Lambeth Palace Library, is a curious mixture of dignified, not to say lofty, sentiments for all the colonial writers used a formula of pious aspiration, and of fierce invective and very petty unworthy gossip; but if England has seen fit to preserve it all, we may quote a representative part of it.

He attributes many of his misfortunes to John Smith, others to Master Archer. His old enemy, Master Crofts, whom we remember as having thriven so well upon the precious preserves and conserves prepared for Wingfield's voyage comes well to the fore in the long discourse addressed to the Council in England. "Master Crofts feared not to say that, if others would join with him, he would pull me out of my seat and out of my skin too. He could hardly have threatened more, but this was not all. I desired justice for a copper kettle which Master Crofts did detain from me. He said I had given it him; I did bid him bring his proof of that. He confessed he had no proof. Then Master President [Ratcliffe] did ask me if I would be sworn I did not give it to him. I said I knew no cause why to swear for mine own. He asked Master Crofts if he would make oath I did give it to him which oath he took and won my kettle from me, that was in that place and time worth half its weight in gold.

He protests against the charge of using the oil, vinegar, and aqua vitse. It is further said I did deny the men and much banquet and rot myself. I allowed a biscuit to every working man for his breakfast by means of provision brought by Captain Newport. I never had but one squirrel roasted whereof I gave part to Master Ratcliffe then sick; yet was that Squirrel given me. I did never heat a fresh pot but when the common pot was so used likewise," and much more to the same purpose. The matter resulted in the impeachment of the President and appointment of Ratcliffe to fill his unfinished term of office. Kendall also, a prime aider and abettor of the deposed President, was afterwards committed about heinous matters which was proved against him."

And so, the fifty colonists had their troubles at home and abroad, but they held on bravely notwithstanding. For some mysterious reason the Indians ceased to molest them, possibly because their own great harvesting time was at hand, and also the hunting season for more profitable game than a few starved Englishmen. However, that may be, they still had their eyes on the intruders, and in order to enter their fort appeared with a present of Bread, Corn, Fish and Flesh in great plenty.

Thus, the representatives of the proudest nation on earth suffered the humiliation of becoming pensioners upon the bounty of savages whose country they had invaded, and whose land they had taken without purchase or permission.

Nothing can exceed the plenty in southern Virginia which swarms in sea and air in the months of October and November. The splendid solangoose, sora, wild ducks, and wild turkey were found in 1607 in even greater plenty than at the present day. No Thanksgiving dinners had thinned their ranks. The rivers literally swarmed with fish. These were all at the command of the settlers. Of corn for bread there was always scarcity, but surely Newport had not forgotten them! They would boil the roots and gather the persimmons until he came. Then, too, some of the disturbers of the peace had been silenced. Kendall had been tried by a jury and shot; Ratcliffe and Archer had attempted to steal the pinnace, and been foiled by Smith's vigilance and resolution.

The helm of affairs had been entrusted to John Smith as Cape Merchant, and he now took the lead. His strong hand was soon recognized in the colony. He set the colonists to work and worked with them, mowing, building, and thatching log cabins, he himself always performing the heaviest tasks. In a short time, shelter was provided for all, now numbering only forty- five individuals, and a church was built on the site to which pilgrims now resort as to a Mecca. [36]

It was not an imposing structure, but it was a regular church. The chronicles describe it as a log building, covered like the cabins with rafts, sedge, and dirt. Thus, the Virginians, despite their enemies, barbarian and Spanish, with all their conflicts, illness, and death, had made a good beginning. They had felled trees, built houses, and erected a church, and were saying their prayers in it, like honest people who were bent on doing their duty in that state of life in which it had pleased Heaven to place them.

Back in England the Council had come to its conclusion, the Colony was worth their investment, despite King Phillip III's spy and informer's protests against the settlement. We find his letter to the King, written March 5, 1609:

On December 12, 1609, I wrote to Your Majesty how two vessels left here for Virginia, and afterwards I heard that they carried up to 150 men most of whom were men of distinction. And likewise, I wrote to Your Majesty on Jan' 17th how they would make still greater efforts, and spoke of sending the Baron de Arundel with a number of people, who has told me that they have excluded him, because in order to go, he asked this King for a Patent and for money, and likewise he tells me he had asked that liberty of conscience should be given in that country. This is what he asserts; but the truth is that they have failed to send him out because he is suspected of being a Catholic. He is dissatisfied and has told me that if Your Majesty would do him the favor to reward him for the services in Flanders, he would be of particular usefulness in this affair. It seems to me he is all jealousy, that they have made the Varon de la Warte [Thomas West, baron De La Warr] general and Governor of Virginia, who is a Kinsman of Don Antonio Sirley [Sherley]. They assure me, he has said that Your Majesty pays no attention, so far, to the people who go there and this has made them so reckless that they no longer send their little by little as heretofore, but they command that Captain Gacht [Sir Thomas Gates] go there, who is a very special soldier and has seen service among the Rebels. He takes 400 to 500 men and 100 women, and all who go have first to take the oath of the supremacy of the King [James I]. He will sail within a month or a month and a half, and as soon as the news of his arrival is received here the baron de la Warr is to sail with 600 or 700 men, and a large part of them principal men and a few women, and when he gets there, the Gacht [Gates] will return here to take more men.

The month of December found the colonists anxiously apprehensive of starvation during the ensuing winter, a winter which was long remembered in Europe as one of unprecedented severity.

Newport had been for many weeks overdue. The weather was already bitterly cold. A great central camp-fire was kept burning, day and night, which they fed from the limbs of the trees they had felled in building their fortifications, church, and humble cabins. Over this fire hung the "common kettle," lately redolent with savory odors of venison and wild fowl, but now relegated to its original uses, the boiling of barley in the grain. Of this only a small portion remained. Captain Smith had carefully laid up some of the autumn's plenty, and "the idlers had as carelessly wasted it." Finding upon measurement that only "fourteen days victuals were left' he sallied forth to tempt the Tappahannocks to trade, sending Captain Martin to the nation of the Paspaheghs on a similar errand.

They found the Indians of those tribe's sulky and reluctant, at that scarce season, to part with their provisions, but they managed to secure from kindlier sources seven hogsheads of corn.

The "idlers" now began to murmur because no effort had been made to explore the country; and complained that the royal order to go in search of the "South Sea", that sea which was to open to them the riches of the East, had not been obeyed. The great sea perhaps lay not far distant. Communication with it would be found, they had heard, through some river running from the northwest. There was the Chickahominy flowing in that direction, why was this river not explored?

The frost and snow had already come. The birds had long ago sought a warmer climate, and the fish would soon be locked in the icebound streams. They dared not wander far from the fort, not even to track the deer or capture the wild-fowl that abound in winter upon the Virginia marshes. More than one of their number had ventured only a short distance away, and been shot full of arrows.

Wherever there was a tangle of grass, or of thick-growing reeds, there would some savage lie in hiding with his evil eye upon the hated white man.

Newport's arrival was a great relief to the disheartened colony. However, the first settlers must have regarded Newport's addition to their number with dismay. There were a *few "labourers," a great many "gentlemen." A jeweller, a perfumer, two refiners, two goldsmiths, and a pipemaker.* These men were sent out to help subdue the wilderness, according to the Virginia Company council. There was not one soldier to aid in protecting the colony against an army of savages- yet there were six tailors. These professors of the fine arts were evidently intended for the service of the "gentlemen."

For a colony that was already starving, and had too many *gentleman*, men that had no idea how to build a sturdy shelter, or plow the ground, you can only imagine how the colonists felt about these new arrivals.

Newport had brought stirring news, and we can imagine the eagerness with which the homesick exiles listened. He had left England with two vessels, but the Phoenix, well equipped with men and supplies, had been separated from his ship in a storm, and he had reason to fear she was lost. He could report the disappointment of the Virginia Company at the failure of the gold test, and their discontent that no immediate return of value seemed likely to reward and reimburse them for all they had adventured. Surely Newport had tarried in Virginia long enough to bring home some treasure, some news of Raleigh's lost colony, or some hope of finding the South Sea.

His Majesty's subjects in the rich new land had evidently been remiss. Of course, letters were received by Percy, Master Hunt, and the "better class." Percy learned that his noble brother, the Duke of Northumberland, was still with Sir Walter Raleigh, confined in the Tower, and that London's learned and scientific men knocked thither to be entertained by them. Will Shakespeare had written a new play, *King Lear*, and although the distinguished prisoners were not allowed to join the ardent crowds at the Globe and Blackfriars, they could read and enjoy the great master as well perhaps in their comfortable apartments in the Tower, as in the *dingy pit under the smoking flambeaux.*

John Smith was especially interested, as his own fatal tragedies he once complained, had been acted on the stage. But the cream of Newport's news was the London gossip. What story could he tell of the court? Was peace concluded with Spain? Was the Guy Fawkes conspiracy forgotten? How did the new King promise, and what nobleman was now in power? The answer to the latter was interesting. A young Scotchman had broken one of his legs at a tilting in the King's presence, and had, with this unfair starting, won more than halfway in the race to royal favor. In one hour, he had found all that is meant by the magic word *favourite.* He was poor, even beyond the limits of Scotch poverty, but he was straight limbed, well-favored, strong-shouldered, and smooth-faced, with some sort of cunning and show of modesty. The King *adored* him, loaded him with jewels and fair raiment, and conferred upon him the honour of knighthood.

People predicted, correctly, that Sir Robert Carr would rise to be a peer of the realm. The highest dignitaries, Cecil, Suffolk, and all, vied with each other which should most engage his favour.

When Lady Raleigh was on her knees, and begged her King not to take her captive husband's estate from her children, he replied, *"I mun have the land! I mun have it for Carr!"*

As to the King, he was continuing to lead a life of indolence and ease, hunting much of the time, and lying in bed the greater part of the day when he had no amusement on hand. His subjects could but rarely gain access to him. They lay in wait for him whenever he stirred abroad, and thrust their "suffixations" into his unwilling hands, to be stuffed unread into convenient pockets. He went so far as to say he would rather return to Scotland than be chained to the Council table.

He dressed in fantastic colors and wore a horn instead of a sword at his side. His queen, however, covered her plain person with jewels and behaved with no more personal dignity than her husband. They were both extravagant beyond precedent, squandering great sums upon their favorites and their own pleasures, and always in want of money. Of course, the king was cordially hated by all except his sycophants and men like himself.

His perpetual refrain was, "I am the King! My subjects must honour and fear me." Your Queen Elizabeth, said Lord Howard, writing to Harrington, did talk of her subjects' love and affection, and in good truth she aimed well: our King talketh of his subjects fear and subjection, and herein I think he doth well too, as long as it holdeth good, all of which seemed a fantastic fairy tale to his Majesty's starving exiles in Virginia.

Some of them, George Percy for example, felt the pressure of 'sorrow's crown of sorrow', remembering happier things, but there were others, always present in the colony, and little better than cutthroats, who exulted in the royal example, and who revelled in the license and freedom of the remote province, safe from swift chastisement at the strong hands of the English law. For these, strong hands, cruel hands, were sent out later.

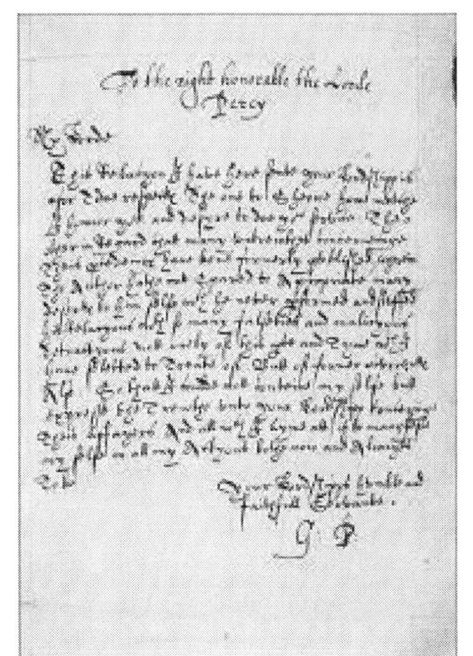

To the right honorable the Lorde Percy

My Lorde

[illegible]

Your Lordships humble and faithfull Servante.

G P

At present, however, the coming of Captain Newport was the occasion of feasting, trading with the sailors, and a general relaxation from all labour.

Powhatan soon heard of Newport's arrival, and sent a present, with an invitation to Werowocomoco. Newport returned his courtesy with presents, and began to prepare the pinnace to visit him.

He was accompanied by Captain Smith and Master Scrivener, a very wise, understanding gentleman, newly arrived and admitted to the Counsell, and thirty or forty chosen men for their guard. But when they reached the point on York River nearest the residence of Powhatan, a wholesome fear of that potentate seized Newport. Would the savage king keep faith?

How about ambuscades, arrows, and tomahawks? What was the meaning of the traplike contrivances over the small streams that must be crossed before audience could be had of the monarch? Newport shook his head, and finally Smith, who feared nothing, dead or living, volunteered, with twenty men, to go ahead and *encounter the worst that can happen.*

To this Newport gladly consented, and while he remained beyond range of arrow-shot in the pinnace with half the escort, Smith set out with his *twenty shot, armed in Jacks*, i.e. quilted jackets then in use which afforded partial protection against Indian arrows. A novel way to accept a house-party invitation to a palace.

Powhatan received Smith with a great show of rejoicing and state. He had much to say to his former captive. "Where is your father [Newport], and where are the guns and grindstone you promised?" Satisfactory answers being ready for these questions, he proceeded to promise Smith corn, wives, and land, provided the twenty men then present would lay their arms at his feet, as did his subjects. "I told him," said the Captain, "that was a ceremonie our enemies desired, but never our friends," so that request, which was to be made perpetually afterwards, was waived for the present.

And now a new disaster awaited our unhappy colonists. I like the temperate, homely words of the old writers, Anas Todkill, William Phetiplace, and others, and I shall again borrow them. "Wee returned to the Fort where this new supply being lodged with the rest, accidentally fired the quarters; and so the Towne, which being but thatched with Reeds, the fire was so fierce as it burnt our Pallizadoes, though ten or twelve yards distant, with all our Arms, Bedding, Apparel, and much private provision.

Good Master Hunt, our Preacher, lost all his Librarie, and all that he had (but the clothes on his back), yet none ever saw him repine at his loss. Upon any alarm, he would be as ready for defense as any; and till he could speak he never ceased to his utmost to animate us constantly to persist: whose soule questionlesse is with God.

Newport remained fourteen weeks at Jamestown. He should have left in fourteen days. Newport's crew again consumed supplies which had been provided for the colony. But a small stream of water issuing from a bank near Jamestown was found to deposit in its channel a glittering sediment which resembled golden ore. The depositation of this yellow stuff was supposed to indicate the presence of a gold mine, and presto, all the little world except Captain Smith went crazy!

The axe was left in the tree, the spade in the corn-hill. There was no more thought of tilling or planting or building. " There was no talke, no hope, no worke, but digge Gold, wash Gold, refine Gold, load Gold; such a bruit of Gold as one mad fellow desired to bee buried in the sand least they should by their art make gold of his bones. Little neede there was and lesse reason the shippe should staye, their wages run on, our victuall consumed," ~These are notes from Samuel Purchas, 'His Pilgrimes," on the opposite page his notes it states, "*Certaine shining yellow sand (I saw it!) with great promises of gold, like the promises yeelding sandy performances."*

Captain Smith set his face like a flint against this gold-fever, which seemed likely to rival Frobisher's experiments and failures in 1577, and declared he was not enamored of the golden promise, nor could he bear to "see necessary business neglected to fraught such a drunken ship with so much gilded dirt." "Till then," continue our historians Anas Todkill, Newport, Percy, and Smith, "we never accounted Captaine Newport a refiner, who being fit to set saile for England, and we not having any use for Parliaments, Playes, Petitions, Admirals, Recorders, Interpreters, Chronologers, Courts of Plea, nor Justices of Peace, sent Master Wingfield and Captaine Archer with him for England, to seeke some place of better imployment." [37]

Newport carried with him twenty turkeys, a present from Powhatan, who received in return twenty swords, the beginning of his acquisition of the arms he so coveted. Newport could hardly have done a more unwise thing. His foolish prodigality prevented all profitable traffic with the Indians thereafter, and he put into their hands the weapons destined to reach the hearts of his own countrymen.

Many of our history has come from writers that lived in Jamestown the first years, and we have no lack of original materials written in the early days. The following chapter is as close to a 'Colonist Diary' as we can hope to find. As with many of the writing in this book, very few spelling, grammer and punctuation changes have been made in order to keep this document as close to original as possible.

1607-1612 The Colonists Diary

This is a historical account written by Captain John Smith and writings from several of the Chief Colonists.

THE PROCEEDINGS OF THE ENGLISH Colony in Virginia, taken faithfully out of the writings of Thomas Studly Cape-merchant, Anas Todkill, Doctor Russell, Nathaniel Powell, William Phetiplace, and Richard Pot, with the laboures of other discreet observers, during their residences.

Proceedings of the English Colonie in Virginia since their first beginning from England in the yeare of our Lord 1606, till this present 1612, with all their accidents that befell them in their journies and discoveries.

Also, the Salvages discourses, orations and relations of the bordering neighbours, and how they became subiect to the English.

Unfolding even the fundamentall causes from whence have sprang so many miseries to the undertakers, and scandals to the business: taken faithfully as they were written out of the writing of Thomas Studley the first prevant maister, Anas Todkill, Walter Russell Doctor of Phisicke, Nathaniell Powell, William Phettyplace. Richard Wiffin, Thomas Abbay, Thomas Hope, Rich Polts and the laboure of many other diligent observers, that were residents in Virginia.

And perused and confirmed by diverse now resident in England that were actors in this busines.
By W. S. AT OXFORD, Printed by Joseph Barnes. 1612.

Long hath the world longed, but to be truely satisfied what Virginia is, with the truth of those proceedings, from whence hath flowne so manie reports of worthy and yet few good effects of the charge, which hath caused suspition in many well wishers that desire yet but to be truely satisfied therein. If any can resolve this doubt it is those that have lived residents in the land: not sailors, or passengers, nor such mercenary contemplators, that only bedeck themselves with others plumes. This discourse is not from such, neither am I the author, for they are many, whose particular discourses are signed by their names. This solid treatise, first was compiled by Richard Pots, since passing the hands of many to peruse, chancing into my hands, (for that I know them honest men, and can partly well witnesses their relations true) I could do no less in charity to the world the reveal, nor in conscience, but approve.

By the advice of many grave and understanding gentlemen, that have pressed it, to the press, it was thought fit to publish it, rather in it own rude phrase then other ways. For that nothing can so purge that famous action from the infamous scandal some ignorantly have conceited, as the plain simple and naked truth. For defect, whereof the business is still suspected, the truth unknown, and the best deservers discouraged, and neglected, some by false reports, others by conjecture, and such power hath flattery to engender of those, hatred and affection, that one is sufficient to beguile more, then 500 can keep from being deceived.

But this discourse is no judge of mens manners, nor catalogue of their former courses; only a reporter of their actions in Virginia, not to disgrace any, accuse any, excuse any, nor flatter any; for which cause there is no wrong done but this, shortness in complaining, & so sparing in commending as only the reader may perceive the truth for his pains, & the action purged of foul slander; it can detract from none that intendeth there to adventure their fortunes; and to speak truly of the first planters, that brake the yee & beat the path, howsoever many difficulties obscured their endeavors, he were worse than the worst of Ingrates, that would not spare them memory that have buried themselves in those foreign regions. From whose first adventures, may spring more good blessings then are yet conceived. So, I rest thine, that will read, peruse, & understand me. If you find false orthography or broken English, they are small faults in soldiers, that not being able to write learnedly, only strive to speak truly, and be understood without an Interpreter.

T. ABBAY.

It might well be thought, a county so faire (as Virginia is) and a people so tractable, would long ere this have been quietly possessed, to the satisfaction of the adventurers, and the eternizing of the memorie of those that affected it. But because all the world doe see a defilement, this following treatise shall give satisfaction to all indifferent readers, how the business hath been carried, where no doubt they will easily understand and answer to their question, how it came to pass there was no better speed and success in those proceedings.

Captaine Bartholomew Gosnold, the first mover of this plantation, having many years solicited many of his friends, but found small assistants; at last prevailed with some Gentlemen, as Mr. Edward-Maria Wingfield, Captain John Smith, and several others who depended a year upon his projects, but nothing could be effected, till by their great charge and industry it came to be apprehended by certain of the Nobility, Gentrie, and Merchants, so that his Maiestie by his letters patents, gave commission for establishing Councels, to direct here, and to govern, and to execute there, to effect this, was spent another yeare, and by that time, three ships were provided, one of 100 Tonns, another of 40, and a Pinnace of 20. The transportation of the company was committed to Captaine Christopher Newport, a Marriner well practised for the westerne parts of America. But their orders for governement were put in a box, not to be opened, nor the governours knowne untill they arived in Virginia.

On the 19 of December, 1606. we set saile, but by unprosperous winds, were kept six weeks in the sight of England; all which time, Mr. Hunt our Preacher, was so weak and sick, that few expected his recovery. Yet although he were but 10 or 12 miles from his habitation (the time we were in the downes) and notwithstanding the stormie weather, nor the scandalous imputations (of some few, little better then Atheists, of the greatest ranke amongst us) suggested against him, all this could never force from him so much as a seeming desire to leave the busines, but preferred the service of God, in so good a voyage, before any affection to contest with his godlesse foes, whose disasterous designes (could they have prevailed) had even then overthrowne the businesse, so many discontents did then arise, had he not with the water of patience, and his godly exhortations (but chiefly by his true devoted examples) quenched those flames of envie, and dissention.

We watered at the Canaries, we traded with the Salvages at Dominica; three weekes we spent in refreshing ourselus amongst these west India Isles; in Gwardalupa we found a bath so hot, as in it we boiled pork as well as over the fire. And at a little Isle called Monica, we tooke from the bushes with our hands, neare two hogshheads full of birds in 3 or 4 houres.

In Mevis, Mona, and the Virgin Isles, we spent some time, where with a lothsome beast like a Crocadile, called a Gwayn, Tortoses, Pellicans, Parrots, & fishes, we daily feasted. Gone from thence in search of Virginia, the company was not a little discomforted, seeing the Marriners had three daies passed their reckoning and found no land, so that Captaine Ratcliffe (Captaine of the Pinnace) rather desired to beare up the helme to returne for England, then make further search. But God the guider of all good actions, forcing tby an extream storme to hull all night, did drive them by his providence to their desired port, beyond all their expectations, for never any of them had seene that coast.

The first land they made they called Cape Henry, where anchoring, Mr Wingfeild, Gosnoll, and Newport, with 30 others, recreating themselves on shore, and were assalted by five Salvages, who hurt two of the English very dangerously. That night was the box opened, and the orders read, in which Barthelomew Gosnoll, Edward Wingfeild, Christopher Newport, John Smith, John Ratliffe, John Martin, and George Kendall, were named to bee the Councell, and to choose a President amongst them for a yeare, who with the Councell should govern.

Matters of moment were to be examined by a Jurie, but determined by the maior part of the Councell in which the Precedent had two voices. Untill the 13th of May they sought a place to plant in, then the Councell was sworne, M. Wingfeild was chosen Precident, & an oration made, while Captaine Smith was not admitted of the Councell as the rest.

Now falleth every man to worke, the Councell contriue the Fort, the rest cut downe trees to make place to pitch their tents. Some provide clapbord to relade the ships, some make gardens, some nets, and The Salvages often visited us kindly.

The Precidents overweening jealousie would admit no exerocise at armes, or fortification, but the boughs of trees cast together in the forme of a halfe moone by the extraordinary paines and diligence of

Captaine Kendall, Newport, with Smith, and twenty others, who were sent to discover the head of the river: by divers small habitations they passed, in six daies they arrived at a towne called Powhatan, consisting of some twelve houses pleasantly seatte down a hill; before it three fertil Isles, about it many of their cornefields, the place is very pleasant, and strong by nature, of this place the Prince is called Powhatan, and his people Powhatans, to this place the river is navigable, but higher within a mile, by reason of the Rockes and Isles, there is not passage for a smal boate, this they call the Falles, the people in all parts kindly intreated them, til being returned within twenty miles of Jamestowne.

They gave just cause of jealousie, but had God not blessed the discoverers otherwise then those at the fort, there had then beene an end of that plantation; for at the fort, where they arived the next day, they found seventeen men hurt, and a boy slaine by the Salvages, and had it not chanced a crosse barre shot from the ships strooke down a bough from a tree amongst them that caused them to retire, our men had all been slaine, being securely all at worke, and their armes in drie fats.

Hereupon the President was contented the Fort should be pallisadoed, the ordinance mounted, his mē armed and exercised, for many were the assaults, and Ambuscadoes of the Salvages, and our men by their disorderly stragling were often hurt, when the Salvages by the nimblenesse of their heeles well escaped. What toile wee had, with so small a power to guard, we worked daies, and watch al night, to resist our enimies and effect our businesse, to relade the ships, cut downe trees, and prepare the ground to plant our corne.

I referre to the readers' consideration. Six weekes being spent in this manner, Captaine Newport (who was hited only for our transportation) was to return with the ships, now Captaine Smith, who all this time from their departure from the Canaries was restrained as a prisoner upon the scandalous suggestions of some of the chiefe envying his repute) who fained he intended to usurpe the governement, murder the Councell, and make himselfe king, that his confederats were dispearsed in all the three ships, and that divers of his confederats that revealed it, would affirme it, for this he was committed, thirteen weekes he remained thus suspected, and by that time the ships should returne they pretended out of their commisserations, to referre him to the Councell in England to receave a check, rather then by particulating his designes make him so odious to the world, as to touch his life, or utterly overthrowe his reputation; but he much scorned their charitie, and publikely defied the uttermost of their crueltie, hee wisely prevented their pollicies, though he could not suppresse their envies, yet so well he demeaned himselfe in this business, as all the company did see his innocencie, & his adversaries malice, and those suborned to accuse him, accused his accusers of subornation; many untruthes were alleaged against him; but being so apparently disproved begat a generall hatred in the harts of the company against such unjust commanders; many were the mischiefes that daily sprung from their ignorant (yet ambitious) spirits; but the good doctrine and exhortation of our preacher Mr Hunt reconciled them, and caused Captaine Smith to be admitted of the Councell.

The next day all receaved the Communion, the day following the Salvages voluntarily desired peace, and Captaine Newport returned for England with newes; leaving in Virginia the 15th of June 1607.

The names of them that were the first planters, were these following.

Mr. Edward Maria Wingfield
Captain Bartholomew Gosnold
Cap. John Smyth
Cap. John Ratliffe
Cap. John Martin
Cap. George Kendall
Mr. Robert Hunt Preacher
Mr. George Percy
Anthony Gosnold
Cap. Gabriell Archer
Robert Ford
William Bruster
Dru Pickhouse
John Brookes
Francis Snarsbrough
Edward Brookes
Richard Dixon
Thomas Sands
John Robinson
Ustis Clovill
Kellam Throgmorton
Nathaniell Powell
Robert Behethland
Jeremy Alicock
Thomas Studley
Richard Croft
Nicholas Houlgrave
Thomas Webbe
John Waller
William Tankard
Thomas Couper, Barber
John Herd, Brick layer
William Garret, Bricklayer
Edward Brinto, Mason

John Martin
George Martin
Anthony Gosnold* listed twice
Thomas Wotton
Thomas Gore
Francis Midwinter
William Laxon
Edward Pising
Thomas Emry
Robert Small
John Capper
Anas Todkill
James Read, Blacksmith
Jonas Profit, Sailer
James Brumfield
Rich Mutton
William Love, Taylor
Nicholas Skot, Drum
John Laydon
William Cassen
George Cassen
Thomas Cassen
William Rods
William White
Ould Edward
Henry Tavin
George Golding
John Dods
William Johnson
William Unger
William Wilkinson. Surgeon
Nathanial Pecock
Samuell Collier

*Complete passenger lists are listed under documents.

What happened till the first supply.

Being thus left to our fortunes, it fortuned that within tennedaies scarse ten amongst us coulde either goe, or well stand, such extreame weaknes and sicknes oppressed us. And thereat none need morvaile, if they consider the cause and reason, which was this; whilest the ships staied, our allowance was somewhat bettered, by a daily proportion of bisket which the sailers would pilser to sell, give or exchange with us, for mony, saxesras, surres, or love. But when they departed, there remained neither taverne, beere-house nor place of relife but the common kettell.

Had we beene as free from all sinnes as gluttony, and drunkennes, we might have bin canonized for Saints; But our President would never have bin admitted, for ingrossing to his private, otemeale, sacke, oile, aquavitae, beefe eggs, or what not, but the kettel; that indeede he allowed equally to be distributed, and that was halfe a pinte of wheat and as much barly boyled with water for a man a day, and this having fryed some 26 weeks in the ships-hold, contained as many wormes as graines; so that we might truely call it rather so much bran then corne, our drinke was water, our lodgings castles in aire, with this lodging and diet, our extreame toile in bearing and planting pallisadoes, so strained and bruised us, and our continuall labour in the extremity of the heate had so weakned us, as were cause sufficient to have made us as miserable in our native counry, or any other place in the world.

From May to September, those that escaped; lived upon Sturgion, and sea-Crabs, 50 in this time we buried, The rest seeing the Presidents projects to escape these miseries in our Pinnas by flight (who all this time had neither felt want nor sickness) so moved our dead spirits, as we deposed him; and established Ratcliffe in his place, (Gosnoll being dead) Kendall deposed, Smith newly recovered, Martin and Ratliffe was by his care preserved and relieved, but now was all our provision spent, the Sturgeon gone, all helps abandoned each houre expecting the fury of the Salvages; when God the patron of all good indeavours in that desperate extreamity so changed the harts of the Salvages, that they brought such plenty of their fruits, and provision as no man wanted.

And now where some affirmed it was ill done of the Council to send forth men so badly provided, this incontradictable reason will shew them plainely they are too ill advised to nourish such ill conceipts; first the fault of our going was our owne, what coulde bee thought fitting or necessary wee had, but what wee should finde, what we should want, where we shoulde be, we were all ignorant, and supposing to make our passage in two monthes, with victuall to liue, and the advantage of the spring to worke; we were at sea five monthes where we both spent our victuall & lost the opportunity of the time, and season to plant.

Such actions have ever since the worlds beginning beene subject to such accidents, and every thing of worth is found full of difficulties, but nothing so difficult as to establish a common wealth so farre remote from men and meanes, and where mens mindes are so untoward as neither do well themselves nor suffer others; but to proceed.

The new President, and Martin, being little beloved; of weake judgement in dangers, and lesse industry in peace, comitted the managing of all things abroad to captaine Smith: who by his owne example, good words, and faire promises, set some to mow, others to binde thatch, some to build houses, others to thatch them, himselfe alwaies bearing the greatest taske for his own share, so that in short time, he provided most of them lodgings neglecting any for himselfe. This done, and seeing the Salvages superfluity beginne to decrease (with some of his workemen) shipped himselfe in the shallop to search the country for trade, the way of the language, knowledge to manage his boat with out sailers, the want of a sufficient power, (knowing the multitude of the Salvages) apparell for his men, & other necessaries, were infinite impediments, yet no discouragement. Being but six or seven in company he went down the river to Kecoughtan, where at first they scorned him, as a starved man, yet he so dealt with them, that the next day they loaded his boat with corne, & in his returne he discovered & kindly traded with the Weraskoyks. In the meane time those at the fort so glutted the Salvages with their commodities as they became not regarded.

Smith perceiving (notwithstanding their late miserie) not any regarded but from hand to mouth, (the company being well recovered) caused the Pinas to bee provided with things fitting to get provision for the yeare following; but in the interim he made three or four journies and discovered the people of Chickahamine, yet what he carefully provided the rest carelesly spent.

Wingfield and Kendall living in disgrace, and seeing althings at randome in the absence of Smith, the companies dislike of their Presidents weaknes, & their small love to Martins never-mending sickness, strengthened themselves with the sailers, and other confederates to regaine their former credit & authority, or at least such meanes abord the Pinas, (being fitted to saile as Smith had appointed for trade) to alter her course and to go for England.

Smith unexpectedly returning had the plot discovered to him, and much trouble he had to prevent it till with store of falcon and musket shot he forced them stay or sinke in the rivers, which action cost the life of captaine Kendall. These brawles are so disgustfull, as some will say they were better forgotten, yet all men of good judgement will conclude, it were better their baseness should be manifest to the world, then the business beare the scorne and shame of their excused disorders.

The President and captaine Archer not long after intended also to have abandoned the country, which project also was curbed, and suppressed by Smith. The Spanyard never more greedily desired gold then he victuall, which finding so plentiful in the river of Chickahamine, where hundreds of Salvages in divers places stood with baskets expecting his coming.

And now the winter approaching, the rivers be came so covered with swans, geese, duckes, & cranes, that we daily feasted with good bread, Virginia pease, pumpions, and putchamins, fish, sowle, and diverse sorts of wild beasts as fat as we could eat them: so that none of our Tustaffaty humorists desired to goe for England. But our comaedies never endured log without a tragedie; so idle exceptions being muttered against Captaine Smith, for not discovering the head of Chickahamine river, and taxed by the Councell, to bee too slow in so worthie an attempt.

The next voyage hee proceeded so farre that with much labour by cutting of trees in sunder he made his passage, but when his Barge could passe no farther, he left her in a broad bay out of danger of shot, commanding none should goe ashore till his returne, himselfe with two English & two Salvages went up higher in a Canowe, but hee was not long absent, but his men went ashore, whose want of government, gave both occasion and opportunity to the Salvages to surprise one George Casson, & much failed not to have cut of the boat & all the rest. Smith little dreaming of that accident, being got to the marshes at the rivers head, twenty myles in the desert, had his two men slaine (as is supposed) sleeping by the Canowe, whilst himselfe by fowling sought them victuall, who finding he was beset with 200 Salvages, two of them hee slew, still defending himselfe with the aid of a Salvage his guide, (whome hee bound to his arme and used as his buckler, till at last slipping into a bogmire they tooke him prisoner.

When this newes came to the fort much was their sorrow for his losse, fewe expecting what ensued. A month those barbarians kept him prisoner, many strange triumphes and coniurations they made of him, yet hee so demeaned himselfe amongst them, as he not only diverted them from surprising the fort, but procured his owne liberty, and got himselfe and his company such estimation amongst them, that those Salvages admired him as a demi God. So returning safe to the Fort, once more staied the Pinnas her flight for England, which till his returne, could not set saile, so extreame was the weather, and so great the frost.

His relation of the plentie he had seene, especially at Werowocomoco, where inhabited Powhatan (that till that time was unknowne) so revived againe their dead spirits as all mens feare was abandoned, Powhatan having sent with this Captaine divers of his men loaded with provision, he had conditioned, & so appointed his trustie messengers to bring but two or three of our great ordenances, but the messengers being satisfied with the sight of one of the discharged, ran away amazed with feare, till meanes was used with gifts to assure them our loves.

Thus, you may see what difficulties still crossed any good indeavour, and the good successe of the businesse, and being thus oft brought to the very period of destruction, yet you see by what strange meanes God hath still delivered it. As for the insufficiencie of them admitted in commission, that errour could not be prevented by their electors, there being no other choice, and all were strangers each to others education, quallities, or disposition; & if any deeme it a shame to our nation, to have any mention made of these enormities, let them peruse the histories of the Spanish discoveries and plantations, where they may see how many mutinies, discords, and dissentions, have accompanied them and crossed their attempts, which being knowne to be particular mens offences, doth take away the generall scorne and contempt, mallice, and ignorance might else produce, to the scandall and reproach of those, whose actions and valiant resolution deserue a worthie respect.

Now whether it had beene better for Captaine Smith to have concluded with any of their severall proiects to have abandoned the Countrie with some ten or twelve of them we cal the better sort, to have left Mr Hunt our preacher, Mr. Anthony Gosnoll, a most honest, worthie, and industrious gentleman, with some 30 or 40 others his countrie men, to the furie of the Salvages, famine, and all manner of mischiefs and inconveniences, or starved himselfe with them for company, for want of lodging, or but adventuring abroad to make them provision, or by his opposition, to preserve the action, and save all their lives, I leave to the censure of others to consider.

Thomas Studley.

The arrivall of the first supply with their proceedings and returne.

ALL this time our cares were not so much to abandon the Countrie, but the Treasurer & Councell in England were as diligent and carefull to supplie us. Two tall ships they sent us, with neere 100 men, well furnished with all things could be imagined necessarie, both for them and us. The one commanded by Captaine Newport: the other by Captaine Nelson, an honest man and an expert marriner, but such was the leewardnesse of his ship, (that though he were within sight of Cape Henry) by stormy contrarie windes, was forced so farre to sea, as the West Indies was the next land for the repaire of his Masts, and reliefe of wood and water. But Captaine Newport got in, and arived at Iames towne, not long after the redemption of Captaine Smith, to whome the Salvages every other day brought such plentie of bread, fish, turkies, squirrels, deare, & other wild beasts, part they gave him as presents from the king; the rest, hee as their market clarke set the price how they should sell.

So he had inchanted those poore soules (being their prisoner) in demonstrating unto them the roundnesse of the world, the course of the moone and starres, the cause of the day and night the largenes of the seas the quallities of our ships, shot and powder, The devision of the world, with the diversity of people, their complexions, customes and conditions. All which hee fained to be under the command of Captaine Newport, whom he tearmed to them his father; of whose arri|val, it chanced he so directly prophecied, as they esteemed him an oracle; by these fictions he not only saved his owne life, and obtained his liberty, but had them at that command, he might command them what he listed. That God that created all these things; they knew he adored for his God, whom they would also tearme in their discourses, the God of Captaine Smith.

The President and Councel so much envied his estimation amongst the Salvages (though wee all in generall equally participated with him of the good therof) that it into their understandings, by their great bounty in giving four times more for their commodities then he appointed; that their greatnesse and authority, as much exceed his, as their bounty, and liberality.

Now the arrivall of his first supply, so overjoyed us, that we could not devise too much to please the mariners. We gave them liberty to track or trade at their pleasures. But in a short time, it followed, that could not be had for a pound of copper, which before was sold for an ounce, Thus ambition, and sufferance, cut the throat of our trade, but confirmed their opinion of Newports greatness, (wherewith Smith had possessed Powhatan) especially by the great presents Newport (often sent him, before he could prepare the Pinas to go and visit him; so that this Salvage also desired to see him. A great bruit there was to set him forwarde: when he went, he was accompanied, with captaine Smith & Mr Scrivener a very wise understanding gentleman newly arrived, & admitted of the Councell, and thirty or fourty chosen men for that guarde.

Arriving at Werowocomo Newports concipt of this great Salvage, bred many doubts, and suspitions of treacheries; which Smith, to make appeare was needlesse, which twenty men well appointed, undertooke to encounter (with that number) the worst that could happen, there names were:

Nathaniell Powell, Robert Beheathland, William Phettiplace, Richard Wyffin, Anthony Gosnoll, John Taverner, William Dier, Thomas Coe, Thomas Hope, Anas Todkell with ten others whose names I have forgotten, these being kindly received a shore, with 200 or 300, salvages were conducted to their towne.

Powhatan strained himselfe to the uttermost of his greatness to entertain us, with great shouts of joy, orations of protestations, and the most plenty of victuall hee could provide to feast us. Sitting upon his bed of mats, his pillow of leather imbroydred (after their rude manner) with pearle & white beades, his attire a faire Robe of skins as large as an Irish mantle, at his head and feet a handsome young woman; on each side his house sat twenty of his concubines, their heads and shoulders painted red, with a great chaine of white beads about their necks, before those sate his chiefest men in like order in his arbor-like house.

With many pretty discourses to reunite their olde acquaintaunce; the great king and our captaine spent the time till the ebbe left our barge a ground, then renuing their feasts and mirth we quartred that night with Powhatan.

The next day Newport came a shore, and received as much content as those people could give him, a boy named Thomas Savage was then given unto Powhatan who Newport called his son, for whom

Powhatan gave him Namontacke his trusty servant, and one of a shrewd subtill capacity, three or four daies were spent in feasting, dancing and trading, wherin Powhatan carried himselfe so prowdly, yet discreetly (in his Salvage manner) as made us all admire his natural gifts considering his education, as scorning to trade as his subjects did, he bespake Newport in this manner.

Captain Newport it is not agreeable with my greatness in this pedalling manner to trade for trifles, and I esteem you a great werowans. Therefore, lay me down all your commodities together, what I like I will take, and in recompence give you that I thinke fitting their value. Captaine Smith being our interpreter, regarding Newport as his father, knowing best the disposition of Powhatan told us his intent was but to cheat us; yet captaine Newport thinking to out brave this Salvage in ostentation of greatness & so to bewitch him with his bounty, as to have what he listed, but so it chanced Powhatan having his desire, valued his corne at such a rate, as I thinke it better cheape in Spaine, for we had not four bushels for that we expected twenty hogsheads.

This bred some unkindness betweene our two captaines, Newport seeking to please the humor of the unsatiable Salvage; Smith to cause the Salvage to please him, but smothering his distast (to avoide the Salvages suspition) glaunced in the eyes of Powhatan many Trifles who fixed his humour upon a few blew beads. A long time he importunatly desired them, but Smith seemed so much the more to affect the, so that ere we departed, for a pound or two of blew beads he brought over my king for two or three hundred bushels of corne, yet parted good friends.

The like entertainement we found of Spechanchynough King of Pamaunke whom also he in like manner fitted, (at the like rates) with blew beads: and so we returned to the fort. Where this new supply being lodged with the rest, accidently fired the quarters, and so the Towne, which being but thatched with reeds the fire was so fierce as it burnt their pallizadoes (though 10 or 12 yardes distant) with their armes, bedding, apparell, and much private provision. Good Mr. Hunt our preacher, lost all his library, and all that he had (but the cloathes on his backe,) yet none ever see him repine at his losse.

This hapned in the winter, in that extreame frost, 1607. Now though we had victuall sufficient, I meane only of oatemeale, meale, and corne, yet the ship staying there fourteen weeks when she might as well have been gone in fourteen daies, spent the beefe, porke, oile, aquavitae, fish, butter, and cheese, beere and such like; as was provided to be landed us. When they departed, what their discretion could spare us, to make a feast or two with bisket, pork beefe, fish, and oile, to relish our mouths, of each somwhat they left us, yet I must confest those that had either money, spare clothes, credit to give bills of payment, gold rings, furres, or any such commodities were ever welcome to this removing taverne, such was our patience to obay such vile commanders, and buy our owne provision at fifteen times the valew, suffering the feast (we bearing the charge) yet must not repine, but fast, and then leakage, ship-rats, and other casualties occasioned the losse, but the vessell and remnants (for totals) we were glad to receive with all our hearts to make up the account, highly commending their providence for preserving that.

For all this plentie our ordinarie was but meale and water, so that this great charge little relieved our wants, whereby with the extreamity of the bitter cold aire more then halfe of us died, and tooke our deathes, in that piercing winter I cannot deny, but both Skrivener and Smith did their best to amend what was amisse, but with the Presidents went the maior part, that their hornes were too short.

But the worst mischiefe was, our gilded refiners with their golden promises, made all men their slaues in hope of recompence, there was no talke, no hope, no worke, but dig gold, wash gold, refine gold, load gold, such a brute of gold, as one mad fellow desired to bee buried in the sandes, least they should by their art make gold of his bones, little need there was and lesse reason, the ship should stay, their wages run on, our victuall consume, fourteen weekes, that the Marriners might say, they built such a golden Church, that we can say, the raine washed neare to nothing in fourteen daies.

Were it that Captaine Smith would not applaud all those golden inventions, because they admitted him not to the sight of their trials, nor golden consultations I knowe not; but I heard him question with Captaine Martin and tell him, except he would shew him a more substantiall triall, hee was not inamored with their durtie skill, breathing out these and many other passions, never any thing did more torment him, then to see all necessarie businesse neglected, to fraught such a drunken ship with so much gilded durt; till then wee never accounted Captaine Newport a refiner; who being fit to set saile for England, and wee not having any use of Parliaments, plaies, petitions, admirals, recorders, interpreters, chronologers, courts of plea, nor justices of peace, sent Mr. Wingfield & Captain Archer with him for England to seeke some place of better imploiment.

The arivall of the Phoenix, her returne, and other accidents.

THE authoritie nowe consisting in resining, Captaine Martin and the still sickly President, the sale of the stores commodities maintained their estates as inheritable revenews. The spring approching, and the ship departed, M. Skriuener and Capt. Smith divided betwixt the, and the rebuilding our towne, the repairing our pallisadoes, and the cutting downe trees, preparing our fields, planting our corne, & to rebuild our Church, and recover our store-house. All men were thus busie at their severall labours, M. Nelson arived with his lost Phoenix (lost I say, for that all men deemed him lost) landing safely his men; so well hee had mannaged his ill hap, causing the Indian Isles to feed his company that his victuall (to that was left us before) was sufficient for halfe a yeare, he had nothing but he freely imparted it, which honest dealing (being a marriner) caused us admire him, wee would not have wished so much as he did for us.

Nowe to relade this ship with some good tidings. The President (yet notwithstanding with his dignitie to leaue the sort) gave order to Captaine Smith and M. Skriuener to discover & search the commodities of Monacans countrie beyound the Falles. Sixty able men was allotted their number, which within six daies exercised, Smith had so well trained to their armes and orders, that they little feared with whome they should encounter. Yet so unseasonable was the time, and so opposite was Capt. Martin to every thing, but only to fraught his ship also with his phantasticall gold, as Captaine Smith rather desired to relade her with Cedar, which was a present dispatch; then either with durt, or the reports of an uncertaine discoverie. Whilst their conclusion was resolving, this happened.

Powhatan to expresse his love to Newport, when he departed, presented him with twenty Turkies, conditionally to returne him twenty swords, which immediatly were sent him. Now after his departure hee presented Captaine Smith with the like luggage, but not finding his humor, obaied in sending him weapons he caused his people with twenty devises to obtain them, at last by ambuseadoes at our very ports they would take them per force, surprise us at work, or any way, which was so long permitted that they became so insolent, there was no rule, the command from England was so straight not to offend thee as our authority bearers (keeping their houses) would rather be any thing thē peace breakers: this charitable humor prevailed, till well it chaunced they medled with captaine Smith, who without farther deliberation gave the such an incounter, as some he so hunted up and downe the Isle, some he so terrified with whipping, beating and imprisonment, as for revenge they surprised two of his forraging disorderly souldiers, and having assembled their forces, boldly threatned at our ports to force Smith to redeliver seven Salvages which for their villanies he detained prisoners, but to try their furies, in lesse then halfe an houre he so hampered their insolencies, that they brought the two prisoners desiring peace without any farther coposition for their prisoners, who being threatned and examined their intents and plotters of their villanies confessed they were directed only by Powhatan, to obtaine him our owne weapons to cut our own throats, with the manner how, where, and when, which wee plainely found most true and apparent.

He sent his messengers and his dearest Daughter Pocahuntas to excuse him, of the iniuries done by his subiects, desiring their liberties, with the assuraunce of his love, after Smith had given the prisoners what correction hee thought fit, used them well a day or two after, & then delivered the Pochahantus, for whose sake only he fained to save their lives and graunt them liberty. The patient councel, that nothing would move to warre with the Salvages, would gladly have wrangled with captaine Smith for his cruelty, yet none was slaine to any mans knowledge but it brought them in such feare & obedience, as his very name wold, sufficiently affright them.

The fraught of this ship being concluded to be cedar, by the diligence of the Master, and Captaine Smith shee was quickly reladed; Mr Scrivener was neither Idle nor slow to follow all things at the fort, the ship falling to the Cedar Isle, captaine Martin having made shift to be sicke neare a yeare, and now, neither pepper, suger, cloves, mace, ginger nor sweet meates in the country (to enjoy the credit of his supposed art) at his earnest request, was most willingly admitted to returne for England. Yet having beene there but a yeare, and not past halfe a year since the ague left him (that he might say somewhat he had seene) hee went twice by water to Paspahegh a place neere seven miles from Jamestowne, but lest the dew should distemper him, was ever forced to returne before night. Thus much I thought fit to expresse, he expresly commanding me to record his journies, I being his man, and he sometimes my master.

Thomas Studly.
Anas Todkill.
Their names that were landed in this supply:

Abots Jefrey
Alberton Robert, Perfumer
Barnes Robert
Bayley William
Beckwith William, Tailor
Belfield Richard, Refiner
Bentley William, Laborer
Bouth John, Laborer
Brislow Richard, Laborer
Burket William, Laborer
Burne James
Cantrill William
Causey William
Coo Thomas
Cotton Robert, Tobacco-pipe-maker
Cutler Robert
Dawson William, Refiner
Dole Richard, Blacksmith
Feld Thomas ,Apothecary
Fetherstone Richard
Forest George
Gittnat Post, Surgeon
Goodyson Raymond, Laborer
Gradon Richard, Laborer
Gryvill William
Gurganay Edward
Miler Richard, Laborer
Molynex Richard
Morton Ralfe
Nelstrop Rowland, Laborer
Nickoles John
Perce William, Laborer
Perkins Francis, Laborer
Phetyplace Michaell
Phetyplace William
Pory Peter
Pots Richard
Powell John, Tailor
Pretty George
Prodger Richard
Ransacke Abraham, Refiner
Rodes Christopher
Russell Doctor
Salvage Richard, Laborer
Salvage Thomas, Laborer
Scrivner, Matthew Council, (drowned in James River Jan 1609)
Sickelmore Michaell
Simons William, Laborer
Speareman John, Laborer
Spence William, Laborer
Stalling Daniell, jeweler
Taverner John

Harford John, Apothecary
Harper John
Hill George
Hope, Thomas Tailor
Johnson William, Refiner
Keffer Peter, Gunner
Killingbeck Richard
Leds Timothy
Lewes John, Couper
May William, Laborer
Towtales Laurence,Tailor
Ven Nicholas, Laborer
Vere Unknown, Laborer
Ward William, Tailor
Watkings James
Worley Richard
Wyffin Richard
Wyles Bishop, Laborer
Yonge William, Tailor
Unknown Michaell, Laborer

*The first supply consisted of two ships, the first was the John and Francis, and the Phoenix. The John and Francis with Captain Christopher Newport left London October 4, 1607, Gravesend October 18th, along with the Phoenix and Captain Francis Nelson in consort, they waited for the winds until November 2 at Falmouth. Reaching Santo Domingo on Dec 9th, Captain Newport reports he lost sight of the Phoenix with her 40 men in a fog. Newport reached Jamestown Saturday evening, Jan 12th. All had thought the Phoenix was lost. Out of the 120 settlers on the two ships, only 100 reached Virginia. The Phoenix arrived some time after the John and Francis. The John and Francis would return to England April 10, 1608, carrying Edward Wingfield, Archer, an Irishman named Francis McGuire, and an Indian, Namontack, arriving in England May 31st.. The Phoenix finally arrived April 20th having wintered over in the West Indies, then left Virginia June 12, 1608 with Captain Nelson and Captain John Martin.

The accidents that happened in the Discoverie of the bay.

The prodigality of the Presidents state went so deepe in the store that Smith and Scrivener had a while tyed both Martin & him to the rules of proportion, but now Smith being to depart, the Presidents authoritie so overswayed Mr Scriveners discretion as our store, our time, our strength and labours was idlely consumed to fulfill his phantasies. The second of June 1608. Smith left the fort to performe his discoverie; with this company.

Walter Russell Doctour of Physicke, Ralph Morton, Thomas Momford, William Cantrill, Richard Fetherstone, James Bourne Michael Sicklemore, Anas Toakill, Robert Small, James Watkins, John Powell, Sould, James Read, Richard Keale, and Jonas Profit

These being in an open barge of two tunnes burthen leaving the Phenix at Cape-Henry we crossed the bay to the Easterne shore & fell with the Isles called Smiths Isles.

The first people we saw were two grimme and stout Salvages upon Cape-Charles with long poles like javelings, headed with bone, they boldly demanded what we were, and what we would, but after many circumstances, they in time seemed very kinde, and directed us to Acawmacke the habitation of the we rowans where we were kindly intreated this king was the comliest proper civill Salvage wee incountred: his country is a pleasant fertill clay-soile.

Hee tolde us of a strange accident lately happened him, and it was two dead children by the extreame passions of their parents, or some dreaming visions, phantasie, or affection moved the againe to revisit their dead carcasses, whose behummed bodies reflected to the eyes of the beholders such pleasant delightfull countenances, as though they had regained their vital spirits. This as a miracle drew many to behold them, all which, (being a great part of his people) not long after died, and not any one escaped.

They spake the language of Powhatan wherein they made such descriptions of the bay, Isles, and rivers that often did us exceeding pleasure. Passing along the coast, searching every inlet, and bay fit for harbours & habitations seeing many Isles in the midst of the bay, we bore up for them, but ere wee could attaine them such an extreame gust of wind, raine, thunder, and lightning happened, that with great daunger we escaped the vnmercifull raging of that ocean-like water. The next day searching those inhabitable Isles (which we called Russels Isles) to provide fresh water, the defect whereof forced us to follow the next Easterne channell, which brought us to the river Wighcocomoco, the people at first with great furie, seemed to assault us, yet at last with songs, daunces, and much mirth, became very tractable, but searching their habitations for water, wee could fill but three, and that such puddle that never til then, wee ever knew the want of good water, we digged and searched many places but ere the end of two daies wee would have refused two barricoes of gold for one of that puddle water of Wighcocomoco.

Being past these Isles, falling with a high land upon the maine wee found a great pond of fresh water, but so exceeding hot, that we supposed it some bath: that place we called Point ployer, being thus refreshed in crossing over from the maine to other Isles, the wind and waters so much increased with thunder, lightning, and raine, that our fore-mast blew overbord and such mightie waves overwrought us in that small barge, that with great labour wee kept her from sinking by freeing out the water, two days we were inforced to inhabit these uninhabited Isles, which for the extremitie of gusts, thunder, raine, stormes, and ill weather we called Limbo.

Repairing our fore saile with our shirts, we set saile for the maine and fell with a faire river on the East called Kuskaranaocke, by it inhabit the people of Soraphanigh, Nause, Arsek, and Nauta quake that much extolled a great nation called Massawomekes, in search of whome wee returned by Limbo, but finding this easterne shore shallow broken Isles, and the maine for most part without fresh water, we passed by the straights of Limbo for the weasterne shore so broad is the bay here, that we could scarse perceiue the great high cliffs on the other side, by them wee ancored that night, and called them Richards Cliffes.

Thirty leagues we sailed more Northwards, not finding any inhabitants, yet the coast well watred, the mountaines very bar, the vallies very fertil, but the woods extreame thicke, full of wolves, beares, deare, and other wild beasts. The first inlet we found, wee called Bolus, for that the clay (in many places) was like (if not) Bole-Armoniacke: when we first set saile, some of our gallants doubted nothing, but that our Captaine would make too much hast home; but hauing lien not above twelve daies in this smal Barge, oft tired at their oares, their bread spoiled with wet, so much that it was rotten (yet so good were their stomacks that they could digest it) did with continuall complaints so importune him now to returne, as caused him bespeake them in this manner.

Gentlemen if you would remember the memorable historie of Sir Ralfe Lane, how his company importuned him to proceed in the discoverie of Morattico, alleaging, they had yet a dog, that being boyled with Saxafras leaves, would richly feed them in their returnes; what a shame would it be for you (that have beene so suspitious of my tendernesse) to force me returne with a months provision scarce able to say where we have been, nor yet heard of that wee were sent to seeke. You cannot say but I have shared with you of the worst is past; and for what is to come of lodging, diet, or whatsoever, I am contented you allot the worst part to my selfe; as for your feares, that I will lose my selfe in these unknowne large waters, or be swallowed up in some stormie gust, abandon those childish feares, for worse then is past cannot happen, and there is as much danger to returne, as to proceed forward.

Regaine therefore your old spirits; for return I will not, (if God assist me) til I have seene the Massawomekes, found Patawomeck, or the head of this great water you conceit to be endlesse three or four days wee expected wind and weather, whose adverse extreamities added such discouragements to our discontents as three or four fell extreame sicke, whose pittiful complaints caused us to returne, leaving the bay some ten miles broad at nine or ten fathom water.

The 16th of June we fell with the river of Patawomeck: feare being gone, and our men recovered, wee were all contented to take some paines to knowe the name of this nine mile broad river, we could see no inhabitants for thirty myles saile; then we were conducted by two Salvages up a little bayed creeke toward Onawmament where all the woods were laid with Ambuscadoes to the number of 3 or 400 Salvages, but so strangely painted, grimed, and disguised, showting, yelling, and crying, as we rather supposed them so many devels, they made many bravadoes, but to appease their furie, our Captaine prepared with a seeming willingnesse (as they) to encounter them. The grazing of the bullets upon the river, with the echo of the woods so amazed them, as down went their bowes & arrowes; (and exchanging hostage) James Watkins was sent six myles up the woods to their kings habitation: wee were kindly used by these Salvages, of whome wee understood, they were commaunded to betray us, by Powhatans direction, and hee so directed from the discontents of Jamestowne.

The like incounters we found at Patawomeck Cecocawone and divers other places, but at Moyaones Nacothtant and Taux, the people did their best to content us. The cause of this discovery, was to search a glistering metal, the Salvages told us they had from Patawomeck, (the which Newport assured that he had tryed to hold halfe silver) also to search what furres, metals, rivers, rockes, nations, woods, fishings, fruits, victuals and other commodities the land afforded, and whether the bay were endlesse, or how farre it extended. The mine we found nine or ten myles up in the country from the river, but it proved of no value.

Some otters, beavers, martins, luswarts, and sables we found, and in diverse places that abundance of fish lying so thicke with their heads above the water, as for want of nets (our barge driving amongst them) we attempted to catch them with a frying pan, but we found it a bad instrument to catch fish with. Neither better fish more plenty or varity had any of us ever seene, in any place swimming in the water, then in the bay of Chesapeack, but there not to be caught with frying-pans. To expresse all our quarrels, treacheries & incounters amongst those Salvages, I should be too tedious. But in briefe at all times we so incontered their insolcties, as they concluded with presents to purchase peace, yet wee lost not a man, at our first meeting our captaine ever observed this order to demand their bowes and arrows, swords, mantles or furres, with some child for hostage; wherby he could quickly perceive when they intended any villany.

Having finished this discovery (though our victuall was neare spent) he intended to have seene his imprisonments, acquaintance upon the river of Toppahannock. But our boate (by reason of the ebbe) chansing to ground upon a many shoules lying in the entrance, we spied many fishes lurking amongst the weedes on the sands, our captaine sporting himselfe to catch them by nailing the to the ground with his sword, set us all a fishing in that manner, by this devise, we tooke more in an houre then we all could eat; but it chanced, the captaine taking a fish from his sword (not knowing her condition) being much of the fashion of a Thornebacke with a longer taile, whereon is a most poysoned sting of two or three inches long, which shee strooke an inch and halfe into the wrist of his arme the which in four houres had so extreamly swollen his hand, arme, shoulder, and part of his body. With much sorrow we concluded his funerall, and prepared his grave in an Isle hard by (as himself appointed) which then we called stingeray Isle after the name of the fish.

Yet by the helpe of a precious oile Doctour Russels applyed, ete night his tormenting paine was so wel asswaged that he eate the fish to his supper, which gaue no lesse ioy and content to us, then ease to himselfe. Having neither Surgeon nor surgerie but that preservatiue oile, we presently set saile for Jamestowne; passing the mouth of pyankatanck, & Pamaunke rivers, the next day we safely arrived at Kecoughtan.

The simple Salvages, seeing our captaine hurt, and another bloudy (which came by breaking his shin) our number of bowes, arrowes, swords, targets, mantles and furs; would needs imagine we had bin at warres, the truth of these accidents would not satisfie them) but impa|ciently they importuned us to know with whom wee fought, finding their aptnes to beleive, we failed not (as a great secret) to tel them any thing that might affright them what spoile wee had got and made of the Masawomeekes, this rumor went faster up the river our barge; that arrived at weraskoyack the 20th of July, where trimming her with painted streamers, and such devises we made the fort jealous of a Spanish frigot; where we all safely arrived the 21st of July.

There wee found the last supply, all sicke, the rest, some lame, some bruised, al unable to do any thing, but complain of the pride and unreasonable needlesse cruelty of their sillie President, that had riotously consumed the store, and to fulfill his follies about building him an unnecessarie pallace in the woods had brought them all to that miserie. Had not we arrived, they had as strangely tormented him with revenge. But the good newes of our discovery, and the good hope we had (by the Salvages relation) our Bay had stretched to the South-sea, appeased their fury; but conditionally that Ratliffe should be deposed, and that captaine Smith would take upon him the government. Their request being effected, hee substituted Mr Scrivener, his deare friend in the Presidencie, equally distributing those private provisions the other had ingrossed; appointing more honest officers to assist Scrivener, (who then lay extreamelie tormented with a callenture) and in regard of the weakness of the company, and heat of the yeare they being unable to worke; he left them to live at ease, but imbarked himselfe to finish his discovery.

Written by
Walter Russell and
Anas Todkill.

<u>What happened the second voyage to discover the Bay.</u>

THE 20th of July Captaine Smith set forward to finish the discovery with 12 men their names were Nathaniell Powell, Thomas Momford,

Richard Faetherstone, Michaell Sicklemore, James Bourne, Anas

Toakill, Edward Pysing, Richard Keale, Anthony Bagnall, James Watkins, William Ward, Jonas Profit

The winde beeing contrary caused our stay two or three days at Kecoughtan the werowances feasting us with much mitth, his people were perswaded we went purposely to be revenged of the Massawomeckes, in the evening we firing two or three rackets, so testified the poore Salvages, they supposed nothing impossible wee attempted, and desired to assist us.

The first night we ancored at Stingeray Isle, the nexte day crossed Palawomecks river, and hasted for the river Bolus, we went not much farther before wee might perceiueiue the Bay to devide in two heads, and arriving there we founde it and devided in four, all which we searched so far as we could saile them; two of them we found uninhabited, but in crossing the bay to the other, wee incountered seven or eight canoes full of Massawomecks. We seeing them prepare to attack us left our oares & made way with our saile to incounter them.

We were only five (with our captaine) for within a daies after wee left Kecoughtan, the rest (being all of the last supply) were sicke almost to death, (untill they were seasoned to the country) having shut them under our tarpawling, we put their hats upon stickes by the barge side to make us seeme many, and so we thinke the Indians supposed those hats to be men, for they rushed with all possible speed to the shoare, and there stayed, staring at the sailing of our barge, till we anchored right against them.

Long it was ere we could drawe them to come unto us, at last they sent two of their company unarmed in a Conowe, the rest all followed to second them if need required. These a being but each presented with all bell, brought aborde all their fellowes, presenting the captain with venison, beares flesh, fish, bowes, arrows, clubs, targets, and beare skins; wee understood them nothing at all but by signes, whereby they signified to us they had been at warres with the Tockwoghs the which they confirmed by shewing their green woods. The night parting us, we imagined they appointed the next morning to meete, but after that we never saw them.

Entring the River of Tockwogh the Saluages all alarmed in a fleet of boates round invironed us, it chanced one of them could speake the language of Powhatan who perswaded the rest to a friendly parly. When they see us furnished with the Massawomeckes weapons, and we faining the invention of Kecoughtan to have taken them perforce;

they conducted us to their pallizadoed towne, mantelled with the barkes of trees, with scaffolds like mounts, brested about with barks very formally, their men, women, and children, with dances, songs, fruits, fish, furres, and what they had kindly entertained us, spreading mats for us to sit on, stretching their best abilities to expresse their loves.

Many hatchets, knives, & peeces of iron, & brasse, we see, which they reported to have from the Sasquesahanockes a mighty people, and mortall enimies with the Massawomeckes. The Sasquesahanocks, inhabit upon the chiese spring of these four two daies journey higher then our Barge could passe for rocks. Yet we prevailed with the interpreter to take with him another interpreter to perswade the Sasquesahanocks to come to visit us, for their language are different.

Three or four daies we expected their returne then sixty of these giant like people came downe with presents of venison, Tobacco pipes, Baskets, Targets, Bowes and Arrows, five of their Werowances came boldly aboard us, to crosse the bay for Tockwogh, leaving their men and Canowes, the winde being so violent that they durst not passe.

Our order was, dayly to have prayer, with a psalm, at which solemnitie the poore Salvages much wondered. Our prayers being done, they were long busied, with consultation till they had contrived their businesse; then they began in most passionate manner to hold up their hands to the sunne with a most feareful song, then imbracing the Captaine, they began to adore him in like manner, though he rebuked them, yet they proceeded til their song was finished, which don with a most strange furious action, and a hellish voice began an oration of their loves. That ended, with a great painted beares skin they covered our Captaine, then one ready with a chaine of white beads (waighing at least 6 or 7 pound) hung it about his necke, the others had 18 mantles made of divers sorts of skinnes sowed together, all these with many other toyes, they laid at his feet, stroking their ceremonious handes about his necke for his creation to be their governour, promising their aids, victuals, or what they had to bee his, if he would stay with them to defend and revenge them of the Massawomecks.

Wee left them at Tockwogh, they much sorrowing for our departure, yet wee promised the next yeare againe to visit them; many descriptions and discourses they made us of Atquanahucke, Massawomecke, and other people, signifying they inhabit the river of Cannida, and from the French to have their hatchets, and such like tooles by trade, these knowe no more of the territories of Powhatan then his name, and he as little of them.

Thus having sought all the inlets and rivers worth noting, we returned to discover the river of Pawtuxunt, these people we found very tractable, and more civill then any, wee promised them, as also the Patawomecks, the next yeare to revenge them of the Massawomecks.

Our purposes were crossed in the discoverie of the river of Toppahannock, for wee had much wrangling with that peevish nation; but at last they became as tractable as the rest. It is an excellent, pleasant, well inhabited, fertill, and a goodly navigable river, toward the head thereof; it pleased God to take one of our sicke (called M. Fetherstone) where in Fetherstons bay we buried him in the night with a volly of shot; the rest, notwithanding their ill diet, and bad lodging, crowded in so small a barge in so many dangers, never resting, but alwaies tossed to and againe all well recovered their healthes.

Then we discovered the river of Payankatank, and set saile for James Towne; but in crossing the bay in a faire calme, such a suddaine gust surprised us in the night with thunder and raine, as wee were halfe imployed in freeing out water, never thinking to escape drowning yet running before the winde, at last we made land by the flashes of fire from heaven, by which light only we kept from the splitting shore, until it pleased God in that black darknes to preserue us by that light to find Point comfort, and arived safe at James Towne, the 7th of September, 1608.

Wee found M. Skriuener and diverse others well recovered, many dead, some sicke. The late President, a prisoner for muteny, by the honest diligence of M. Skriuener the harvest gathered, but the stores, provision, much spoiled with raine. Thus was that yeare (when nothing wanted) consumed and spent and nothing done; (such was the government of Captain Ratcliffe) but only this discoverie; wherein to expresse all the dangers, accidents, and incounters this small number passed in that small barge, with such watrie diet in these great waters and barbarous Countries (til then to any Christian utterly unknowne) I rather referre their merit to the censure of the courteous and experienced reader, then I would be tedious, or partiall, being a partie;
By
Nathaniell Poell, and
Anas Todkill.

The Presidencie surrendred to Captaine Smith, the arrivall and returne of the second supply: and what happened.

The 10th of September 1608. by the election of the Councel & request of the company Captaine Smith received the letters patents, and tooke upon him the place of President, which till then by no meanes he would accept though hee were often im|portuned therevnto. Now the building of Ratcliffes pallas staide as a thing needlesse. The church was repaired, the storehouse recouered; building prepared for the supply we expected. The fort reduced to the forme of this figure, the order of watch renued, the squadrons (each setting of the watch) trained. The whole company every Satturday exercised in a fielde prepared for that purpose; the boates trimmed for trade which in their journey encountred the second supply, that brought them back to discover the country of Monacan, how, or why, Captaine Newport obtained such a private commission as not to returne without a lumpe of gold, a certainty of the south-sea or one of the lost company of Sir Walter Rawley, I know not, nor why he brought such a five pieced barge, not to beare us to that south sea, till we had borne her over the mountaines: which how farre they extend is yet unknowne) as for the coronation of Powhatan & his presents of Bason, Ewer, Bed, Clothes, and such costly novelties, they had bin much better well spared, then so ill spent.

For we had his favour much better, only for a poore peece of Copper, till this stately kinde of soliciting made him so much overvalue himselfe, that he respected us as much as nothing at all. As for the hiring of the Poles and Dutch to make pitch and tarre, glasse, milles, and sope-ashes, was most necessarie and well. But to send them and seventy more without victuall to worke, was not so well considered; yet this could not have hurt us, had they bin 200 (though we were 130 that wanted for our selves.) For we had the Salvages in that Decorum, (their harvest beeing newly gathered) that we feared not to get victuall sufficient had we bin 500. Now there no way to make us miserable but to neglect that time to make our provision, whilst it was to be had; the which was done to performe this strange discovery, but more strange coronation; to loose that time, spend that victuall we had, tire & starve our men, having no means to carry victuall, munition, the hurr or sicke, but their owne backs, how or by whom they Were invented I know not; But Captaine Newport we only accounted the author, who to effect these proiects had so gilded all our hopes, with great promises, that both compa|ny and Councel concluded his resolution. I confesse we little vnderstood then our estates, to conclude his conclusion, against al the inconveniences the foresee|ing President all eadged. There was added to the cou]cell one Captaine Waldo, and Captaine Winne two an|cient souldiers and valiant gentlemen, but ignorant of the busines (being newly arrived) Rateliffe was also permitted to have his voice, & Mr Scrivener desirous to see strange countries, so that although Smith was President, yet the Councell had the authoritie, and ru|led it as they listed; as for cleering Smiths obiections, how pitch, and tarre, wanscot, clapbord, glasse, & sope ashes, could be provided to relade the ship; or provisi|ongot to liue withal, when none was in the Country and that which we had, spent before the ships depar|ted; The answer was, Captaine Newport vndertook to fraught the Pinnace with corne, in going and returning in his discoverie, and to refraught her againe from Werawocomoco; also promising a great proportion of victuall from his ship, inferring that Smiths proposi|tions were only devises to hinder his iourney, to effect it himselfe; and that the crultie Smith had used to the Salvages, in his absence, might occasion them to hinder his designes; For which, all workes were left; and 120 chosen men were appointed for his guard, and Smith, to make cleere these seeming suspicions, that the Salvages were not so desperate, as was pretended by Captaine Newport, and how willing he was to further them to effect their proiects, (because the coronation would consume much time) undertooke their message to Powhatan; to intreat him to come to James Towne to receive his presents, accompanied only with Captaine Waldo, M. Andrew Buckler, Edward Brinton, & Samuell Collier; with these 4 hee went over land, against Werawacomoco, there passed the river of Pa|mavuke in the Salvages Canowes, Powhatan being 30 myles of, who, presently was sent for, in the meane time his women entertained Smith in this manner.

In a faire plaine field they made a fire, before which he was sitting upon a mat; suddainly amongst the woods was heard such a hideous noise and shriking, that they betooke them to their armes, supposing Powhatan with all his power came to surprise them; but the beholders which were many, men, women, & children, satisfied the Captaine there was no such matter, be|ing presently presented with this anticke, 30 young women camenaked out of the woods (only covered behind and before with a few greene leaues) their bodies all painted, some white, some red, some black, some partie colour, but every one different, their leader had a faire paire of stagges hornes on her head, and an ot|ter skinne at her girdle, another at her arme, a quiver of arrowes at her backe, and bow and arrowes in her hand, the next in her hād a sword, another a club, ano|ther a pot-stick, all hornd alike, the rest every one with their severall devises. These feindes with most hellish cries, and shouts rushing from amongst the trees, cast themselues in a ring about the fire, singing, and daun|cing with excellent ill varietie, oft falling into their infernall passions, and then solemnely againe to sing, and daunce. Having spent neere an houre, in this maskardo, as they entered; in like manner departed; hauing reaccommodated themselves, they solemnely invited Smith to their lodging, but no sooner was hee within the house, but all these Nimphes more tormented him then ever, with crowding, and pressing, and hanging upon him, most tediously crying, love you not mee. This salutation ended, the feast was set, consisting of fruit in baskets, fish, & flesh in wooden platters, beans and pease there wanted not (for twenty hogges) nor any Salvage daintie their invention could devise; some attending, others singing and dancing about them; this mirth and banquet being ended, with firebrands (instead of torches) they conducted him to his lodging.

The next day, came Powhatan; Smith delivered his * message of the presents sent him, and redelivered him Namontack, desiring him come to his Father New|port to accept those presents, and conclude their revenge against the Monacans, wherevnto the subtile Salvage thus replied.

If your king have sent me presents, I also am a king, and this my land, eight daies I will stay to receaue them, your father is to come to me, not I to him, nor yet to your fort, neither will I bite at such a baite: as for the Monacans, I can revenge my owne iniuries, and as for Atquanuchuck, where you say your brother was slain, it is a contrary way from those parts you suppose it.

But for any salt water beyond the mountaines, the re¦lations you have had from my people are false, wherupon he began to draw plots upon the ground (according to his discourse) of all those regions; many other discourses they had (yet both desirous to give each other content in Complementall courtesies) and so Captaine Smith returned with this answer.

Upon this Captaine Newport sent his presents by water, which is neare 100 miles, with 50 of the best shot, himselfe went by land which is but 12 miles, where he met with our 3 barges to transport him over. All things being fit for the day of his coronation, the presents were brought, his bason, ewer, bed & fur|niture set up, his scarlet cloake and apparel (with much adoe) put on him (being perswaded by Namontacke they would doe him no hurt.) But a fowle trouble there was to make him kneele to receaue his crowne, he neither knowing the maiestie, nor meaning of a Crowne, nor bending of the knee, indured so many perswasions, examples, and instructions, as tired them all.

At last by leaning hard on his shoulders, he a little stooped, and Newport put the Crowne on his head. When by the warning of a pistoll, the boates were prepared with such a volly of shot, that the king start up in a horrible feare, till he see all was well, then re|membring himselfe, to congratulate their kindnesse, he gave his old shoes and his mantle to Captain Newport. But perceiuing his purpose was to discover the Monacans, hee laboured to divert his resolution refusing to lend him either men, or guids, more then Namontack, and so (after some complementall kindnesse on both sides) in requitall of his presents, he presented Newport with a heape of wheat eares, that might contain some 7 or 8 bushels, & as much more we bought ready dressed in the towne, wherewith we returned to the fort.

The ship having disburdened her selfe of 70 persons, with the first gentlewoman, and woman servant that arrived in our Colony; Captaine Newport with al the Councell, and 120 chosen men, set forward for the discovery of Monacan, leauing the President at the fort with 80. (such as they were) to relade the shippe. Arriving at the falles, we marched by land some forty myles in two daies and a halfe, and so returned downe to the same path we went.

Two townes wee discovered of the Monacans, the people neither using us well nor ill, yet for our securitie wee tooke one of their pettie Werowances, and lead him bound, to conduct us the way. And in our returne searched many places wee supposed mynes, about which we spent some time in refining, having one William Callicut a refiner, fitted for that purpose, from that crust of earth wee digged hee perswaded us to beleeue he extracted some small quantitie of silver (and not unlikely better stuffe might bee had for the digging) with this poore trial being contented to leave this faire, fertill, well watred countrie. Coming to the Falles, the Salvages fained there were diverse ships come into the Bay to kill them at James Towne. Trade they would not, and find their corn we could not, for they had hid it in the woods, and being thus deluded we arrived at James Towne, halfe sicke, all complaining, and tired with toile, famine, and discontent, to have only but discovered our gilded hopes, and such fruitlesse certaineties, as the President foretold us.

No sooner were we landed, but the President dispersed many as were able, some for glasse, others for pitch, tarre and sope ashes, leaving them, (with the fort) to the Councels oversight. But 30 of us he conducted five myles from the fort to learn to make clapbord, cut downe trees, and lye in woods; amongst the rest he had chosen Gabriell Beadell, & John Russell the only two gallants of this last supply, and both proper gentlemen: strange were these pleasures to their conditions, yet lodging eating, drinking, working, or playing they doing but as the President, all these things were carried so pleasantly, as within a weeke they became Masters, making it their delight to heare the trees thunder as they fell, but the axes so oft blistered there tender fingers, that commonly every third blow had a lowd oath to drowne the eccho; for remedy of which sin the President devised howe to have everie mans oathes numbred, and at night, for every oath to have a can of water powred downe his sleeue, with which every offender was so washed (himselfe & all) that a man should scarse heare an oath in a weeke.

By this, let no man think that the President, or these gentlemen spent their times as common wood-hackers at felling of trees, or, such like other labours, or that they were pressed to any thing as hirelings or common slaves, for what they did (being but once a little inured) it seemed, and they conceited it only as a pleasure and a recreation.

Yet 30 or 40 of such voluntary Gentlemen would doe more in a day then 100 of the rest that must bee prest to it by compulsion. Master Scrivener, Captaine Waldo, and Captaine Winne at the fort, every one in like manner carefully regarded their charge. The President returning from amongst the woodes, seeing the time con|sumed, and no provision gotten, (and the ship lay Idle, and would do nothing) presently imbarked himselfe in the discovery barge, giving order to the Councell, to send Mr Persey after him with the next barge that ar|rived at the fort; two barges, he had himselfe, and twenty men but arriving at Chickahamina that dogged nation, was too well acquainted with our wants, refusing to trade, with as much scorne and insolencie as they could expresse.

The President perceiving it was Powhatans policy to starve us, told them he came not so much for their corne, as to revenge his imprisonment, and the death of his men murdered by them, & so landing his men, and ready to charge them, they immediatly fled; but then they sent their imbassadours, with corne, fish, fowl, or what they had to make their peace, (their corne being that year bad) they complained extream|ly of their owne wants, yet fraughted our boats with 100 bushels of corne, and in like manner Mr Persey, that not long after us arrived; they having done the best they could to content us, within four or five daies we returned to James Towne.

Though this much contented the company (that then feared nothing but starving) yet some so envied his good successe, that they rather desired to starve, these paines should prove so muchmore effectuall then theirs; some proiects there was, not only to have deposed him but to have kept him out of the fort, for that being President, he would leaue his place, and the fort without their consents; but their hornes were so much too short to effect it, as they themselues more narrowly escaped a greater mischiefe.

All this time our old taverne, made as much of all them that had either mony or ware as could bee desired; and by this time they were become so perfect on all sides (I meane Souldiers, Sailers, and Salvages,) as there was ten-times more care, to maintaine their da]nable and private trade, then to provide for the Colony things that were necessary, neither was it a small pollicy in the mariners, to report in England wee had such plenty and bring us so many men without victuall, when they had so many private factors in the fort, that within six or seven weekes after the ships returne, of 2 or 300 hatchets, chissels, mattocks, and pickaxes scarce 20 could be found, and for pike-heads, knives, shot, powder, or any thing (they could steale from their own fellowes) was uendible.

They knew as well (and as secretly) how to convay them to trade with the Salvages, for furres, baskets, mussaneekes, young beastes or such like commodities, as exchange them with the sailers, for butter, cheese, biefe, porke, aquavitae, beere, bis|ket, and oatmeale; and then faine, all was sent them from their friends. And though Virginia afford no furs for the store, yet one mariner in one voyage hath got so many, as hee hath confessed to have solde in England for 30l.

Those are the Saint-seeming worthies of Virginia, that have notwithstanding all this, meate, drinke, and pay, but now they begin to grow weary, their trade being both perceived and prevented; none hath bin in Virginia (that hath observed any thing) which knowes not this to be true, and yet the scorne, and shame was the poore souldiers, gentlemen and carelesse governours, who were all thus bought and solde, the ad|venturers cousened, and the action overthrowne by their false excuses, informations, and directions, by this let all the world judge, how this businesse coulde prosper, being thus abused by such pilfering occasions.

The proceedings and accidents, with the second supply.
Mr Scrivener was sent with the barges and Pinas to Werawocomoco, where he found the Salvages more ready to fight then trade, but his vigilancy was such, as prevented their proiectes, and by the meanes of Namontack got three or four hogsheads of corne, and as much Red paint which (then) was esteemed an excellent die.

Captaine Newport being dispatched with the tryals of pitch, tarre, glasse, frankincense, and sope ashes, with that clapoord and wainscot could bee provided met with Mr Scrivener at point Comfort, & so retur|ned for England, leaving us in all 200. with those hee brought us.

The names of those in this supply are these.
Captaine Peter Winne, Captaine Richard Waldo, were appointed to bee of the Councell.

Abbey Thomas
Bedle Gabriell
Bedle John
Bell Henry, Tradesman
Bradley Thomas, Tradesman
Burras Anne, maid to Mistress Forrest
Burras John, Tradesman
Burton George
Chroshaw Rawley
Hardwin Unknown, Laborer
Haryson Harmon
Hellyard Unknown
Hoult John
Hugh David ap, Tradesman
Hunt Master
Lavander Thomas, Tradesman
Ley Henry
Lowicke Michaell

Clarke John, Tradesman
Collings Henry
Dauxe John
Dowman William
Dowse Thomas, Laborer
Ellys David, Tradesman
Forest Thomas
Forrest Mistress
Fox Thomas, Laborer
Gipson Thomas, Tradesman
Graves Thomas
Gudderington John
Hancock Nicholas, Laborer
Mallard Thomas, Laborer
Maxes Thomas
Milman Unknown
Morrell Unknown, Laborer
Norton Thomas
Oconor Dionis, Tradesman
Phelps Thomas, Tradesman
Philpot Henry
Powell Unknown Master, Trade
Prat John, Tradesman
Rose Unknown, Laborer
Russell John
Russell William, escaped Indian ambush Dec 1609
Sambage William
Scot Unknown, Laborer
Shortridge Jefry, Tradesman, escaped Indian ambush Dec 1609
Taler William, Laborer
Tucker Daniell, left Virinia 1612, adventurer, Coldham pg 4
Waldo Captaine Richard, Council, drowned in James River Jan 1609
Walker Unknown, Laborer
West Master Francis
Williams Unknown, Laborer
Winne, Captaine Peter, Council, died about April 1609
Wollystone Hugh
Wynne Hugh, Tradesman
Yarington George

Mistresse Forest and Anne Buras her maide, 8 Dutchmen, and Poles with divers to the number of 70 persons.

Those poore conclusions so affrighted us all with famine; that the President provided for Nansamund, tooke with him Captaine Winne & Mr Scrivener (them returning from Captaine Newport), these people also long denied him trade, (excusing themselues to bee so comanded by Powhatan) til we were constrained to begin with them perforce, and then they would rather sell us some, then wee should take all; so loading our boats, with 100 bushels we parted friends, and came to James Towne, at which time, there was a marriage betweene John Laydon and Anna Burrowes, being the first marriage we had in Virginia.

Long he staied not, but fitting himselfe & captaine Waldo with two barges, from Chawopo, weanocke and all parts there, was found neither corne nor Salvage, but all fled (being jealous of our intents) till we discovered the river and people of Appametuck, where we founde little that they had, we equally devided, betwixt the Salvages and us (but gaue them copper in consideration) Mr Persie, and Mr Scrivener went also abroad but could finde nothing.

The President seeing this procastinating of time, was no course to liue, resolved with Captaine Waldo, (whom he knew to be sure in time of need) to surprise Powhatan, and al his provision, but the vnwillingnes of Captaine Winne, and Mr Scrivener (for some private respects) did their best to hinder their proiect: But the President whom no perswasions could perswade to starue, being invited by Powhatan to come vnto him, & if he would send him but men to build him a house, bring him a grinstone, fifty swords, some peeces, a cock and a hen, with copper and beads, he would loade his shippe with corne, the President not ignoraunt of his devises, yet unwilling to neglect any opportunity, presently sent three Dutchmen and two English (having no victuals to imploy them, all for want therof being idle) knowing there needed no better castel, that house to surprize Powhatan, to affect this proiect he took order with Captaine Waldo to second him if need required; Scrivener he left his substitute; and set forth with the Pinnas two barges and six and forty men which only were such as volentarily offered themselues for his journy, the which (by reason of Mr Scriveners ill successe) was censured very desperate, they all knowing Smith would not returne empty howsoever, caused many of those that he had appointed, to finde excuses to stay behinde.

Captaine Smiths Journey to Pamavnke

THE 29th of December hee set forward for Werawocomoco, his company were these:
In the Discovery barge, himselfe, Robert Behethland, Nathaniell Powell, John Russell, Rawly Crashaw, Michaell Sicklemore, Richard

Worlie, Anas Todkill, William Love, William Bentley, Geoffery Shortridge, Edward Pising, and William Warde

In the Pinnace.
Mr George Persie, brother to the Earle of Northumberland, Mr Frauncis West, brother to the Lord De-la-Ware.
William Phetiplace Captaine of the Pinnas, Jonas Profit Master, Robert Ford clarcke of the councell, Michaell Phetiplace, Geoffery Abbot Serg., William Tankard, George Yarington, James Bourne, George Burton, Thomas Coe, John Dods.
Edward Brinton, Nathaniel Peacocke, Henry Powell, David Ellis, Thomas Gipson, John Prat, George Acrigge, James Reade, Nicholas Hancocke, James Watkins, Anthony Baggly, Thomas Lambert, Edward Pising, with four Dutchmen and Richard Salvage were sent by land, to build the house for Powhatan against our arrivall.

This company being victualled but for three or four daies lodged the first night at Weraskoyack; where the President tooke sufficient provision; This kind Salvage did his best to divert him from seeing Powhatan, but perceiving he could not prevaile, he advised in this maner Captaine Smith, you shall finde Powhatan to use you kindly, but trust him not, and bee sure hee have no opportunitie to seaze on your armes, for hee hath sent for you only to cut your throats. The Captaine thanked him for his good counsell, yet the better to try his love, desired guides to Chowanoke, for he would send a present to that king to bind him his friend.

To performe this journey, was sent Michael Sicklemore, a very honest, valiant, and painefull souldier, with him two guids, and directions howe to search for the lost company of Sr Walter Rawley, and silke grasse: then wee departed thence, the President assuring the king his perpetuall love, and left with him Samuell Collier his page to learne the language.

The next night being lodged at Kecoughtan, the extreame wind, raine, frost, and snowe, caused us to keepe Christmas amongst the Salvages, where wee were never more merrie, nor fedde on more plentie of good oysters, fish, flesh, wildfoule, and good bread, nor never had better fires in England in the drie warme smokie houses of Kecoughtan. But departing thence, when we found no houses, we were not curious in any weather, to lie 3 or 4 nights together upon any shore vnder the trees by a good fire, 148 fowles the President, Anthony Bagly, and Edward Pising, did kill at three shoots. At Kiskiack the frost forced us three or four daies also to suppresse the insolencie of those proud Salvages; to quarter-in their houses, and guard our barge, and cause them giue us what wee wanted, yet were we but 12 with the President, and yet we never wanted harbour where we found any houses.

The 12th of Januarie we arrived at Werawocomoco, where the river was frozen neare halfe a mile from the shore; but to neglect no time, the President with his barge, so farre had approached by breaking the Ice as the eb left him amongst those oozie shoules, yet rather then to lie there frozen to death, by his owne example hee taught them to march middle deepe, more then a flight shot through this muddie frozen ooze; when the barge sloted the appointed 2 or 3 to returne her abord the Pinnace, where for want of water in melting the salt Ice they made fresh water, but in this march M. Russell (whome none could perswade to stay behind) being somewhat ill, and exceeding heavie, so overtoiled him selfe, as the rest had much adoe (ere he got a shore) to regaine life, into his dead benummed spirits, quartering in the next houses we found, we sent to Powhatan for provision, who sent us plentie of bread, Turkies, & Venison.

The next day hauing feasted us after his ordinarie manner, he began to aske, when we would beegon, faining hee sent not for us, neither had hee any corne, and his people much lesse, yet for 40 swords he would procure us 40 bushels. The President shewing him the men there present, that brought him the message and conditions, asked him how it chaunced he became so forgetful thereat the king concluded the matter with a merry laughter, asking for our commodities, but none he liked without gunnes and swords, valuing a basket of corne more pretious then a basket of copper, saying he could eate his corne, but not his copper.

Captaine Smith seeing the intent of this subtil Salvage; began to deale with him after this manner, Powhatan, though I had many courses to have made my provision, yet beleeving your promises to supply my wants, I neglected all, to satisfie your desire, and to te|stifie my love, I sent you my men for your building, neglecting my owne: what your people had you have engrossed, forbidding them our trade, and nowe you thinke by consuming the time, wee shall consume for want, not hauing to fulfill your strange demandes, as for swords, and gunnes, I told you long agoe, I had none to spare And you shall knowe, those I have, can keepe me from want, yet steale, or wrong you I will not, nor dissolue that friendship, wee have mutually promised, (except you constraine mee by your bad usage.

The King having attintively listned to this discourse; promised, that both hee and his Country would spare him what they could, the which within two daies, they should receaue, yet. Captaine Smith, (saith the king) some doubt I have of your coming hither, that makes me not so kindly seeke to relieve you as I would; for many do informe me, your comming is not for trade, but to invademy people and possesse my Country, who dare not come to bring you corne, seeing you thus armed with your men. To cleere us of this feare, leave abord your weapons, for here they are needlesse we being all friends and for ever Powhatans.

With many such discourses they spent the day, quartring that night in the kings houses, the next day he reviewed his building, which hee little intended should proceed; for the Dutchmen finding his plenty, and knowing our want, and perceived his preparation to surprise us, little thinking wee could escape, both him, and famine, (to obtaine his favour) revealed to him as much as they knew of our estates and proiects, and how to prevent them; one of them being of so good a iudgement, spirit, and resolution, & a hireling that was certaine of wages for his labour, and ever well used, both he and his countrimen, that the President knewe not whome better to trust, & not knowing any fitter for that imploiment, had sent him as a spie to discover Powhatans intent, then little doubting his honestie, nor could ever be certaine of his villany, till neare halfe a yeare after.

Whilst we expected the comming in of the countrie, we wrangled out of the king ten quarters of corne for a copper kettle, the which the President perceived him much to effect, valued it at a much greater rate, but (in regard of his scarcety) hee would accept of as much more the next yeare, or else the country of Monacan, the king exceeding liberall of that hee had not yeelded him Monacan. Wherewith each seeming well contented; Powhatan began to expostulate the difference betwixt peace and war, after this manner.

Captaine Smith you may understand, that I, having seene the death of all my people thrice, and not one living of those three generations, but my selfe, I knowe the difference of peace and warre, better then any in my Countrie. But now I am old, & ere long must die, my brethren, namely Opichapam, Opechankanough, and Kekataugh, my two sisters, and their two daughters, are distinctly each others successours, I wish their experiences no lesse then mine, and your love to them, no lesse then mine to you; but this brute from Nansamund that you are come to destroy my Countrie, so much affrighteth all my people, as they dare not visit you; what will it availe you, to take that perforce, you may quietly have with love, or to destroy them that provide you food? what can you get by war, when we can hide our provision and flie to the woodes, whereby you must famish by wronging us your friends; & whie are you thus jealous of our loves, seeing us unarmed, and both doe, & are willing still to feed you with that you cannot get but by our labours?

Think you I am so simple not to knowe, it is better to eate good meate, lie well, and sleepe quietly with my women & children and laugh and be merrie with you, have copper, hatchets, or what I want, being your friend; then bee forced to flie from al, to lie cold in the woods, feed upon acorns roots, and such trash, and be so hunted by you, that I can neither rest, eat, nor sleepe; but my tired men must watch, and if a twig but breake, everie one crie there comes Captaine Smith, then must I flie I knowe not whether, and thus with miserable feare end my miserable life; leaving my pleasures to such youth as you, which through your rash vnadvisednesse, may quickly as miserably ende, for want of that you never knowe how to find? Let this therefore assure you of our loves and everie yeare our friendly trade shall furnish you with corne, & now also if you would come in friend|ly manner to see us, and not thus with your gunnes & swords, as to invade your foes. To this subtil discourse the President thus replied.

Seeing you will not rightly cōceaue of our words, wee striue to make you knowe our thoughts by our deeds. The vow I made you of my love, both my selfe * and my men have kept, as for your promise I finde it everie daie violated, by some of your subiects, yet wee finding your love and kindnesse (our custome is so far from being vngratefull) that for your sake only, wee have curbed our thirsting desire of revenge, else had they knowne as wel the crueltie we use to our enimies as our true love and curtefie to our friendes. And I thinke your iudgement sufficient to conceiue as well by the adventures we have vndertaken, as by the ad|vantage we have by our armes of yours: that had wee intended you anie hurt, long ere this wee coulde have effected it; your people coming to me at Jamestowne, are entertained with their bowes and arrowes without exception; we esteeming it with you, as it is with us, to weare our armes as our apparell. As for the da]gers of our enimies, in such warres consist our chiefest pleasure, for your riches we have no use, as for the hi|ding your provision, or by your flying to the woods, we shall so vnadvisedly starue as you conclude, your friendly care in that behalfe is needlesse; for we have a rule to finde beyond your knowledge.

Manie other discourses they had, til at last they began to trade, but the king seing his will would not bee admitted as a lawe, our gard dispersed, nor our men disarmed, he (sighing) breathed his mind, once more in this manner.

Captaine Smith, I never used anie of Werowances, so kindlie as your selfe; yet from you I receave the least kindnesse of anie. Captaine Newport gave me swords, copper, cloths, a bed, tooles, or what I desired, ever taking what I offered him, and would send awaie his gunnes when I intreated him: none doth denie to laie at my feet (or do) what I desire, but only you, of who I can have nothing, but what you regard not, and yet you will have whatsoever you demand. Captain Newport you call father, and so you call me, but I see for all us both, you will doe what you list, and wee must both seeke to content you: but if you intend so friendlie as you saie, sende hence your armes that I may beleeue you, for you see the love I beare you, doth cause mee thus nakedlie forget my selfe.

Smith seeing this Salvage but trifled the time to cut his throat: procured the Salvages to breake the ice, (that his boat might come to fetch both him and his corne) and gaue order for his men to come ashore, to have surprised the king, with whom also he but trifled the time till his men landed, and to keepe him from suspition, entertained the time with this reply.

Powhatan, you must knowe as I have but one God, I honour but one king; and I live not here as your subject, but as your friend, to pleasure you with what I can by the gifts you bestowe on me, you gaine more then by trade; yet would you visite mee as I doe you, you should knowe it is not our customes to sell our curtesie as a vendible commoditie.

Bring all your Country with you for your gard, I will not dislike of it as being over iealous. But to content you, to morrow I will leaue my armes, and trust to your promise. I call you father indeed, and as a father you shall see I will love you, but the smal care you had of such a child, caused my men perswade me to shift for my selfe.

By this time Powhatan having knowledge, his men were readie: whilst the ice was breaking, his luggage women, and children fledde, and to avoid suspition, left two or three of his women talking with the Captaine, whilst he secretly fled, and his men as secretlie beset the house, which being at the instant discovered to Captain Smith, with his Pistol, Sword & Target, he made such a passage amongst those naked divels, that they fled be sore him some one waie some another, so that with|out hurt he obtained the Corps du-guard; when they perceived him so well escaped, and with his eight men (for he had no more with him.)

To the uttermost of their skill, they sought by excuses to dissemble the matter, and Powhatan to excuse his flight, and the suddaine co]ming of this multitude, sent our Captaine a greate bracelet, and a chaine of pearle, by an ancient Orator that bespoke us to this purpose, (perceiving then from our Pinnace, a barge and men departing & comming unto us.) Captaine Smith, our Werowans is fled, fearing your guns, & knowing when the ice was broken there would come more men, sent those of his to guard his corne from the pilfrie, that might happen without your knowledge, now though some bee hurt by your misprision, yet he is your friend, and so will continue: and since the ice is open hee would have you send awaie your corne; and if you would have his companie send also your armes, which so affrighteth this people, that they dare not come to you, as he hath promiseed they should: nowe having provided baskets for our men to carrie the corne, they kindlie offered their service to gard our armes, that none should steale them.

A great manie they were, of goodlie well appointed fellowes as grim as divels; yet the verie sight of cocking our matches against them, and a few words, caused them to leaue their bowes & arrowes to our gard, and beare downe our corne on their own backes; wee needed not importune them to make quick dispatch. But our own barge being left by the ebb, caused us to staie, till the midnight tide carried us safe abord, having spent that halfe night with such mirth, as though we never had suspected or intended any thing, we left the Dutchmen to build, Brinton to kill fowle for Powhatan (as by his messengers he importunately desired) and left directions with our men to give Powhatan all the content they could, that we might enjoy his company at our returne from Pamaunke.

How we escaped surprising at Pamaunke

WEE had no sooner set saile, but Powhatan returned, and sent Adam and Francis (two stout Dutch men) to the fort, who faining to Captaine Winne that al things were well, and that Captaine Smith had use for their armes, wherefore they requested newe (the which were given them) they told him their co]ming was, for some extraordinary tooles and shift of apparell, by this colourable excuse, they obtained six or seven more to their confederacie, such expert theefes, that presently furnished them with a great many swords, pike-heads, peeces, shot, powder and such like, they had Salvages at hand ready to carry it away, the next day they returned unsuspected, leaving their confederates to follow, and in the interim, to convay them a competencie of all things they could, for which service they should liue with Powhatan as his chiefe affected: free from those miseries that would happen the Colony. Samuell their other consort, Powhatan kept for their pledge, whose diligence had provided them, 300. of their kinde of hatchets, the rest, 50 swords, 8 peeces, and 8 pikes.

Brinton, & Richard Salvage seeing the Dutchmen so strangly diligent to accommodate the Salvages these weapons attempted to have got to James Towne, but they were apprehended; within two or three daies we arrived at Pamavnke, the king as many daies, entertained us with feasting and much mirth: & the day he appointed to begin our trade, the President with Mr Persey, Mr West, Mr Russell, Mr Beheathland, M Powell, Mr Crashaw, Mr Ford, and some others to the number of 15 went up to Opechancanougs house (near a quarter of a mile from the river,) where we founde nothing, but a lame fellow and a boy, and all the houses about, of all things abandoned; not long we staide ere the king arrived, and after him came divers of his people loaded with bowes and arrowes, but such pinching commodities, and those esteemed at such a value, as our Captaine beganne with him in this manner.

Opechancanough the great love you professe with your tongue, seemes meere deceipt by your actions; last yeare you kindly fraughted our ship, but now you have invited me to starue with hunger. You know my want, and I your plenty, of which by some meanes I must have part, remember it is fit for kings to keepe their promise, here are my commodities, wherof take your choices; the rest I will proportion, fit bargaines for your people.

The king seemed kindly to accept his offer; and the better to colour his proiect, sold us what they had to our own cōtēt; promising the next day, more cōpany, better provided; (the barges, and Pinnas being committed to the charge of Mr Phetiplace) the President with his old 15 marched up to the kings house, where we found four or five men newly come with great baskets, not long after came the king, who with a strained cheerefulnes held us with discourse, what paines he had take to keepe his promise; til Mr Russell brought us in news that we were all betraied: for at least 6 or 700 of well appointed Indians had invironed the house and beset the fields.

The king coniecturing what Russell related, we could wel perceiue how the extremity of his feare bewrayed his intent: whereat some of our companie seeming dismaide with the thought of such a multitude; the Captaine incouraged us after this manner.

Worthy countrymen were the mischiefes of my seeming-friends, no more then the danger of these enemies, I little cared, were they as many more, if you dare do, but as I. But this is my torment, that if I escape them, our malicious councell with their open mouthed minions, will make mee such a peace-breaker (in their opinions) in England, as wil break my neck; I could wish those here, that make these seeme Saints, and me an oppressor.

But this is the worst of all, wher in I pray aide me with your opinions; should wee begin with them and surprize this king, we cannot keep him and defend well our selues, if we should each kill our man and so proceede with al in this house; the rest will all fly, then shall we get no more, then the bodies that are slaine, and then starue for victuall: as for their fury it is the least danger; for well you know, (being alone assaulted with two or 300 of them) I made them compound to save my life, and we are now sixteen & they but 700 at the most, and assure your selves God will so assist us, that if you dare but to stande to discharge your peeces, the very smoake will bee sufficient to affright them; yet howsoever (if there be occasion) et us fight like men, and not die like sheep; but first I will deale with them, to bring it to passe, we may fight for some thing, and draw them to it by conditions. If you like this motion, promise me youle be valiant. The time not permitting any argument, all vowed, to execute whatsoever he attempted, or die; whereupon the captaine, approaching the king bespoke him in this manner.

I see Opechancanough your plot to murder me, but I feare it not, as yet your men and mine, have done no harme, but by our directions. Take therefore your arms; you see mine; my body shalbe as naked as yours; the Isle in your river is a fit place, if you be contented: and the conqueror (of us two) shalbe Lord and Master over all our men; otherwaies drawe all your men into the field; if you have not enough take time to fetch more, and bring what number you will, so everie one bring a basket of corne, against all which I will stake the value in copper; you see I have but fifteen men, & our game shalbe the conquerer take all.

The king, being guarded with 50 or 60 of his chiefe men, seemed kindly to appease Smiths suspition of unkindnesse, by a great present at the dore, they intreated him to receiue. This was to draw him without the dore where the present was garded with (at the least 200 men and 30 lying vnder a greate tree (that lay thwart as a Barricado) each his arrow nocked ready to shoot; some the President commanded to go & see what kinde of deceit this was, and to receiue the present, but they refused to do it, yet divers offered whom he would not permit; but commanding Mr Persie and Mr West to make good the house, tooke Mr Poell and Mr Beheathland to guard the dore, and in such a rage snatched the king by his vambrace in the midst of his men, with his pistoll ready bent against his brest: thus he led the trembling king, (neare dead with feare) amongst all his people, who delivering the Captaine his bow and arrowes, all his men were easily intreated to cast downe their armes, little dreaming anie durst in that manner have used their king; who then to es|cape himselfe, bestowed his presents in goodsadnesse. And hauing caused all his multitude to approach difarmed; the President argued with them to this effect.

I see you Pamavnkies the great desire you have to cut my throat; and my long suffering your iniuries, have inboldened you to this presumption. The cause I have forborne your insolences, is the promise I made you (before the God I serue) to be your friend, till you giue me iust cause to bee your enimie. If I keepe this vow, my God will keepe me, you cannot hurt me; if I breake it he will destroy me. But if you shoot but one arrow, to shed one drop of blood of any of my men, or steale the least of these beades, or copper, (I spurne before me with my foot) you shall see, I wil not cease revenge, (if once I begin) so long as I can heare where to find one of your nation that will not deny the name of Pamavnke; I am not now at Rasseneac (halfe drownd with mire) where you tooke me prisoner, yet then for keeping your promise, and your good usage, & saving my life, I so affect you, that your denials of your treacherie, doth half perswade me to mistake my selfe.

But if I be the marke you aime at, here I stand, shoote hee that dare. You promised to fraught my ship ere I departed, and so you shall, or I meane to load her with your dead carkases; yet if as friends you wil come and trade, I once more promise not to trouble you, ex|cept you giue me the first occasion. Upon this away went their bowes and arrowes, and men, women, and children brought in their commodities, but two or three houres they so thronged about the President, and so overwearied him, as he retired himself to rest, leaving Mr Beheathland and Mr Powel to accept their presents; but some Salvage perceiving him fast asleepe, and the guard carelesly dispersed, 40 or 50 of their choice, each with an English sword in his hand, began to en|ter the house, with two or 300 others that pressed to se|cond them. The noise and hast they made in, did so shake the house, as they awoke him from his sleep, & being halfe amazed with this suddaine sight, betooke him straight to his sword and target, Mr Crashaw and some other charging in like manner, they thronged faster backe, then before forward. The house thus clensed, the king and his ancients, with a long oration came to excuse this intrusion. The rest of the day was spent with much kindnesse, the company againe reuniting their presents of their best provision. And what soever we gaue them, they seemed well contented with it.

Now in the meane while since our departure, this hapned at the fort, Mr Scriuener willing to crosse the surprizing of Powhatan; 9 daies after the Presidents departure, would needs visit the Isle of hogges, and took with him Captaine Waldo (though the President had appointed him to bee readie to second his occasions) with Mr Anthony Gosnoll and eight others; but so violent was the wind (that extreame frozen time) that the boat sunke, but where or how, none doth knowe, for they were all drowned; onlie this was knowne, that the Skiffe was much overloaded, & would scarse have lived in that extreame tempest, had she beene emptie; but by no perswasion hee could bee diverted, though both Waldo and 100 others doubted as it happened.

The Salvages were the first that found their bodies, which so much the more encouraged them to effect their proiects. To advertise the

President of this heavie newes, none could bee found would undertake it, but the journey was often refused of all in the fort, untill Mr Wiffin undertooke alone, the performance thereof; wherein he was encountred with many dangers & difficulties, and in all parts as hee passed (as also that night he lodged with Powhatan) perceived such prepa|ration forwarre, that assured him, some mischiefe was intended, but with extraordinarie bribes, and much trouble, in three daies travell at length hee found us in the midst of these turmoiles. This unhappie newes, the President swore him to conceale from the rest, & so dissembling his sorrow, with the best countenance he could, when the night approached, went safely abord with all his companie.

Now so extreamely Powhatan had threatned the death of his men, if they did not by some meanes kill Captaine Smith, that the next day they appointed the Countrie should come to trade unarmed: yet unwilling to be treacherous, but that they were constrained hating fighting, almost as ill as hāging, such feare they had of bad successe. The next morning the sunne had not long appeared, but the fieldes appeared covered with people, and baskets to tempt us ashore.

The President determined to keepe abord, but nothing was to bee had without his presence, nor they would not indure the sight of a gun; then the President seeing many depart, and being unwilling to lose such a booty, so well contrived the Pinnace, and his barges with Ambuscadoes, as only with Mr Persie, Mr West, & Mr Russell armed, he went ashore, others unarmed he appoin ted to receive what was brought; the Salvages flocked before him in heapes, and (the bancke serving as a trench for retreat) hee drewe them faire open to his ambuscadoes, for he not being to be perswaded to go to visit their king, the King came to visit him with 2 or 300 men, in the forme of two halfe moons, with some 20 men, and many women loaded with great painted baskets; but when they approached somewhat neare us, their women and children fled; for when they had environed and beset the fieldes in this manner, they thought their purpose fure; yet so trembled with fear as they were scarse able to nock their arrowes; Smith standing with his 3 men readie bent beholding them, till they were within danger of our ambuscado, who, upon the word discovered themselues, and he retiring to the banke; which the Salvages no sooner perceived but away they fled, esteeming their heeles for their best advantage.

That night we sent to the fort Mr Crashaw and Mr Foard, who (in the mid-way betweene Werawocomoco and the fort) met four or five of the Dutch mens confederates going to Powhatan, the which (to excuse those gentlemens Suspition of their running to the Salvages returned to the fort and there continued.

The Salvages hearing our barge depart in the night were so terriblie affraide, that we sent for more men, (we having so much threatned their ruine, and the ra|sing of their houses, boats, and canowes) that the next day the king, sent our Captaine a chaine of pearle to alter his purpose; and stay his men, promising (though they wanted themselves) to fraught our ship, & bring it abord to avoid suspition, so that 5 or 6 daies after, from all parts of the countrie within 10 or 12 miles, in the extreame cold frost, and snow, they brought us provision on their naked backes.

Yet notwithstanding this kindnesse and trade; had their art and poison bin sufficient, the President with Mr West and some others had been poysoned; it made them sicke, but expelled it selfe; Wecuttanow a stout yonng fellow, knowing hee was suspected for bringing this present of poison, with 40 or 50 of his choice companions (seeing the President but with a few men at Potavncat) so prowdlie braved it, as though he expected to incounter a revenge; which the President perceiving, in the midst of his companie did not onlie beat, but spurned him like a dogge, as scorning to doe him anie worse mischiefe; whereupon all of them fled into the woods, thinking they had done a great mat|ter, to have so well escaped; and the townsmen remaining, presentlie fraughted our barge, to bee rid of our companies, framing manie excuses to excuse Wecuttanow (being son to their chiefe king but Powhatan) and told us if we would shew them him that brought the poyson, they would deliver him to us to punish as wee pleased.

Men maie thinke it strange there should be this stir for a little corne, but had it been gold with more ease we might have got it; & had it wanted, the whole collonie had starved. We maie be thought verie patient, to indure all those iniuries; yet onlie with fearing them, we got what they had. Whereas if we had taken revenge, the by their losse we should have lost our selves.

We searched also the countries of Youghtanund and Mattapamient, where the people imparted that little they had, with such complaints and tears from women and children; as he had bin too cruell to be a Christian that would not have bin satisfied, and moved with conpassion. But had this happened in October, November, and December, when that unhappie discoverie of Monacan was made, we might have fraughted a ship of 40 tuns, and twice as much might have bin had; from the rivers of Toppahannock, Patawomeck, & Pawtuxunt. The maine occasion of our temporizing with the Salvages was to part friends, (as we did) to give the lesse cause of suspition to Powhatan to fly; by whom we now returned, with a purpose, to have surprised him & his provision, for effecting whereof, (when we came against the towne) the President sent Mr Wiffin and Mr Coe, a shore to discover and make waie for his intended project. But they found that those damned Dutch-men had caused Powhatan to abandon his new house, and werawocomoco, and to carrie awaie all his corne & provision; and the people, they found (by their means so ill affected, that had they not stood well upon their guard, they had hardlie escaped with their lives. So the President finding his intention thus frustrated, & that there was nothing now to be had, and therefore an vnfit time to revenge their abuses, helde on his course for Iames Towne; we having in this Iornie (for 25l of copper 50l of Iron and beads) kept 40 men 6. weekes, and dailie feasted with bread, corne, flesh fish, and fowle, everie man having for his reward (and in consideration of his commodities) a months provision; (no trade being allowed but for the store;) and we delivered at James Towne to the Cape-Marchant 279 bushels of corne.

Those temporall proceedings to some maie seeme too charitable; to such a dailie daring trecherous peo|ple: to others vnpleasant that we washed not the ground with their blouds, nor shewed such strange in ventions, in mangling, murdering, ransaking, and destroying, (as did the Spaniards) the simple bodies of those ignorant soules; nor delightful because not stuf|fed with relations of heaps, and mines of gold and silver, nor such rare commodities as the Portugals and Spaniards found in the East & West Indies. The what wherof hath begot us (that were the first undertakers) no lesse scorne and contempt, then their noble conquests & valiant adventures (beautified with it) praise and honor. Too much I confesse the world cannot attribute to their ever-memorable merit. And to cleare us from the worlds blind ignorant censure, these fewe words may suffise to any reasonably understanding.

It was the Spaniards good hap to happen in those parts, where were infinite numbers of people, whoe had manured the ground with that providence, that it afforded victuall at all times: and time had brought them to that perfection, they had the use of gold and silver, and the most of such commodities, as their countries afforded, so that what the Spaniard got, was only the spoile and pillage of those countrie people, and not the labours of their owne hands.

But had those fruitfull Countries, beene as Salvage as barbarous, as ill peopled, as little planted, laboured and manured as Virginia, their proper labours (it is likely) would have produced as small profit as ours. But had Virginia bin peopled, planted, manured, and adorned, with such store of pretious jewels, & rich commodities, as was the Indies: then had we not gotten, and done as much as by their examples might bee expected from us, the world might then have traduced us and our merits, & have made shame and infamy our recompence and reward.

But we chanced in a lande, even as God made it. Where we found only an idle, improvident, scattered people; ignorant of the knowledge of gold, or silver, or any commodities; & carelesse of any thing but from hand to mouth, but for bables of no worth; nothing to encourage us, but what accidentally wee found na|ture afforded. Which ere wee could bring to recompence our paines, defray our charges, and satisfie our adventurers, we were to discover the country, subdue the people, bring them to be tractable, civil, and industrious, and teach them trades, that the fruits of their labours might make us recompence, or plant such colonies of our owne that must first make provision how to live of themselves, ere they can bring to perfection the commodities of the countrie, which doubtles will be as commodious for England, as the west Indies for Spaine, if it be rightly managed; notwithstanding all our home-bred opinions, that will argue the contrarie, as formerly such like have done, against the Spaniards and Portugals. But to conclude, against all rumor of opinion, I only say this, for those that the three first yeares began this plantation, notwithstanding al their factions, mutenies, and miseries, so gently correct and well prevented) peruse the Spanish Decades, the relations of M. Hacklut, and tell mee how many ever with such smal meanes, as a barge of two Tunnes; sometimes with 7. 8. 9, or but at most 15 men did ever discover so many faire and navigable rivers; subiect so many severall kings, people, and nations, to obedience, & contribution with so little bloud shed.

And if in the search of those Countries, wee had hapned where wealth had beene, we had as surely had it, as obedience and contribution, but if wee have overskipped it, we will not envy them that shall chance to finde it. Yet can wee not but lament, it was our ill fortunes to end, when wee had but only learned how to begin, and found the right course how to proceed.

By
Rich. Wiffin,
William Phettiplace, and
Anas Todkill.
CHAP. 10.

How the Salvages became subiect to the English

When the shippes departed, al the provision of the store (but that the President had gotten) was so rotten with the last somers rain, and eaten with rats, and wormes, as the hogs would scarsely eat it, yet it was the souldiers diet, till our returnes: so that wee found nothing done, but victuall spent, and the most part of our tooles, and a good part of our armes convayed to the Salvages. But now, casting up the store, & finding sufficient till the next harvest, the feare of starving was abandoned; and the company divided into tennes, fifteenes, or as the businesse required four houres each day was spent in worke, the rest in pastimes and merry exercise; but the untowardnesse of the greatest number, caused the President to make a generall assembly, and then he advised them as followeth.

Countrimen, the long experience of our late miseries, I hope is sufficient to perswade every one to a present correction of himselfe; and thinke not that ei|ther my pains, or the advēturers purses, will ever main|taine you in idlenesse and sloth; I speake not this to you all, for diverse of you I know deserue both honor and reward, better then is yet here to bee had: but the greater part must be more industrious, or starue, howsoever you have bin heretofore tolerated by the au|thoritie of the Councell from that I have often commanded you, yet seeing nowe the authoritie resteth wholly in my selfe; you must obay this for a law, that he that will not worke shall not eate (except by sick|nesse he be disabled) for the labours of 30 or 40 honest and industrious men, shall not bee consumed to maintaine 150 idle varlets.

Now though you presume the authoritie here is but a shaddow, and that I dare not touch the liues of any, but my own must answer it; the letters patents each week shall be read you, whose contents will tell you the contrary. I would wish you therefore without contempt seeke to obserue these orders set downe: for there are nowe, no more Councells to protect you, nor curbe my indeauors. Therefore hee that offendeth let him assuredly expect his due punish ment. Hee made also a table as a publike memoriall of every mans deserts, to encourage the good, and with shame to spurne on the rest to amendment. By this many became very industrious, yet more by severe punishment performed their businesse; for all were so tasked that there was no excuse could prevaile to de|ceiue him, yet the Dutchmens consorts so closely still convaid powder, shot, swords, and tooles, that though we could find the defect, we could not find by whom it was occasioned, till it was too late.

All this time the Dutchmen remaining with Powhatan, received them, instructing the Salvages their use. But their consorts not following them as they expected, (to knowe the cause, they sent Francis their companion (a stout young fellow) disguised Salvage like) to the glasse-house, (a place in the woods neere a myle from James Towne) where was the randavus for all their unsuspected villany, 40 men they procured of Powhatan to lie in Ambuscadoe for Captaine Smith, who no sooner heard of this Dutchman, but hee sent to apprehend him, who foūd he was gon, yet to crosse his returne to Powhatan, Captaine Smith presently dispatched 20 shot after him, and then returning but from the glasse-house alone, hee incountred the king of Paspaheigh, a most strong stout Salvage, whose perswasions not being able to perswade him to his ambush, seeing him only armed but with a fauchion, attempted to have shot him; but the President prevented his shot by grapling with him, and the Salvage as well prevented him for drawing his fauchion, and perforce bore him into the river to have drowned him; long they struggled in the water, from whence the king perceiving two of the Poles upon the sandes would have fled; but the President held him by the haire & throat til the Poles came in; then seeing howe pittifully the poore Salvage begged his life, they conducted him prisoner to the fort.

The Dutchman ere long was also brought in, whose villany, though all this time it was suspected, yet he fained such a formall excuse, that for want of language, Win had not rightly vnderstood them, and for their dealings with Powhatan, that to saue their liues they were constrained to accommo|date his armes, of whome he extreamely complained to have detained them perforce; and that hee made this escape with the hazard of his life, and meant not to have returned, but only walked in the woods to gather walenuts: yet for all this faire tale (there was so smal appearance of truth) hee went by the heeles; the king also he put in fetters; purposing to regaine the Dutch-men, by the saving his life; the poore Salvage did his best, by his daily messengers to Powhatan, but all returned that the Dutchmen would not returne, neither did Powhatan stay them, and bring them fiftie myles on their backes they were not able; daily this kings wiues children, and people, came to visit him with presents, which hee liberally bestowed to make his peace, much trust they had in the Presidents promise, but the king finding his gard negligent (though fettered) yet escaped.

Captaine Win thinking to pursue him, found such troopes of Salvages to hinder his passages, as they exchanged many volies of shot for flights of arrowes. Captaine Smith hearing of this, in returning to the fort tooke two Salvages prisoners, the one called Kemps, the other Kinsock, the two most exact villaines in the countrie; with those, Captaine Win, and 50 chosen men attempted that night to have regained the king, and revenged his iniurie (and so had done if he had followed his directions, or bin advised by those two villaines, that would have betraied both their king and kindred for a peece of copper, but hee trifling away the night, the Salvages the next morning by the rising of the sunne, braved him come a shore to fight, a good time both sides let flie at other, but wee heard of no hurt, only they tooke two Canows, burnt the kings house and so returned.

The President fearing those bravadoes, would but incourage the Salvages, begun himselfe to trie his cōclusions; whereby six or seven Salvages were slaine, as many made prisoners; burnt their houses, tooke their boats with all their fishing weares, and planted them at Iames Towne for his owne use; and nowe resolved not to cease till he had revenged himselfe upon al that had iniured him, but in his journey passing by Paspaheigh towards Chickahamina, the Salvages did their best to draw him to their ambuscadoes; but seeing him regardlesly passe their Countrey, all shewed thēselues in their bravest manner, to rrie their valours, he could not but let flie, and ere he could land, the Salvages no sooner knewe him, but they threw downe their armes and desired peace; their Orator was a stout young man called Ocanindge, whose worthie discourse deserveth to be remembred; and this it was.

Captaine Smith, my master is here present in this company thinking it Captaine Win, and not you; and of him hee intended to have beene revenged, having never offended him: if hee have offended you in escalping your imprisonment; the fishes swim, the fowles flie, and the very beastes striue to escape the snare and live; them blame not him being a man, hee would entreat you remēber, your being a prisoner, what paines he tooke to save your life; if since he hath iniured you he was compelled to it, but howsoever, you have revenged it with our too-great losse, we perceiue & well knowe you intend to destroy us, that are here to intreat and desire your friendship, and to enioy our houses and plant our fields, of whose fruit you shall participate, otherwise you will have the worst by our absence, for we can plant any where, though with more labour, and we know you cannot liue if you want our harvest, and that reliefe wee bring you; if you promise us peace we will beleeue you, if you proceed in revenge, we will abandon the Countrie. Upon these tearmes the President promised them peace, till they did us injurie, upon condition they should bring in provision, so all departed good friends, & so continued till Smith left the Countrie.

Ariving at James Towne, a complaint was made to the President that the Chickahaminos, who all this while continued trade, and seemed our friendes, by colour thereof were the only theaves, and amongst other things, a pistol being stolne, and the theese fled, there were apprehended two proper young fellows that were brothers, knowne to be his cōfederats. Now to regain this pistoll, the one we imprisoned, the other was sent to returne againe within twelve houres, or his brother to be hanged, yet the President pittying the poore naked Salvage in the dungeon, sent him victuall and some charcole for fire; ere midnight his brother returned with the pistoll, but the poore Salvage in the dungeon was so smothered with the smoke he had made, and so pittiously burnt, that wee found him dead, the other most lamentably bewailed his death, and broke forth in such bitter agonies, that the Presidēt (to quiet him) told him that if herafter they would not steal. he wold make him aliue againe, but little thought hee could be recovered, yet (we doing our best with aquavitae & vineger) it pleased God to restore him againe to life, but so drunke and affrighted that he seemed lunaticke, not vnderstanding any thing hee spoke or heard, the which as much grieved and tormented the other, as before to see him dead; of which maladie (upon promise of their good behaviour afterward) the President promised to recover him and so caused him to be laid by a fire to sleepe, who in the morning (having well slept) had recovered his perfect senses; and then being dressed of his burning, and each a peece of copper gi|ven them, they went away so well contented, that this was spread amongst all the Salvages for a miracle, that Captaine Smith could make a man alive that is dead; these and many other such pretty accidents, so amazed and affrighted both Powhatan and all his people that from all parts with presents they desired peace, returning many stolne things which wee neither demaunded nor thought of. And after that, those that were taken stealing (both Powhatan and his people) have sent them backe to James Towne to receive their punishment, and all the countrie became absolutely as free for us, as for themselves.

What was done in three monthes having victuall. The store devoured by rats, how we lived three monthes of such naturall fruits as the countrie afforded.

NOW wee so quietly followed our businesse, that in three monthes we made 3 or 4 last of pitch and tarre, and soap ashes, produced a triall of glasse, made a well in the forte of excellent sweete water (which till then was wanting) built some twenty houses, recovered our Church, provided nets and weares for fishing (& to stop the disorders of our disorderly theeues & the Salvages) built a blocke house in the necke of our Isle, kept by a garrison to entertaine the Salvages trade, & none to passe nor repasse, Salvage, nor Christian, with out the Presidents order, 30 or 40 acres of ground we digged, and planted; of three sowes in one yeare increased 60 and odg pigges, and neere 500 chickens brought up themselves (without having any meate given them) but the hogges were transported to hog Isle, where also we built a blocke house with a garrison, to give us notice of any shipping, and for their exercise they made clapbord, wainscot, and cut downe trees against the ships comming.

We built also a fort for a retreat, neare a convenient river upon a high commanding hill, very hard to be assaulted, and easie to be defended; but ere it was halfe finished this defect caused a stay; in searching our casked corne, wee found it halfe rotten, the rest so consumed with the many thousand rats (increased first from the ships) that we knewe not how to keepe that little wee had. This did driue us all to our wits ende, for there was nothing in the countrie but what nature afforded. vntill this time Keinps and Tassore, were fettered prisoners, and daily wrought, and taught us how to order and plant our fields.

Whome now (for want of victuall) we set at libertie, but so wel were they used, that they little desired it; and to express their loves, for 16 daies continuance, the Countrie brought us (when least) 100 a daie of squirrils, Turkies, Deare, and other wild beastes; but this want of corne occasioned the end of all our workes, it being worke sufficient to provide victuall. 60 or 80 with Ensigne Laxon were sent downe the river to liue upon oysters, & 20 with leiftenant Percie to trie for fishing at point comfort, but in six weekes, they would not agree once to cast out their net.

Mr West with as many went up to the falles, but nothing could bee found but a fewe berries and acornes; of that in the store every one had their equall proportion. Till this present (by the hazard and endeavour of some 30 or 40) this whole number had ever been fed. Wee had more Sturgeon that could be devoured by dogge and man; of which the in dustrious, by drying and pownding, mingled with caviare, sorrel, and other wholsome hearbs, would make bread and good meate; others would gather as much Tockwough roots in a day, as would make them bread a weeke, so that of those wilde fruites, fish and berries, these lived very well, (in regard of such a diet) but such was the most strange condition of some 150, that had they not beene forced nolens volens perforce to ga|ther and prepare their victuall they would all have starved, and have eaten one another. Of those wild fruites the Salvages often brought us: and for that the President would not fulfill the unreasonable desire of those distracted lubberly gluttons, to sell, not only our kettles, howes, tooles, and iron, nay swords, peeces, & the very ordenance, and houses, might they have prevailed but to have beene but idle, for those salvage fruits they would have imparted all to the Salvages, especially for one basket of corne they heard of, to bee at Powhatans. Fifty myles from our fort, though he bought neere halfe of it to satisfie their humours, yet to have had the other halfe, they would have sold their soules, (though not sufficient to have kept them a weeke) thousands were their exclamations, suggestions, and devises, to force him to those base inventions, to have made it an occasion to abandon the Countrie. Want perforce constrained him to indure their exclaiming follies till he found out the author, one Dyer, a most craftie knave, and his ancient maligner, whom he worthely punished, and with the rest he argued the case in this manner.

"Fellow souldiers, I did little thinke any so false to report, or so many so simple to be perswaded, that I either intend to starue you, or that Powhatan (at this present) hath corne for himselfe, much lesse for you; or that I would not have it, if I knewe where it were to be had. Neither did I thinke any so malitious as now, I see a great many, yet it shall not so much passionate me, but I will doe my best for my worst maligner. But dreame no longer of this vaine hope from Powhatan, nor that I will longer forbeare to force you from your Idlenesse, and punish you if you raile, you cannot deny that by the hazard of my life, many a time I have saved yours, when, might your owne wills have prevailed, you would have starved, and will doe still whether I will or no.

But I protest by that God that made me, since necessitie hath not power to force you togather for your selves, those fruits the earth doth yeild, you shall not only gather for your selves, but for those that are sicke: as yet I never had more from the store then the worst of you. All my English extraordinarie provision that I have, you shall see mee devide among the sick. And this Salvage trash, you so scornfully repine at, being put in your mouthes your stomacks can digest it, and therefore I will take a course you shall provide it. The sicke shall not starve, but equally share of all our labours, and every one that gathereth not every day as much as I do, the next daie shall be set beyond the river, and for ever bee banished from the fort, and live there or starve."

This order many murmured, was very cruell, but it caused the most part so well bestir themselves, that 200 men (except they were drowned) there died not past seven or eight. As for Captaine Winn, and Mr Ley, they died, ere this want happened, and the rest died not for want of such as preserved the rest. Many were billitted among the Salvages, whereby we knewe all their passages, fieldes, and habitations, howe to gather and use their fruits, as well as themselves.

So well those poore Salvages used us, (that were thus Billited) as divers of the souldiers ran away, to search Kemps our old prisoner. Glad was this Salvage to have such an occasion to testifie his love for insteed of entertaining them, & such things as they had stolen with all the great offers and promises they made them to revenge their injuries upon Captaine Smith.

First he made himselfe sport, in shewing his countrymen (by them) how he was used; feeding them with this law: *who would not worke must not eat,* till they were neere starved, continuallie threatening to beate them to death, neither could they get from him, till perforce he brought them to our Captaine, that so we contented him, and punished them. As manie others that intended also to have followed them, were rather contented to labour at home, then adventure to live Idle among the Salvages, (of whom there was more hope to make better christians and good subiects, then the one halfe of those that counterfeited themselves both.)

For so afeard were all those kings and the better sorte of their people, to displease us, that some of the baser sort that we have extreamelie hurt and punished for their villanies, would hire us, we should not tell it to their kings or countrymen, who would also repunish them, and yet returne them to James Towne to content the President, by that testimonie of their loves.

Mr Sicklemore well returned from chawonock, but found little hope and lesse certainetie of them were left by Sir Walter Rawley. So that Nathaniell Powell & Anas Todkill, were also, by the Quiyoughquohanocks, conducted to the Mangoages to search them there. But nothing could we learne but they were all dead, this honest, proper, good promise keeping king, of all the rest did ever best affect us, and though to his false Gods he was yet very zealous, yet he would confesse, our God as much exceeded his, as our guns did his bowe and arrows. He often sending our President manie presents to praie to his God for raine, or his corne would perish, for his Gods were angrie all this time.

To reclaime the Dutchmen, and one Bentley and other fugitive, we imployed one William Volda (a Switzer by birth) with pardons and promises to regaine them. Little we then suspected this double villanie, of anie villanie, who plainlie taught us, in the most trust was the greatest treason. For this wicked hypocrit, by the seeming hate he bore to the lewd condition of his cursed countrymen, and having this opportunitie by his emploiment to regaine them, conveighed them everie thing they desired to affect their project to destroy the colonie.

With much devotion they expected the Spanyard, to whom they intended to have done good service. But to begin with the first oportunitie, they seeing necessittie, thus inforced us to disperse our selves; importuned Powhatan to lend them but his forces, and they would not only destroie our hogs, fire, our towne, and betraie our Pinnas; but bring to his service and subiection the most part of our companies.

With this plot, they had acquainted many discontents and many were agreed to their divelish practise. But on Thomas Douese & Thomas Mallard, whose Christian hearts much relenting at such an unchristian act, voluntarily revealed it to Captaine Smith. The Captain did his best it might be concealed, perswading Douese and Malard to proceed in the confederacie: onlie to bring the irreclaimable Dutchmen, and inconstant Salvages in such a maner amongst his ambuscadoes, as he had prepared, as not manie of them shoulde ever have returned from out our penisula. But this brute coming to the ears of the impatient multitude, they so importuned the President to cut off those Dutchmen, as amongst manie that offered to cut their throates before the face of Powhatan. Mr Wiffin and Jefrey Abots were sent to stab or shoot them; but these Dutchmen made such excuses, accusing Volda whom they supposed had revealed their project, as Abot would not, yet Wiffin would, perceiving it but deceipt.

The king understanding of this, their emploiment, sent presentlie his messengers to Captaine Smith to signifie it was not his fault to detaine them, nor hinder his men from executing his command, nor did he nor would he maintaine them, or anie to occasion his displeasure.

But ere this bussiness was brought to a point, God having seene our misery sufficient, sent in Captaine Argall to fish for Sturgion with a ship well furnished with wine and bisket, which though it was not sent us. Such were our occassions we tooke it at a price, but left him sufficient to returne for England, still dissembling Valdo his villany, but certainlie hee had not escaped had the President continued.

By this you may see, for all those crosses, treacheries, and dissentions, howe he wrastled and overcame (without bloud shed) all that happened. Also, what good was done, how few died, what food the country naturally affordeth, what small cause there is men shoulde starve, or be murdered by the Salvages, that have discretion to manage this courage and industry.

The two first years though by his adventures he had oft brought the Salvages to a tractable trade, yet you see how the envious authority ever crossed him, and frustrated his best endeavours. Yet this wrought in him that experience and estimation among the Salvages, as otherwaies it had bin impossible he had ever effected that he did, though the many miserable yet generous and worthy adventures, he had long, and oft indured as well in some parts of Africa, and America, as in the most partes of Europe and Asia by land or sea had taught him much, yet in this case he was againe to learne his lecture by experience.

Which with, thus much a doe having obtained, it was his ill chance to end, when hee had but onlie learned how to begin. And though hee left these vnknowne difficulties, (made easie and famil|liar) to his unlawfull successors, whoe onlie by living in James Towne, presumed to know more then all the world could direct them though they had all his souldiers with their triple power, and twise triple better meanes, by what they have done in his absence, the world doth see: and what they would have done in his presence, had he not prevented their indiscretions: it doth justlie approve what cause he had to send them for England.

They have made it more plaine since their returne, having his absolute authoritie freely in their power, with all the advantages, and opportunity that his labours had effected. As I am sorry their actions have made it so manifest, so I am unwilling to say what reason doth compell me, to make apparant the truth, least I should seeme partial, reasonlesse, or malitious.

The Arivall of the third supply

TO redresse those iarres & ill proceedings, the Councell in England altered the governement & devolved the authoritie to the Lord De-la-ware. Who for his deputie, sent Sr Thomas Gales, & Sr George Somers, with nine ships & 500 persons.

They set saile from England in May 1609, a small catch perished at sea in a Herycano. The Admirall, with 150 men, with the two knights, & their new commission, their bills of loading with all manner of directions, and the most part of their provision arrived not.

With the other 7 (as Captaines) arived Ratliffe, whose right name was Sickelmore, Martin, and Archer. Who as they had been troublesome at sea, beganne againe to marre all ashore. For though, as is said, they were formerly deposed & sent for England: yet now returning againe, graced by the title of Captaines of the passengers, seeing the admirall wanting, and great probabilitie of her losse: strengthned themselves with those newe companies. So railing and exclaiming against Captaine Smith, that they mortally hated him, ere ever they see him. Who understanding by his scouts, the arivall of such a fleet (little dreaming of any such supply) supposing them Spaniards, hee so determined and ordered his affaires, as wee little feared their arivall, nor the successe of our incounter, nor were the Salvages any way negligent or unwilling, to aide and assist us with their best power, had it so beene, wee had beene happy. For we would not have trused them but as our foes, whereas receiving those as our countriemen and friends, they did their best to murder our President, to surprise the store, the fort, and our lodgings, to usurp the governement, and make us all their servants, and slaves to our owne merit, to 1000 mischiefes those lewd Captaines led this lewd company.

Wherein were many unruly gallants packed thether by their friends to escape ill destinies, and those would dispose and determine of the governement, sometimes one, the next day another, to day the old commission, to morrow the new, the next day by neither. In fine, they would rule all or ruine all; yet in charitie we must endure them thus to destroy us, or by correcting their follies, have brought the worlds censure upon us to have beene guiltie of their bloods.

Happy had we been had they never arrived; and we for ever abandoned, & (as we were) left to our fortunes, for on earth was never more confusion, or miserie, then their factions occasioned.

The President seeing the desire those braves had to rule, seeing how his authoritie was so unexpectedly changed, would willingly have left all and have returned for England, but seeing there was small hope this newe commission would ariue, longer hee would not suffer those factious spirits to proceed. It would bee too tedious, too strange, and almost incredible, should I particularly relate the infinite dangers, plots, & practises, hee daily escaped amongst this factious crue. The chiefe whereof he quickly laid by the heeles, til his lea sure better served to doe them justice; & to take away all occasions of further mischiefe, Mr Persie had his request granted to returne for England. Mr West with 120 went to plant at the falles. Martin with neare as many to Nansamund, with their due proportions, of all provisions, according to their numbers.

Now the Presidents yeare being neere expired, he made Martin President, who knowing his own insufficiencie, and the companies scorne, and conceit of his unworthinesse, within three houres resigned it againe to Captaine Smith, and at Nansamund thus proceeded.

The people being contributers used him kindly: yet such was his jealous feare, and cowardize, in the midst of his mirth, hee did surprize this poore naked king, with his monuments, houses, and the Isle he inhabited; and there fortified himselfe, but so apparantly distracted with fear, as imboldned the Salvages to assalt him, kill his men, redeeme their king, gather and carrie away more then 1000 bushels of corne, hee not once daring to intercept them. But sent to the President, to send to the Falles 30 good shotte, which from Jamestowne immediatly were sent him, but hee so well imploid them, as they did just nothing, but returned, complaining of his childishnesse, that with them fled from his company, and so left them to their fortunes.

Mr West having seated his men at the Falles, presently returned to revisit James Towne, the President met him by the way as he followed him to the falles: where he found this company so inconsiderately seated, in a place not only subiect to the rivers inundation, but round invironed with many intollerable inconveniences. For remedy whereof, he sent presently to Powhatan, to sell him the place called Powhatan, promising to defend him against the Monacans, and these should be his conditions (with his people) to resigne him the fort and houses and all that countrie for a proportion of copper: and that all stealing offenders should bee sent him, there to receive their punishment: that every house as a custome should pay him a bushell of corne for an inch square of copper, and a proportion of Pocones as a yearely tribute to King James, for their protection as a dutie: what else they could spare to barter at their best discreation.

But both this excellent place and those good conditions did those furies refuse, contemning both him, and his kind care and authoritie. The worst they could to shew their spite, they did. I doe more then wonder to thinke how only with five men, he either durst, or would adventure as he did, (knowing how greedy they were of his blood) to land amongst them and commit to imprisonment the greatest spirits amongst them, till by their multitudes being 120.

They forced him to retire, yet in that retreate hee surprised one of the boates, wherewith hee returned to their shippe, wherein was their provisions, which also hee tooke. And well it chaunced hee found the marriners so tractable and constant, or there had beene small possibility he had ever escaped. Notwithstanding there were many of the best, I meane of the most worthy in judgement, reason or experience, that from their first landing hearing the generall good report of his old souldiers, and seeing with their eyes his actions so well managed with discretion, as Captaine Wood, Captaine Webb, Captaine Mone, Captaine Phitz-James, Mr Partridge, Mr White, Mr Powell and divers others.

When they perceived the malice and condition of Ratliffe, Martin, and Archer, left their factions; and ever rested his faithfull friends: But the worst was, the poore Salvages that dailie brought in their contribution to the President, that disorderlie company so tormented those poore naked soules, by stealing their corne, robbing their gardens, beating them, breaking their houses, & keeping some prisoners; that they dailie complained to Captaine Smith. Smith had brought them for protectors, worse enimies then the Monocans themselves; which though till then, (for his love) they had indured: they desired pardon, if hereafter they defended themselves, since he would not correct them, as they had long expected he would. So much they importuned him to punish their misdemeanores, as they offered (if hee would conduct them) to fight for him against them. But having spent nine daies in seeking to reclaime them, shewing them how much they did abuse themselves, with their great guilded hopes, of seas, mines, commodities, or victories they so madly conceived.

Then (seeing nothing would prevaile with them) he set saile for James Towne: now no sooner was the ship under saile but the Salvages assaulted those 120 in their fort, finding some stragling abroad in the woods they slew manie, and so affrighted the rest, as their prisoners escaped, & they scarse retired, with the swords & cloaks of these they had slaine. But ere we had sailed a league our shippe grounding, gave us once more libertie to summon them to a parlie. Where we found them all so stranglie amazed with this poore simple assault, as they submitted themselves upon any tearmes to the Presidents mercie. Who presentlie put by the heeles six or seven of the chiefe offenders, the rest he seated gallantlie at Powhatan, in their Salvage fort they presently built and fortified with poles and barkes of trees sufficient to have defended them from all their Salvages in Virginia, drie houses for lodgings, 300 acres of grounde readie to plant, and no place so strong, so pleasant and so delightful in Virginia, for which we called it nonsuch.

The Salvages also he presentlie appeased; redelivering to every one their former losses. Thus all were friends, new officers appointed to command, and the President againe readie to depart. But at that instant arrived Mr West, whose good nature with the perswasions and compassion of those mutinous prisoners was so much abused, that to regaine their old hopes new turboiles arose. For the rest being possessed of all their victuall munition and everie thing, they grow to that height in their former factions, as there the President left them to their fortunes, they returning againe to the open aire at west fort, abandoning Nonsuch, and he to James Towne with his best expedition, but this happened him in that Journie.

Sleeping in his boat, for the ship had returned only two dayss before, accidentally, Captain Smith fired his powder bag, which tore his flesh from his bodie and thighes, nine or ten inches square in a most pittifull manner, to quench the tormenting fire, frying him in his cloaths he leaped over board into the deep river, before they could recover him, he was near drowned. In this condition, without either Chirurgio, or Chirurgery he was to go near 100 miles.

Arriving at Jamestowne causing all things to be prepared for peace or wars to obtain provision, whilest those things were providing, Martin, Ratliffe, and Archer, being to have their trials their guiltie conciences fearing a just reward for their deserts, seeing the President unable to stand, & near bereaved of his senses by reason of his torment, they had plotted to have murdered him in his bed. But his heart did fail him that should have given fire to that merciless pistol. So, not finding that course to be the best they joined together to usurp the government, thereby to escape their punishment, and excuse themselves by accusing him.

The President, had notice of their plans, and through his old souldiers pressured them and did not permit them to resist. They promised that they would not resist his command. He sent for the masters of the ships and tooke order with them for his returne for England, seeing there was no surgeon in the fort to cure his hurt, and the ships were to depart the next day, his commission to be suppressed he knew not why, himselfe and souldiers to be rewarded he knew not how, and a new commission granted they knew not to whom, the which so disabled that authority he had, as made them presume so oft to those mutinies and factions as they did.

So grievous were his wounds, & so cruell his torment, few expected he could live, nor was he able to follow his business to regain what they had lost, suppresse those factions and range the countries for provision as he intended, and well he knew in those affaires his owne actions and presence was as requisit as his experience, and directions, which now could not be, he went presently aboard, resolving there to appoint them govenors, and to take order for the mutiners and their confederates.

Who seeing him gone, perswaded Mr Percy (to stay) and be their President, and within lesse then an houre was this mutation begun and concluded. For when the company understood Smith would leave them and see the rest in armes, called Presidents and councellors, many began to fawne on those new commanders, that now bent all their wits to get him resigne them his commission, who after many salt and bitter repulses, that their confusion should not be attributed to him for leaving the country without government and authority; having taken order to bee free from danger of their malice. He was not unwilling they should steale it from him, but never consented to deliver it to any. But had that unhappy blast not happened, he would quickly have quallified the heate of those humors and factions, had the ships but once left them and us to our fortunes, and have made that provision from among the Salvages, as we neither feared Spanyard, Salvage, nor famine: nor would have left Virginia, nor our lawfull authoritie, but at as deare a price as we had bought it, and paid for it.

What shall I say? but thus we lost him, that in all his proceedings, made justice his first guide, and experience his second; ever hating basenesse, sloth, pride, and indignitie, more then any dangers; that never allowed more for himselfe, then his souldiers with him; that upon no danger would send them where he would not lead them himselfe; that would never see us want what he either had, or could by any meanes get us; that would rather want then borrow, or starve then not pay; that loved actions more than wordes, and hated falshood worse then death: whose adventures were our lives, and whose losse our deathes.

Captain Smith left us with three ships, seven boates, commodities ready to trade, the harvest newly gathered, ten weekes provision in the store, *490 odd persons,* 24 peeces of ordinances, 300 muskets, snaphanches, and fire lockes, shot, powder, and match sufficient, curats, pikes, swords, and moryons more then men. The Salvages language & habitations well knowne to 100 well trained and expert souldiers; nets for fishing, tooles of all sortes to worke, apparell to supply our wants, six mares and a horse, 5 or 600 swine, as many hens and chicken; some goates, some sheep, what was brought or bread there remained, but they regarded nothing but from hand to mouth, to consume that we had, tooke care for nothing but to perfit some colourable complaints against Captaine Smith. For effecting whereof, three weekes longer they stayed the 6 ships till they could produce them that time and charge might much better have beene spent, but it suited well with the rest of their discreations.

Now all those, Smith had either whipped, punished, or any way disgraced, had free power and liberty to say or sweare any thing, and from a whole armefull of their examinations this was concluded.

The mutiners at the Falles, complained hee caused the Salvages to assalt them, for that hee would not revenge their losse, they being but 120, and he five men and himselfe, and this they proved by the oath of one hee had oft whipped for perivrie and pilfering. The dutchmen that he had appointed to bee stabbed for their treacheries, swore he sent to poison them with rats baine.

The prudent Councel, that he would not submit himselfe to their stolene authoritie. Coe & Drer, that should have murdered him, were highly preferred for swearing, they heard one say, he heard Powhatan say, that he heard a man say: if the king would not send that corne he had, he should not long enjoy his copper crowne, nor those robes he had sent him: yet those also swore hee might have had corne for tooles but would not.

The truth was, Smith had no such ingins as the king demanded, nor Powhatan any corne. Yet this argued he would starve them. Others complained hee would not let them rest in the fort (to starve) but forced them to the oyster bankes, to live or starve, as he lived himselfe. For though hee had of his owne private provisions sent from England, sufficient; yet hee gave it all away to the weake and sicke, causing the most untoward (by doing as he did) to gather their food from the unknowne parts of the rivers & woods, that they lived (though hardly) that otherwaies would have starved, ere they would have left their beds, or at most the sight of James Towne to have got their own victuall.

Some propheticall spirit calculated hee had the Salvages in such subjection, hee would have made himselfe a king, by marrying Pocahontas, Powhatans daughter. It is true she was the very nomparell of his kingdome, & at most not past 13 or 14 yeares of age. Very oft shee came to our fort, with what shee could get for Captaine Smith, that ever loved and used all the Countrie well, but her especially he ever much respected: & she so well requited it, that when her father intended to have surprized him, shee by stealth in the darke night came through the wild woods and told him of it. But her marriage could no way have intitled him by any right to the kingdome, nor was it ever suspected hee had ever such a thought, or more regarded her, or any of them, thē in honest reason, & discreation he might. If he would he might have married her, or have done what him listed. For there was none that could have hindred his determination. Some that knewe not any thing to say, the Councel instructed, and advised what to sweare.

So diligent they were in this businesse, that what any could remember, hee had ever done, or said in mirth, or passion, by some circumstantiall oath, it was applied to their fittest use, yet not past eight or nine could say much and that nothing but circumstances, which all men did knowe was most false and untrue.

Many got their passes by promising in England to say much against him. I have presumed to say this much in his behalfe for that I never heard such foule slaunders, so certainely beleaved, and urged for truthes by many a hundred, that doe still not spare to spread them, say them and sweare them, that I thinke doe scarse know him though they meet him, nor have they ether cause or reason, but their wills, or zeale to rumor or opinion.

For the honorable and better sort of our Virginian adventurers I think they understand it as I have writ it. For instead of accusing him, I have never heard any give him a better report, then many of those witnesses themselves that were sent only home to testifie against him. Richard Pots, W. P.

When the ships departed C. Davis arived in a small Pinnace with some 16 proper men more, to those were added a company from James Towne under the command of Captaine Ratliffe to inhabit Point comfort. Martin and Mr West having lost their boates, and neere halfe their men amongst the Salvages, were returned to James Towne, for the Salvages no sooner understood of Captaine Smiths losse, but they all revolted, and did murder & spoile all they could incounter.

Now were we all constrained to live only of that which Smith had only for his owne company, for the rest had consumed their proportions. And now have we 20 Presidents with all their apprtenances, for Mr Percy was so sicke he could not goe nor stand.

Before all was consumed, M. West and Ratliffe, each with a pinnace, and 30 or 40 men well appointed, sought abroad to trade, how they carried the businesse I knowe not, but Ratliffe and his men were most slaine by Powhatan, those that escaped returned neare starved in the Pinnace. And Mr West finding little better successe, set saile for

England. Now wee all found the want of Captaine Smith, yea his greatest maligners could then curse his losse.

Now for corne, provision, and contribution from the Salvages; wee had nothing but mortall wounds with clubs and arrowes. As for our hogs, hens, goats, sheep, horse, or what lived, our commanders and officers did daily consume them, some small proportions (sometimes) we tasted till all was devou|red then swords, arrowes, peeces; or any thing we traded to the Salvages, whose bloody fingers were so imbrued in our bloods, that what by their crueltie, our Governours indiscreation, and the losse of our ships;

Of 500, within six monthes after there remained not many more then 60 of the most miserable and poore creatures. It were to vile to say what we endured; but the occasion was only our owne, for want of providence, industrie, and governement, and not the barrennesse and defect of the countrie, as is generally supposed, for till then in 3 yeares (for the numbers were landed us) we had never landed sufficient provision for 6 months such a glutton is the sea, and such good fellowes the marriners, wee as little tasted of those great proportions for their provisions, as they of our miseries, that notwithstanding ever swaid and overruled the business. Though we did live as is said, three yeares chiefly of what this good countrie naturally affordeth: yet now had we beene in Paradise it selfe, and with those governours it would not have beene much better with us, yet was there some amongst us, who had they had the governement, would surely have kept us from those extremities of miseries, that in ten daies more would have supplanted us all by death.

But by Gods grace, that we would not be unplanted, sent Sir Thomas Gates, and Sir George Sommers, with a ship of 150 men, most happily preserved by the Berondoes to preserve us, strange it is to say how miraculously they were preserved, in a leaking ship, in those extreame stormes and tempests in such overgrowne seas three daies and three nights by bappling out water. And having given themselves to death, how happily when least expected that worthy Captaine Sir George Somers, having line all that time cuning the ship before those swollowing waves, discovered those broken Isles, where how plentifully they lived with fish & flesh, what a paradice this is to inhabit, what industrie they used to build their two ships, how happily they did transport them to James Towne in Virginia, I refer you to their owne printed relations.

But when those noble knights did see our miseries (being strangers in the country) and could understand no more of the cause but by their coniecture, of our clamors and complaints, of accusing or excusing one another, they imbarked us with themselves, with the best means they could, and abandoning James Towne set saile for England.

But yet God would not so have it, for ere wee left the river; we met the Lord De-la-ware, then governour for the countrie, with three ships exceeding well furnished with al necessaries fitting, who againe returned them to the abandoned James Towne, the 9th of June, 1610.

Accompanied with Sir Ferdinando Wainman, and divers other gentlemen of sort. Sir George Somers, and Captaine Argall he presentlie dispatcheth to require the Bermondas to furnish them with provision: Sir Thomas Gates for England to helpe forward their supplies: himselfe neglected not the best was in his power for the furtherance of the busines and regaining what was lost. But even in the beginning of his proceedings, his Lords had such an incounter with a scurvy sickenesse, that made him unable to weld the state of his body, much lesse the affaires of the colonie, so that after eight monthes sicknesse, he was forced to save his life by his returne for England.

In this time, Argall not finding the Bermondas, having lost Sir George Somers at sea, fell on the coast of Sagadahock, where refreshing himselfe, found a convenient fishing for God. With a tast whereof hee returned to Jamestowne, from whence the Lord De-la-ware sent him to trade in the river of Patawomecke, where finding an English boy those people had preserved from the furie of Powhatan, by his acquaintance had such good usage of those kind Salvages, that they fraughted his ship with corne, wherewith he returned to James Towne, and so for England with the Lord governour, yet before his returne, the adventurers had sent Sr Thomas Dale with three ships, men and cattell, and all other provisions necessarie for a yeare, all which arrived the 10th of May, 1611.

Againe, to second him with all possible expedition there was prepared for Sr Thomas Gates, six ships with 300 men, and 100 kyne, with other cattel, with munition and all manner of provision could bee thought needfull, and they arived about the 1st of August next after safely at Jamestowne.

Sir George Somers all this time was supposed lost: but thus it happened missing the Bermondas, hee fell also as did Argall with

Sagadahock, where being refreshed, would not content himselfe with that repulse, but returned againe in the search; and there safely arived. But overtoiling himselfe on a surfeit died. And in this Cedar ship built by his owne directions, and partly with his owne hands, that had not in her any iron but only one bolt in her keele, yet well endured thus tossed to and againe in this mightie Ocean, til with his dead body she arived in England. At Whitchurch in Dorsetshire, his body by his friends was honourably buried, with many volies of shot, and the rights of a souldier. And upon his Tombe was bestowed this Epitaph:

Hei mihi Virginia, quod tam cito praeterit aestas,
Autumnus sequitur, saeuiet inde & hyems.
At ver perpetuum nascetur, & Anglialaeta
Decerpit flores, Floryda terra tuos.

Since there was a ship fraughted with provision, and 40 men, and another since then with the like number and provision to stay in the Countrie twelve months with Captaine Argall.

The Lord governour himselfe doth confidently determine to goe with the next, or as presently as hee may in his owne person, with sundry other knights & gentlemen, with ships & men so farre as their meanes will extend to furnish. As for all their particular actions since the returne of Captaine Smith, for that they have beene printed from time to time, and published to the world, I cease farther to trouble you with any repetition of things so well knowne, more then are necessarie.

To conclude the historie, leauing this assurance to all posteritie, howe unprosperously things may succeed, by what changes or chances soever. The action is honorable and worthie to bee approved, the defect whereof hath only beene in the managing the businesse; which I hope now experience hath taught them to amend, or those examples may make others to beware, for the land is as good as this booke doth report it.

CAptaine Smith I returne you the fruit of my labours, as Mr Croshaw requested me, which I bestowed in reading the discourses, & hearing the relations of such which have walked, & observed the land of Virginia with you. The pains I took was great: yet did the nature of the argument, and hopes I conceaved of the expedition, give me exceeding content. I cannot finde there is any thing, but what they all affirme, or cannot contradict: the land is good: as there is no citties, so no sonnes of Anak: all is open for labor of a good and wise inhabitant: and my prayer shall ever be, that so faire a land, may bee inhabited by those that professe and love the Gospell.[38]

Your friend W. S.

Part Four

Rising and falling from ashes

The church that was burned in the Jamestown fire of January 17, 1608, was the wretched affair of logs, sedge, and dirt, built by the colonists to take the place of the awning between two trees under which they first worshipped.

In a map of the Virginia settlement, sent by Zuniga to King Philip the Third in September of 1608, the site of a church is indicated enclosed within the fort. Captain Newport employed his mariners in rebuilding this church, "all which works they finished cheerfully and in short time."

The time, it appears, was short indeed. Anas Todkill and his collaborators assert that it was "little need they should stay and consume victuall for fourteene days, that the Mariners might say they built such a golden Church, that we can say the raine washed neere to nothing in fourteene days."

Our "Doctor of Divinitie" duly records that when Newport departed "Captain Smith and Master Scrivener divided betwixt them the rebuilding Jamestown, the repairing our Palliza, the cutting down trees, preparing our fields for planting corne, and rebuilding our Church."

This, at best only a flimsy affair, was the second Church, we suppose the mariners' work was mended, not destroyed, and the good preacher, Master Hunt, was still alive. The day of his death is not known. He was certainly living in December, 1608, for somebody, and doubtless in the church, married John Laydon to Ann Burras. We know of no minister who came over until 1610. In the interval between his death and the arrival of Mr. Bucke, daily prayers, and homilies on Sunday, were said in the church, although there was no minister.

We are aware that it behooves us to be pretty careful in this matter of churches, now that the shovels and picks of the Association for the Preservation of Virginia Antiquities are busy with the foundations of the Jamestown churches. They will never find the foundation of the first one, nor of the second, for the very good reason that they had none.

The 20th of April, all hands were at work hewing down trees and planting corn, when an alarm from the guard caused every man to drop axe and hoe and take up arms, each one expecting an assault from the savages. But presently a trumpet blast reached the ear, and a ship was seen sailing up the James with the red cross of St. George flying from the masthead.

This was the Pheonix, a marine pheonix, rising from the sea after "many perrills of extreame storms and tempests." This happy arrival of Captain Nelson, "having been three months missing after Captain Newport's arrivall, being to all our expectations lost, having been long crossed with tempestuous weather and contrary winds, did so ravish us with exceeding joy that now we thought ourselves as well fitted as our hearts could wish both with a competent number of men as also for all other needful provisions till a further supply could come to us."

Captain Francis Nelson, an honest man and expert mariner, turned his back on the fantastical gold and freighted his ship for her return voyage with cedar. When he sailed for home he took with him the gold-hunting Captain Martin, and Smith's "True Relation of Virginia." The first book written by an Englishman in America, used throughout this book and every history book written about America.

Captain Smith felt the restless stirrings of his adventurous spirit. He had long wished to explore the great bay, and he now accompanied the Phoenix as far as the capes. As the ship "bore up the helm," and entered her long path on the great sea, he turned the prow of his little barge northward to the mysterious unexplored waters of the Chesapeake. Relying upon Indian information, he had sent, by Captain Newton, almost a pledge that he would find the outlet to the South Sea through the northern waters, rather than the James or Chickahominy rivers.

Personally, he had nothing to gain, and the crown would be sure to claim everything, but it behooved him to satisfy the London Company. Christians and patriots had swelled his sails with psalms and prayers when he left England, but he had reason to fear that the existence of the colony did not depend upon the Christian who thought of nothing but the coming of God's Kingdom on earth, nor upon the patriot who sought only the honour of old England. Rather upon a King and company seeking the present gold, and a path whereby gold-bearing regions might be reached in future.

The colonists had always been reluctant to cultivate food products, and were by consequence always starving. This was, in part, because they were not allowed to plant on their own account, except upon condition of contributing part of their crops and one month's service annually for the benefit of the London Company.

Neither could they leave the country without special permission. Private letters from England were constantly intercepted. It is narrated that a passport from the King for the return of one of the colonists was sewed in a garter to ensure its delivery. The settlers were, as a matter of fact, *slaves and prisoners*, chained hand and foot to a life of privation and peril.

Their true position was concealed for a while from the English people, but the secret was kept for a short time only. *Banishment to Virginia was worse than death.*

Scott makes his profligate apprentice consider the alternative of suicide or life in Virginia. "I may save the hangman a labour or go the voyage to Virginia, said Jin Vincent." Three thieves, under sentence of death, were offered pardon and transportation to Virginia. One of the three preferred hanging. The other two were sent to the long-suffering colonists.

"The first country in America," says Stith, "is under the unjust scandal of being another Siberia, fit only for the vilest of people."

In October, an unexpected ship appears on the broad bosom of the James. The London Company has hurriedly fitted out the Mary Margaret, and sent Newport back to hasten Smith's discovery of the northward passage to the South Sea. As the ship approaches, the keen eyes of the crowd on shore discern something besides the red cross of St. George fluttering in the autumn breeze. What means this white pennon like a flag of truce? The amazed watchers rub their eyes and gaze again. "It looks like, but no, that cannot be, it certainly looks like-yes, it is- an apron" Sure enough, on the forward deck a small slip of a maiden stands beside a matron in ruff and farthingale, and the little maid's apron signals a greeting to the shore. This is little fourteen year old Ann Burras. Her brother, "John Burras, Tradesman," is on board. She is going to be a famous woman very soon.

She is going to marry John Laydon, and hers will be the first marriage, and her little daughter will be the first English child born in Virginia, and the London Company will be proud of her and look to her dower, and so she and her John will found the genuine, first family of Virginia. She is very unconscious of all this as she stands in her ruff and short petticoat, beside her mistress, Madame Forrest, who is brave in a farthingale, long, pointed bodice, lace ruff, and broad-banded hat. Her husband, "Thomas Forrest, Gentleman," is on board, but the gentleman and his Madam signify very little beside the rosy English maiden who serves them. We will soon get to the first wedding and ceremony in Jamestown.

In the meantime, the news brought by Newport on his return voyage from England was too exciting to leave room for interest in Zuniga's hysterics and the court happenings. Ratcliffe had written home by the last mail that Smith and his followers intended to seize the country and divide it among themselves. This would not be the last time that dissention of power in Jamestown affected the decision made in London. I am sure that they were unaware that their squabbles would result in such a harsh response, had they thought that, perhaps they would have settled their disputes among themselves. The council of the Virginia Company and the King himself, was ready and willing to believe, having been enlightened, by the disgraced Wingfield. The orders were now explicit.

There were to be no more evasions, no more apologies, no more subterfuge. The Virginia colonists were to discover and return one of the lost Roanoke men, to send back a lump of gold, and to find the South Sea, both eastward or northward, or beyond the mountains. Moreover, the returning ship was to be freighted with goods, the sale of which would reimburse the company for its present outlay. Failing in obedience to these orders, the settlers must "consider themselves an abandoned colony and remain in Virginia as banished men."

This was the ultimate ultimatum. It would not be the last that the Colonists of Virginia would ultimately face from the mother county or their Sovereign. Yet, this is possibly the first demand that could have been the first domino to fall, ultimately leading to the War of Independence.

Up until this moment, the Colonists had viewed themselves as adventurers, discoverers whose names would go down in history as the founding fathers of the New World, the great New Britain. Little bye little they realized that their sacrifice and suffering mattered not to their King, nor their countrymen. They were little more than the slaves.

In order to facilitate the progress to the South Sea, the company had kindly sent out a barge in sections, to be borne on the men's backs across the intervening mountains, and to be pieced together when the river running into the South Sea should be reached.

Captain Smith suspected Newport of having instigated these orders, and a violent quarrel ensued. Smith threatened to send the Mary & Margaret home, and keep Newport for a year, put him to work, and let him see for himself how matters stood at Jamestown. However, differences were smoothed over for the present[39]. Apparently, Ratcliff went unnoticed.

King James the First had foolishly amused himself by causing a trumpery crown of copper to be made for Powhatan the First, and sent it with instructions for a formal coronation ceremony. Various presents were to accompany the crown, a bedstead, scarlet cloak, ewer, and basin. Smith was sent overland to invite the Emperor to come to Jamestown for his coronation.

When Smith arrived at Werowocomoco, to his surprise, he found Powhatan gone on a journey to one of his several country houses. A messenger was dispatched to fetch him. Meanwhile a great fire was kindled in a field near a wood, and before it mats were spread for the party of Englishmen. They were probably smoking comfortably, after the manner of tired men, when they heard such a hideous noise and shrieking that the five Englishmen betook themselves to their arms and seized two or three old men by them, supposing Powhatan with all his power was come to surprise them.

But presently Pocahontas came, willing them to kill her if any hurt were intended; and the beholders, which were men, women, and children, satisfied the Captain there was no such matter.

In all our descriptions of Indian ceremonies, it must not be forgotten that we describe the fashions of the Sylvan Court, or, the

Court Barbarian.

Masques were in high vogue at this time at the Court of St. James. Here, also, in the western wilderness was to be a masque, the melodrama to be produced by an amateur company in private theatricals.

Presently, thirty young women came naked out of the woods (only covered before and behind with a few green leaves, their bodies all painted, some white, some red, some black, some partly-colored, but every one different. Their leader had a faire pair of staggers homes on her head, and an otter skin at her girdle, another at her arm, a quiver of arrows at her back, and bow and arrows in her hand.

The next held in her hand a wooden sword; another a club; another a pot-stick: all horned alike. The rest every one with their several devises.

These fiends, with most hellish cries and shouts rushing from amongst the trees, cast themselves in a ring about the fire, singing and dancing with excellent ill variety, or falling into their infernal passions and then solemnly again to sing and dance. Having spent near an hour in this maskarade, as they entered in like manner they departed.

The Earl of Southampton in a letter to the Earl of Salisbury wrote in 1609:

My Lord,

Talking with the King by chance I told him of the Virginia squirrels which they say will fly, whereof there are now divers brought into England, and he presently and very earnestly asked me if none of them was provided for him, saying that he was sure you would get him one of them. I would not have troubled you with this but that you know so well how he is affected by these toys, and with a little enquiry of any of your folks you may furnish yourself to present him at his coming to London which will not be before Wednesday next the Monday, before Theobald's and the Saturday before that to Royston.

Your lordships most assuredly to do your service,

H. Southampton.

Captain Smith indulged himself in writing an imprudent, sharp letter to the, 'Right Honorables,' in London. He entitled his epistle "A Rude Answer," in which he exhibited in caustic terms the preposterous folly of expecting a present profitable return from Virginia. As to gold, he had from the first discouraged all hope of it. The pieced barge for the South Sea? That, at least, was a feasible project. True, it could not be borne many hundreds of miles and over mountains on the backs of his men, but he could burn it and have the ashes carried over in a bag! He then rallies the company for its prodigality in giving Newport a hundred pounds a year for carrying news, and informs them that he sends Ratcliffe home unless the colonists should cut his throat.

All this did but little good to our Captain, as he had cause to realize afterward. 'Had Newport suspected the character of the Rude answer,' says Cooke, it is probable he would have dropped it into the Atlantic. But he duly took it to England and the Right Honorables no doubt gasped at its truculence.'

In December, 1608, there were two hundred men within the palisades at Jamestown, although the weather was delightful, 'affrighted with famine.' The little wooded peninsula, small and marshy as it was, might with proper foresight and industry have yielded corn and garden products, but as Captain Smith in his *Rude Answer* had stated: *'One-half of us are sicke, the other little better. Our diet is usually a little meale and water, and not sufficient of that. Though there be fish in the sea, fowles in the aire, and beasts in the woods, their bounds are so large, they so wilde, and we so weake and ignorant, we cannot trouble them. And we must long lodge and feed the men you send before they can be made good for anything.*

In over-toyling our weake unskilful bodies, we can scarce recover ourselves from one supply to another. If you would send out carpenters, husbandmen and diggers-up of trees' roots, they would be worth more than a thousand of such as we have.'

It was always the old, question of bread and cheese, which has settled adversely many a good cause. Smith, however, did his best with the effeminate gentlemen who had come in Newport's latest ship. He himself shrank from no toil, no exposure. Neither danger nor labour discouraged his manhood, and with his example before them, grappling as he did with the hardest tasks, his followers were deprived of all excuse for complaint or discontent.

Two very choice gallants, Gabriel Beadle and John Russell, both proper gentlemen, were among the thirty whom he invited to join him in the noble art of woodcraft, felling trees, splitting them with wedges, and shaping them with hatchets into clapboards for the additional shelter needed by themselves. In the meantime, they were to lie in the woods at night. The Mary & Margaret had brought over six mares and a horse, so these new "gentlemen" would not be forced, as were their predecessors, to bear this timber on their backs out of the forest.

The novelty had its charm of pleasurable excitement. [40]"Strange were these pleasures to their conditions, yet lodging, eating, drinking, working or playing, they doing but as the President, all these things were carried so pleasantly as within a weeke they became Masters; making it their delight to heare the Trees thunder as they fell. Axes so oft blistered their tender fingers that commonly every third blow had a lowd Oath to drowne the Echo."

Captain Smith rarely indulged in the courtly luxury of profane swearing, and was not inclined to grant privileges to others he did not allow himself. He resolved to have none of it in his Majesty's colony. As for himself he did not need it. He could command vigorous English without it, and so he set about the reformation of the *Gallants and proper Gentlemen,* who had lately come from the English court. He adopted, as a remedial agent, a novel punishment. "He had every man's Oathes numbered, and at night for every oath a can of water was poured down his sleeve, with which every offender was so washed himself and all that a man should scarce heare an oath in a week." And so, we gather, the Captain was after all sometimes overtaken, as well as other people.

The narrator of this incident, Richard Potts, wishes us to make no mistake. "By this he continues, let no man think the President or these Gentlemen spent their times as common woodhackers, felling Trees or such like labours, or that they were pressed to anything as hirelings or common slaves, for what they did, being but a little inured, it seemed they conceited it only a pleasure and a recreation. Yet thirty or forty of such Gentlemen would do more in a day than one hundred of the rest that must be prest by compulsion. "

The numbers at the plantation had again been reduced by sickness to about two hundred people, who were at war with the Indians, and in need of ammunition.

Many of the laborors were taken off the streets, or kidnapped. Some were convicts for petty crimes, judges had made deals with Captains for their delivery in exchange of land in the New World. Many died on the ship, and many more died within the first year. Children, even toddlers were sentence to

'The hand of God was heavy on the Colony, and the hand of God reacheth all the earth.'

Who can avoid it or dispute with him? The Indians had heard of the powder accident from which Captain Smith had suffered so much, and missing him from the fort, concluded he was dead. They saw their opportunity. "They all revolted and did spoil and murther all they encountered." Powhatan resolved to press the war in earnest. All now felt the loss of the strong, fearless captain. Beverley, the old historian, says, "as soon as he left them, all went to ruin."

George Percy, enfeebled from illness, was utterly unable to cope with the difficulties falling on him. His crew at home was a motley one, some thirty "true men," some honest labourers, the rest detrimental in every particular. There were now outlying forts and plantations to be cared for.

At Jamestown,[41]"there was but one Carpenter (John Laydon) and three others who were only learners; two Blacksmiths; two saylers; and those we write 'laborers' were for the most part footmen, and such as they that were adventurers brought to attend them, or such as they could perswade to goe with them, that never did know what a daye's work was. All the rest were poore gentlemen, tradesmen, serving-men, libertines and such like; ten times more fit to spoyle a commonwealth than either begin one or but helpe to maintaine one. For when neither the feare of God, nor the law, nor shame, nor displeasure of their friends could rule them in England, there is small hope ever to bring one in twentie of them ever to be good in Virginia."

There was one way to remedy this state of things, and but one, annihilation! Many died from yellow fever, many from the London plague, or Indian attack. The rest hastened to destruction from starvation.

'The hand of God was heavy, who could avoid it or dispute with Him?"

As the days passed on, the disorder increased, and the inevitable dissolution hastened. Martin's men at Nansemond and West's at the Falls were assailed by the savages and took refuge in Jamestown. Percy was now so ill he could neither goe nor stand. Lord Delaware's kinsman had sailed in despair for England. With every passing hour, the prospect grew darker. Thirty men seized one of the vessels and became buccaneers. Utter hopelessness took possession of those left behind. [42]Every day death visited some house, and when the master was buried, the house was pulled down for firewood, the living not being able to gather fuel in the woods. Parts of the defending palisade were burnt, although the inmates trembled with fear of the Indians. Only the blockhouse was the safety of the few who lived.

The Indians knew all this weakness and forebore to assault the fort or hazard themselves in a war on those whom they were assured in a short time would of themselves perish, yet they killed all stragglers found beyond bounds. Every particle of food was devoured, and the miserable women and children begged from the savages, to receive insult and mortal wounds. Roots, acorns, and the skins of horses were boiled for food. At last dead Indians were dug up and devoured "by the baser sort."

A horrible, ghastly tragedy froze the blood of the "better sort." A man killed his wife, and had devoured part of her body, when he was discovered. He was executed, but that only added horror to horror.

This time marked one of two terrible epochs, the starving time, and the great massacre of 1622. Nearly five hundred persons had lately been landed at Jamestown, and six months afterward "there remained not past sixty men, women and children, most miserable and poor creatures." Of five hundred, more than four hundred had perished, either dead of starvation or brained by the Indian tomahawk.

In May, 1607, the Englishmen had landed in what they termed "a paradise." Over the mossgreen earth- bespred with faire flowers, the branches of the stately trees threw lacelike shadows. Flowering vines hung from their boughs, brilliant birds darted among them, or swooped down to dip their blue and crimson wings in the clear rivulets. All was happiness, activity, and hope.

Now, in May, 1610, the earth was trampled bare of all verdure, ragged stumps of the felled trees were rotting in the ground, noisome vapours rose from the neglected, filthy yards of a pestilence-smitten town. Men, women, and children, gaunt and wild-eyed from famine, perishing by inches slowly but surely, lay about the town, moaning and despairing. The last agony was near. They knew that without help they could not survive many hours. Long ago they had ceased to expect it.

We can imagine the frantic joy when two vessels appeared on the river! These were the cedar ships we left Admiral Somers and Sir Thomas Gates building at Bermuda, the Deliverance and the Patience. The Admiral and Sir Thomas cast anchor and at once went on shore.

The scene that ensued baffles description. The two mariners looked upon wretchedness and desolation indescribable. The shipwreck on sea looked into the eyes of the shipwrecked-on land. Jamestown was in ruins, the town encumbered with filth. The torn-down palisades, the gates swinging to and from on rusty hinges, the church ruined and unfrequented, the dismantled houses, the emaciated faces, the hollow hungry eyes, and voices hardly able to articulate the prayer to be " taken home to die," these were the piteous sights and sounds which greeted the commanders as they landed from their cedar ships. All hope of Virginia was over forever!

Even the stout hearts that had borne storm and wreck in the Sea Venture were appalled by the spectacle.

Gates and Somers had heard at Algernoune Fort of the sad condition of the colony. Captain Percy had happened to be in the fort directing the preparations for its abandonment.

'From hence,' says Strachey, 'in two days only by the help of Tydes and no wind stirring, we plyed it sadly up the river, and the three and twentieth of May we cast Anchor before Jamestowne where we landed, and our much grieved Governour first visiting the church caused the Bell to be rung, at which all such as were able to come out of their houses repayred to the church where our Maister Bucke made a zealous and sorrowful Prayer, finding all things so contrary to our expectation, so full of misery and misgovernment.

After service our Governour caused me to read his commission, and Captain Percy delivered up to him his commission, the old Patent and the Councell Sealed. There was another witness to this scene besides the actors therein. Namontack, Powhatan's man, had returned to England with Newport before the sailing thence of the fleet, and with him Machumps, the brother of the king's favourite, wife Winganuskie. [43]'These two Indians were on the Sea Venture when she was wrecked at Bermuda. There, in a lonely spot, the two had quarrelled and fought, and Machumps killed Namontack, buried him, and kept the secret from his own people. He revealed it, however, to his English friends, and told how he had buried Namontack, the whole of him, finding he could dig only a small grave, he had taken the trouble to cut off his legs and very neatly lay them in order beside him.

Machumps was much esteemed by the colonists. He aided the first explorers of the James River, and they had named a creek "Machump's Creek," in his honour. He lived a year or more at Jamestown with Kemps, a former prisoner, who had also become a friend. The two were more intimate in their relations to the

Englishmen than any other Indians except Pocahontas and Chanco. John Rolfe, "an honest gentleman and of good behaviour," was also a passenger in one of the cedar ships. The little "Bermuda" had died, perhaps on the voyage, and his wife died soon after, so he was left free for the romance, a few years later, of his marriage with Pocahontas.

Upon reckoning up the stores brought in the tiny cedar ships, the Admiral and Gates perceived there were only enough to last sixteen days, allowing two cakes a day to each person. They accordingly, to the joy of the colonists, concluded to abandon Jamestown and sail for England via Newfoundland, where English fishing vessels were supposed to be in condition to victual the company for England. The wretched remnant of the colony was overjoyed at this decision. The fort was dismantled and the cannon buried at the gate. There was little else to take away.

Some of the unhappy sufferers wished to set fire to the houses where they had endured so much, but the commanders elected otherwise; and to prevent the destruction of the houses, church, and palisades, Sir Thomas Gates remained on shore with a party to preserve order, and was the last man to step into the boat. On June 7, every man, woman, and child, at the beating of the drum, repaired aboard the Discovery, the Deliverance, the Patience, and the Virginia, and at noon a salvo of small arms announced to the listening echoes that all was over, all the hope, expectation, struggle, and despair.

That night they fell down the tide to Hogg Island, and bright and early next morning set sail again with glad hearts, the tide bringing them to Mulberry Island. There, to their amazement, they met Captain Edward Brewster in a rowboat, his sailors bending to the oars in great haste to intercept their farther advance. Lord Delaware was at Point Comfort with three vessels laden with all things needful, and hearing there of the movements of Somers and Gates, sent his long boat to command their return to Jamestown. Had the latter been a few moments earlier, or Captain Brewster a trifle later, they would not have met. "This was the arm of the Lord of Hosts who would have his people pass through the Red Sea and the Wilderness, and then possess the Land of Canaan," exclaims the old writer, who bursts forth into exclamations of " thanks and praise for the Lord's infinite goodness! Never had poor people more cause to cast themselves at his very footstool."

The poor people themselves felt differently at the time. "Sir

Thomas Gates the next day, to the great grief of all his company, as wind and weather gave leave, returned his whole company with charge to take possession again of those poor ruinated habitations at Jamestown which they had formerly inhabited. Himself in a boat proceeded down to meet his Lordship, who making all speed up shortly arrived at Jamestown."

Meanwhile the Deliverance, Discovery, Patience, and Virginia "bore up the helm," went in advance, and relanded that night. The fires were rekindled, the guns dug up, and preparation hastily made to receive his Lordship.

[44]Lord Delaware reached Jamestown on Sunday, June 10, 1610, and in the afternoon he went ashore, landing at the south gate of the palisade. Sir Thomas Gates caused his company in arms to stand in order and make guard, William Strachey acting on this special occasion as colourbearer. As soon as the Lord Governor landed, he fell upon his knees before them all, and made a long and silent prayer to God. Then arising, he marched up into the town, Strachey bowing with the colours as he entered the gate, and let them fall at his Lordship's feet, who passed on into the chapel, where evening service was read, followed by a sermon by Rev. Richard Bucke, and after that- caused his ensign to read his commission as Lord Governour and Captaine Generall during the life of the Colony and Plantation in Virginia, upon which Sir Thomas Gates delivered up to his lordship his own commission and the counsell sealed His Lordship. They then delivered some few words of warning and encouragement to the colony, and as no fitting house could be had for him in the town, repaired again to his ship for his lodging.

Events had followed each other like scenes in a theatre. The curtain had slowly descended upon a desolate picture of death, darkness, and despair; it rose with the morning sun on an animated scene of hope and activity. In the space of three days the Virginia colony had perished and come to life again.

The government was now invested in one over whose deliberations there could be no control, and with whom there could consequently be no rivalry.[45] Steady obedience was required and enforced. Things soon assumed a wholesome and active appearance. Every man had his own duty and officers were appointed to see that duty done; and it was not long before the disturbances and confusion which had been the natural consequences of disaffection and revolt were succeeded by the happy fruits of peaceful industry and order.

Let it never be forgotten that in all the time of sore distress there were steadfast souls who never lost their trust in God or failed in their religious duties. They were never without a church, in less that six years they had built or re-built five. In their darkest hour, they had built a church. In it, although the edifice during the starving time fell into a "ruinous condition," they held daily prayers; and in the absence of a minister met on Sunday for "prayers and homilies."

At their lowest estate, they had faith to pray to be delivered from "battle and murder, plague, pestilence, and famine," and to implore help in all their "time of tribulation." Although to their human apprehension the supplication was not answered, the faith of these pious souls failed not. A prayer for daily use was sent to them from the mother church in England, a petition for strength to bear their heavy burdens, for a blessing on all their work, for the conversion of the savages, and ending with a fervent invocation, "God bless England, our sweet native county!"

Lord Delaware repaired the church, and in it Pocahontas was baptized and married. The edifice was of wood, and it was known as the third church. It was sixty feet long by twenty-four wide, and before the arrival of Lord Delaware was probably plainly furnished within. He had it fitted with a chancel of cedar and a communion table of black walnut.

"All the pews and pulpit were of cedar, with fair, broad windows, also of cedar, to shut and open as the weather should occasion. The font was hewn hollow like a canoe, and there were two bells in the steeple at the west end. The church was so cast as to be very light within, and the Lord Governor caused it to be kept passing sweet, trimmed up with divers flowers."

There was a sexton in charge of the church, and every morning the bell rang for prayers at ten and again at four in the afternoon. There was also a sermon every Thursday, and two on Sunday. "Every Sunday when the Lord Governour went to church, he was accompanied with all the councillors, captains, other officers, and all the gentlemen, and with a guard of fifty halberdiers, all in his Lordship's livery, in fair red cloaks." His Lordship sat in the choir in a green velvet chair, and the council, captains, and officers on each side of him.

We have the two pictures, a starved, ragged handful, prostrate before the altar, responding in feeble accents, "Good Lord, deliver us";

and the light and colour, the corps de garde in crimson, the Lord Governor kneeling on his green velvet cushion, the bright flowers filling the chancel. They are all gone now! "Whose souls questionless whether proud or humble, are with God." Jamestown Island is a graveyard.

After Lord Delaware landed with his accessions to the colony, 900 persons had been sent from England to Virginia, of whom 700 had perished. [46]In 1619 it was estimated that 2540 immigrants had landed at Jamestown, of whom 1640 had died.

The total mortality in less than twenty years was 6040, out of 7280. "Around the church thousands are buried, the victims of the first season of starvation and those of the last: good Master Hunt, hardy adventurers, knights and ladies, paupers and gentlemen, gentle and simple, and on the island also Kemps, the Indian, the poor victim of military execution; and Opechancanough, the savage instigator of three massacres, friend and foe they all lie together. The kind mother earth covers them all. In winter, they lie beneath the pure snows from heaven, and the summer daisies look up to God from their ashes: and so they all sleep together, untill the generall day."

The hidden truths of* Importing Slave Labor *found in Colonial Documents:

There are no records in existance that lay out the conditions of those taken to Virginia, traded, sold or bartered. The men in the first years were merely called 'laborors'. It was their job to cut trees, build, or farm the land. The great debabte of white slavery would not be a debate if the documents were so cut and dry as most of the discoveries and Company corraspondance has been.

Four Hundred and ten years ago, when Jamestown was founded, the colonist were extremely diligent in recording their memoirs, unfortunately the memoirs of the laborers is scarcely mentioned throughout those documents. Many of which have been used in this book, and many are similar in details and events.

To learn about the laborers however, we are going to have to do some digging inside those documents. Many of the English laborers who were on board the ships bound for Virginia are recorded as passengers. However, passengers from other regions such as Ireland are not as easy to find in documents that have been preserved.

This chapter is dedicated to the memory of those laborers whose existance has been questioned, and even recently been termed, *The Irish Myth.* They are not a myth, theyre not even all Irish! The following pages will prove that although the Colonist may not have readily mentioned them, and ship passenger lists do not exist, they have not been completely left out, and are sporadically documented.

These souls, who were brought to Virginia for the mere purpose of industry and gain for both England and Virginia, worked hard to build this country. I believe that they deserve as much credit, perhaps more so, and deserve to have their memory preserved for what they sacrificed founding America.

Robert Johnson was an advocate for the Jamestown Colony, he was a London alderman and the deputy treasurer of the Virginia Company of London in early 1609. Johnson presented his economic discourse at a company meeting and on February 28, 1609, it was submitted for publication as *"Nova Brittania."* Johnson writes: *"We have already provided and sent thither skillful workmen from forraine parts, which may teach and set ours in the way, whereby we may set many thousands a worke, in these such like services."*

This statement backs up the narrative the Colonist wrote, that is printed in full in this book, about Francis McGuire. In all the ship passenger lists, letters and accounts of the colony sent to England, McGuire does not appear on any of them. However, McGuire is listed as a passenger that *left Virginia for England April 10, 1608, carrying Edward Wingfield, Captain Archer, an Irishman named Francis Mcguire, and an Indian, Namontack.* This makes it very likely he was one of the original 1607 settlers, although he is not listed on John Smith's list of settlers.

Francis Maguel (or McGuire, Maguire) provided a deposition to a fellow Irishman about his eight months spent in "this fort, which the English call James Fort." His account described the sea voyage from England to Virginia, the James River and James Fort, natural resources to be found and used in Virginia, the Powhatan Indians, three purported routes from Jamestown to the coveted South Sea (Pacific Ocean) and China, and the execution at the fort of Captain George Kendall, a Catholic, accused of plotting "to get to Spain, in order to reveal to His Majesty all about the country and many plans of the English."

Ironically, Maguel/Maguire was also Catholic, which went undiscovered by the Protestant English at Jamestown, and his report served as a Spanish spy document enclosed in a letter dated 21 July 1610, from Spanish King Philip III to his ambassador in London, Don Alonso de Velasco.

Maguel/McGuire swore all he reported was true, and he was willing to return to Virginia "To serve His Catholic Majesty, by showing to the eye all that he says, if His Majesty should be pleased to employ him in this service." [47] Francis Maguel, "Report of what Francisco Maguel, and Irishman, learned in the state of Virginia during his eight months that he was there, July 1, 1610"

Haile claims the letter containing Maguel's report was sent by Ambassador Velasco to his king, nevertheless, no matter who sent the Maguel report it is obvious both King Philip III and Velasco considered it to be vital intelligence about the English colony at Jamestown.

As stated earlier, Spanish ambassadors in England were continually seeking information about the Virginia colony to report to their king, none more aggressively than Don Pedro de Zuñiga who incessantly advocated the destruction of Jamestown.

The Spanish ambassadors in England from 1606-1624, the period of existence of the Virginia Company of London, were Don Pedro de Zuñiga (1605-May 1610), Don Alonso de Velasco (1610-1613), Don Diego Sarmiento de Acuña, Count de Gondomar (August 1613-April 1622, being absent from England from July 1618 to March 1620 and his duties assumed by acting ambassador, Spanish Secretary Julian Sanchez de Ulloa), and finally Don Carolo de Columbo.[48]

In a letter dated 22 November 1621, Virginia"s governor, Sir Francis Wyatt, noted the safe arrival at Jamestown of the ship, The Flying Harte, from Ireland. The ship transported its sponsor, Daniel Gookin, who brought with him aboute 50 more upon that Adventure besides some 30 other Passengers, wee have Accordinge to their desire seated them at Newports news, and we doe conceave great hope (if the Irish Plantacone prosper) frome Ireland greate multitudes of People wilbe like to come hither.[49]

Gookin, an Englishman who owned an estate in Ireland, contracted with the Virginia Company to transport not only settlers but Irish cattle to the colony with the understanding he would be given land to establish his own particular plantation. The Virginia Company eventually granted his land patent, totaling 1,831 acres, in present-day Newport News. How many of Gookin's passengers were Irish is hard to determine, as none of the 20 inhabitants identified as living at his "Newportes Newes" muster in 1625 are listed by nationality.

Nonetheless, notes of a Virginia Company meeting held in London, April 3, 1622, document Gookin's safe arrival in Virginia and the interest of certen gentlemen of Ireland nowe in Towne beinge much encouraged made an offer to undertake the like performance as Mr. Gookin had donn …to transport out of Ireland 20 or 30 able youths of 16 or 17 yeares of age to Virginia to be Apprentices for 6 or 7 yeares in the Companies service.[50]

In an August 1609 letter, Sir Richard Moryson recommended the following course of action for Virginia to the Earl of Salisbury, High Treasurer and Chief of State to James I, as well as the patron of the Jamestown colony, "Should his Lordship please to allow of them to be employed in the intended plantation of Virginia, …he thinks good use might be made of them for the present there, both in defending them now in the beginning, if they be disturbed in their first settling, and in relieving their wants from time to time."[51]

Ironically, as these "certen gentlemen of Ireland" and Virginia Company officials were discussing sending more settlers to Virginia, they were unaware of the numerous Powhatan Indian attacks launched upon many of the English settlements scattered along both banks of the James River on 22 March 1622. Among the names of the 347 settlers listed as being killed that day was "Francis, an Irishman."[52] An additional tabulation of the dead in the colony entitled, "A List of the names of the Dead in Virginia since April last; [F]ebruary 16, 1623[1624]," contains the names of two deceased Irishmen, James and John, residents of Elizabeth City, perhaps brought to Virginia by Gookin.[53]

A letter written by William Hobart to his father, dated 12 April 1623, claimed Gookin's plantation had suffered further losses since the March 22 attacks: He [Hobart] found at his landing out of the Abigail, The Gouernor & lady [Mr. and Mrs. Wyatt] at Mr. Gookin's Plantacon. But of all Mr. Gookin's men which he sent out the last yeare we found but 7: being all killd by the Indians and his plantacon ready to fall to decay.[54]

If this account is correct, several of the dead listed for Elizabeth City on February 16, 1623/24, were probably residents of Gookin's plantation, and except for James and John, no other Irish persons are identified. Perhaps this was an oversight on the part of the chronicler; conceivably further research of records in England or Ireland would reveal that Gookin's plantation was predominately an Irish one.[55]

One other documented Irish arrival in Virginia is of an unnamed youth in January 1622. The ship Tiger, transporting settlers to Virginia, was attacked and boarded by Turks on its way to Virginia. Two English boys were removed by the Turks and substituted with a French and Irish youth. Their fate after arriving in Virginia is undocumented.[56]

The arrival of additional settlers at Jamestown on the Mary & Margaret in September 1608 added to the multi-national make-up of the colony's population. Aboard this ship were men from Germany and Poland and a new member of the governing council, Captain Peter Winne (Wynne). Captain John Smith wrote, *"Of this supply there was added to the council one Captain Waldo and Captain Wynne, two ancient soldiers and valiant gentlemen, but yet ignorant of the business, being but newly arrived."*[57]

Captain Winne was Welsh, as was another of the new arrivals, David ap Hughes.[58] ("ap" is a Welsh idiom meaning, "son of.") In a letter dated the November 26, 1608, Winne described an exploratory trip he took into Monacan Indian territory, west of Jamestown:

I traveled between 50 or 60 miles by land into a country called Monacon, who owe no subjection to Powaton [...]. The people of Monacon speak a far differing language from the subjects of Powaton, their pronunciation being very like Welch, so that the gentlemen in our company desired me to be their interpreter.[59]

Unfortunately for Captain Winne, his reputation with John Smith so deteriorated that Smith claimed Winne was plotting to "hinder their project."[60] It is believed Winne died in Virginia in the spring of 1609.[61]

Records do not identify any early Jamestown settler as being Scottish; however, the Spanish ambassador to England, Don Pedro de Zuñiga, in a letter to his king dated 5 October 1607, suggests there was a possibility, and fear they would be given opportunity. King James I was also King James VI of Scotland before becoming the King of England following the death of Queen Elizabeth I in March 1603. His Scottish peers were anxious to exploit their relationship with the new king in order to gain wealth and prominence over their English counterparts. It would appear, according to Zuñiga, this Scottish scramble for advantage extended to the colonization of Virginia.[62]

Zuñiga writes:

A man has told me to-day, a man who usually tells me the truth, that these men [English] are complaining of what the King [James I] does for the Scotch who may go there [Virginia], and that he favors them more than themselves.[63]

As earlier stated, with the arrival of the Mary & Margaret at Jamestown in September 1608, John Smith recorded the landing of "eight Dutchmen [Germans] and Poles."[64]

The Virginia Company was beginning its active recruitment of people from "forraine parts" to begin industries in Virginia it hoped would prove financially beneficial to the company, the colony and England. Many of these industries required the expertise of skilled artisans found in other parts of Europe.

As early as the 14th century, England was importing skilled craftsmen to make the country as self-sufficient as possible in manufacturing. Every European power, in order to increase its wealth and not the wealth of its competitors, attempted to minimize its importation of other nation"s natural resources and finished products.

Competition between European countries for natural resources, manufactured goods, trade and consumption of goods was one of the driving forces behind colonization. England wanted colonies to ensure her economic independence and power in Europe, especially against Spain. The Virginia Company of London, in its attempt to make Jamestown financially successful, mimicked the Mother Country"s long-held policy of encouraging its companies and manufacturers to import foreign artisans.[65]

One of the first manufacturing endeavors tried at Jamestown was glass production; the reason German or "Dutch" glassblowers were shipped to the colony in September 1608.[66] John Smith provided the first names of three Germans ("Dutchmen") who arrived in 1608: Adam, Francis and Samuel. When Captain Newport sailed back to England on the Mary & Margaret in December 1608, he transported "Trials of pitch, tar, glass, frankincense, soap-ashes, with the clapboard and wainscot that could be provided."[67]

Perhaps Adam, Francis and Samuel were the glassblowers responsible for this trial of glass. Smith further relates he dispatched "three Dutchmen and two English," after Newport"s departure, to Chief Powhatan"s village, Werowocomoco, to build the chief an English-style house, which he had requested of Smith. The three "Dutchmen" sent were Adam, Francis and Samuel.[68] Does this indicate, as some scholars claim, that these three were carpenters and not glassblowers?

German glassmaking records specify that glassmakers worked in teams of two or three, the "Meister" or master, and the "Knecht" or assistant. In addition, these professional artisans required the assistance of workers to do manual labor, such as cutting wood to fire the glass furnaces and build their working area, or glasshouse.[69]

In 1610, William Strachey described this "glasshouse" area:

For should they [Powhatan Indians] have broad and open windows in the quarters of their houses, they knew not well how upon any occasion to make them close and let in the light too, for glass they know not—though the country wants not salsodiac [sal soda, a hydrated sodium carbonate] enough to make glass of, and of which we have made some store in a goodly house set up for the same purpose, with all offices and furnaces thereto belonging, a little without the island where James town stands.[70]

Did the three named Germans have multiple jobs; building the glasshouse facilities, producing the trial of glass, and building Chief Powhatan"s house, or were they the laborers sent to assist the real glassblowers?

Unfortunately, the second attempt at establishing glassmaking at Jamestown was a fiasco, as described in a letter written by the colony"s treasurer, George Sandys, in March 1623: The ill successe of ye glasse workes is almost equall unto this: first the coveringe of ye house, ere fully finished, was blowne downe, by a tempest noe sooner repaired but ye Indians came upon us, which for a while deferd ye proceedinges.

Then they built up ye furnace, which after one forthnight yt ye fire was put in, flew in peeces: yet ye wife of one of ye Italians (whom I have now sent home, haveinge received many wounds from her husband at severall times, & murder not otherwise to be prevented, for a more damned crew hell never vomited) reveald in her passion it was Vincentio crackt it with a crow of iron: yet dare wee not punish theise desperate fellowes, least ye whole dessigne through theire stubbornesse should perish.

The summer cominge on, Capt: Norton dyed with all saving one of his servants, & hee nothinge worth: The Italians fell extremely sicke: yet recoveringe in the ye beginninge of ye winter, I hyred some men for yt service, assisted them with mine owne, rebuilt the furnace, ingaged my selfe for provisions for them, & was in a manner a servant unto them. The fier hath now beene six weekes in ye furnace, and yett nothinge effected. They complaine yt ye sand will not run. Though themselves made choise therof, and like it then well enough & now I am sendinge up ye river to provide them with better, if it bee to bee had. But I conceave that they would gladly make the worke to appeare unfeasible, yt they might by yt meanes be dismissed for England. Much hath beene my truble herein, and not a little my patience, haveinge beene called rascall to my face for reprovinge them of theire ryot, negligence & dissension, for the debt which I am in, for theire sustentation I hope ye adventurers will see it discharged.[71]

In another letter written by George Sandys in April 1623, he explains to Virginia Company officials that he was still trying to make the glassmaking project successful by locating sources

"For sand for the Glassemen, all the servants are dead."47 Only five Italians were listed among the living at the "the glasse howse" in February 1623/24. Vincentio, mentioned by Sandys in his letter-

Bernardo, "Ould Sheppard, his sonn;" Mrs. Bernardo and Richard Tarborer. The only other Italian mentioned in the lists of 1623/24 was deceased: "Symon, an Italian." Vincentio and Bernardo were probably glassblowers because their wives had come with them to Virginia, but Tarborer's and Symon's occupation and/or relation to them is unclear.

A letter dated 15 June 1625, from the governing council at Jamestown explains that Sandys "glassmaking efforts were for naught as, the glass woorkes geven in by Mr. George Sandys, we herewith send you, the death of one of ye princypall woorkmen, an other beinge subject to the falinnge sicknese, and many defects which render the woorke unservable, Hath moved us to Condescende to the importunate suite of the glasse men of returninge for England.[72] It is unknown how many, if any, of the remaining Italians survived to return to England or decided to remain in Virginia.

John Smith, who is usually critical of others efforts at Jamestown, especially when on the subject of work, wrote, that many of the settlers never did know what a day's work was, except the Dutchmen and Poles and some dozen other."[73]

Virginia might allow them to escape religious persecution, while others, such as the French Catholics in Nova Scotia, were brought against their will to Jamestown and made residents by force. The majority of the non-English Europeans who came to Virginia from 1607-1625 were sent by the Virginia Company of London to use their skills to create financially successful commercial enterprises, imitating the English business tradition of using non-English craftsmen. Some of the same investors and managers of these English businesses and overseas trading companies were also stockholders and governing officials in the Virginia Company of London. It was sound business practice to combine their effort at colonization, with all of its desired economic benefits, with the home-grown businesses of England. But, despite the efforts of imported craftsmen to Virginia, none of their enterprises were successful enough to create profits for themselves or the Virginia Company of London. Yet, in spite of these failed colonial economic adventures, these people contributed to the colony"s ultimate survival against what seemed, at times, insurmountable odds.

Terming Slavery

Under the arbitrary rule of Governor Argall this system was to some extent revived. "Three years' slavery" to the colony was the penalty for a violation of his edicts, and absence from church was punished with " slavery " from a week to a year and a day. [74]

No freedom was granted from the common servitude until March, 1617, when the three-year contract made by Dale with the men of Charles City Hundred had expired and they demanded their "long desired freedom from that general and common servitude." Governor Yeardley willingly assented to this reasonable request, as they had now served the colony for nine or ten years.[75] No further extensive grant of freedom was made until he came as Governor in 1619, bringing a proclamation of freedom to most of the ancient planters. Whenever it was obtained before this it was only at an "extraordinary payment," and throughout the first ad' ministration of Yeardley and that of Argall the great majority of the colonists remained in their former condition, which the ancient planters with little exaggeration termed " no way better than slavery."[76] Their rights as Englishmen, guaranteed by the first charter of the company, had practically no recognition before the arrival of Yeardley.

The numerous letters sent by the Governor and General Assembly, 1621-1623, to prevent a re-establishment of Sir Thomas Smith's government in the Company, while expressed in extravagant language, bear witness to the very arbitrary treatment of the colonists during the first twelve years of the Company. Facts were attested by many persons who had been actual sufferers, and affirm that many of those whose lives had been recklessly sacrificed were not of mean rank, as alleged by Smith and Alderman Johnson, but of " ancient houses and born to estates of 1,000 by the year, some more, some less who likewise perished by famine, those who survived who had both adventured their estates and persons were constrained to serve the colony (as if they had been slaves) seven or eight years for their freedoms who underwent as hard service and labors as the basest fellow that was brought out of Newgate. Rather than be reduced to live under like government," they say, "we desire his Majesty that Commissioners may be sent over with authority to hang us." [77]

In 1618 the popular party in the Virginia Company triumphed

over the court party, and Sir Thomas Smith was ousted from the governorship and Sir Edwin Sandys elected in his stead. An almost complete change of policy was the result; a new Governor was sent in the person of Yeardley to supplant the rapacious Argall. Yeardley carried with his commission an important concession of rights to the Virginia planters. A new regime of freedom and representative government, coupled with full rights of private property in land and a responsible governorship, now began in the colony. Yeardley did not bring freedom to all the ancient planters, but only to all those who had gone at their own charge previous to the departure of Dale in 1616, and to those who, sent at the Company's charge, had already served the full time of their servitude to the colony. [78] Many were, however, still retained in servitude until the end of their terms, and the Company, until its dissolution in 1624, continued to send others at the Company's charge on terms of servitude modified to suit the changed conditions in the colony.

We see, then, that the colonist, while in theory only a Virginia member of the London Company, and entitled to equal rights and privileges with other members or adventurers, was, from the nature of the case, practically debarred from exercising these rights. As a planter absent in Virginia he could not sit nor have a voice in the councils of the Company; he was entirely dependent on the Company's good faith for the performance of its obligations, and had recourse to no means to enforce their performance.

He was kept by force in the colony,[79] and could have no communication with his friends in England. His letters were intercepted by the Company and could be destroyed if they contained anything to the Company's discredit. He was completely at the mercy of the edicts of arbitrary governors, and was forced to accept whatever abridgment of his rights and contract seemed good to the Governor and the Company. [80]

His true position was that of a common servant working in the interest of a commercial company. In lieu of his support, or of his transportation and support, he was bound to the service of this company for a term of years. Under the arbitrary administration of the Company and of its deputy governors he was as absolutely at its disposal as a servant at his master's. His conduct was regulated by corporal punishment or more extreme measures. He could be hired out by the Company to private persons, or by the Governor for his personal advantage.

Suggested by the policy of the Company, there gradually grew up after the year 1616 and the establishment of separate plantations, the practice on the part of societies of planters, and later of private persons, of transporting servants to settle and work their lands very much on the same conditions of service as those made by the Company. [81] This developed, as property began to be acquired by the planters generally, into the common mode of transporting servants on contracts by indenture for a limited time of service, varying in individual cases according to the terms of the contract. [82]

In 1619, under the new Governor of the Company, an important modification was introduced regarding its servants in Virginia and colonists who should be afterwards transported at the common charge. The plan instituted by Dale of making a part of the colonists farmers or tenants at a fixed rent, and others servants on a large tract of land for the Company's use, had worked successfully in raising revenues for the government, and the Company now proposed, by an extension of this experiment, to relieve the colonists, "forever of all taxes and public burthens," by setting apart large tracts of "public land," to be worked by a system of tenant ship-at-halves.

Such a system had been commended to Governor Argall in 1617, and orders had been issued setting apart various tracts of land, but the provisions were not carried out until the governorship of Yeardley. Tracts of three thousand acres were set apart in each of the four boroughs, and a special tract of like size was reserved for the Governor at Jamestown. These were for the *general revenue* of the government.

Other tracts of half the size, called "borough lands," were given as common lands to each borough for the support of their " particular magistrates and officers and of all other charges." For endowing a " university and college " ten thousand acres were allotted in the territory of Henrico. [83]Men were to be placed on the land as tenants-at-halves on contract, and to remain there seven years, returning half the profits of their labor to the Company and enjoying the other half themselves. They were apportioned as the revenues to be raised demanded, and increased from time to time.

Within less than a year, 500 persons were sent on these terms.[84] Not only were the old public offices, such as the governor's and secretary's, to be thus supported by the allotment of a fixed number of tenants, which must be kept intact by successive incumbents, but whenever a new office was created or any project of public importance undertaken, this became the common mode of insuring its support. [85]

By a special application of the English system of apprenticeship, well established in England after the Statute of Apprentices of Elizabeth, 1563, which put a premium upon agricultural apprenticeship, an attempt was made to round out this tenantship and insure its perpetuity.

One hundred poor boys and girls who were about to starve in the streets of London were sent in 1619, by the aid of the mayor and council of the city, to be bound to the tenants for a term of years, at the end of which they were to become themselves tenants-at-halves on the public lands, with an allowance of stock and corn to begin with. Industrial apprenticeship was also provided for to encourage trade and to stop the excessive planting of tobacco.

The term was usually limited to seven years, or in the case of girls, upon marriage or becoming of age. Apprentices soon began to be disposed of to the planters on their reimbursing the Company for the charges of their outfit and transportation, and the records in several cases suggest a suspicion of speculation. [86]

The intent was probably to establish a kind of metayage system[87], though the tenant was at liberty at the expiration of his term to remove to " any other place at his own will and pleasure." It was supposed that the terms were sufficiently advantageous to induce him to enter into further contracts for successive periods of seven years. The success of the earlier plan introduced by Dale led the Company to hope rot only for the support of the government, but for large returns in excess, and the design was to make it a permanent and certain source of all the necessary revenues.

It was frustrated, however, by the maladministration of the system in the part of the government and officers. The tenants were frequently seated on remote and barren lands, or defrauded in their contracts, being taken from their places and hired by the year to planters, so that almost from the beginning the system was a failure, and instead of providing a revenue it was not even self-supporting. The public tenants were particularly neglected in favor of those belonging to the officers, and several propositions were made at different times for a change in the terms of tenantship, but it was never effected. The system practically came to an end with the dissolution of the Company in

1624, but even as late as 1642 some few tenants remained, showing that the Company's plan of renewal of terms had been practiced. [88] It had degenerated by this time into the payment of a fixed rent or into planting for the benefit of the owner. [89]

The growth of a class of strictly indented servants was also a factor in the failure of this tenant-ship. Servants were much less costly, and rapidly became more profitable. [90] Fifty servants were sent to serve the public in 1619, and in the next year a hundred more, say the records, "to be disposed of among the old planters which they exceedingly desire and will pay the Company their charges with very great thanks." [91] These men had been selected with great care, but the Company was unfortunate in being forced by the repeated orders of King James to add a number of dissolute persons whom he was determined, by the exercise of mere prerogative, to remove from England as an undesirable class. [92]

The new life which began in Virginia in the year 1619 greatly encouraged industry and husbandry, and led to a large increase of independent proprietaries within a few years. Special incentives were offered by large grants of land and exceptional privileges to associations of planters and adventurers for the establishing of separate plantations. Liberal grants were also made to tradesmen and to members of the Company in proportion to their shares. To encourage immigration additional grants were made to them for every person transported to the colony in the next seven years. [93]

A large number of servants and tenants was needed on these plantations, and for some time the importation by private persons was larger than that by the Company. [94] In 1619 the number of tenants and servants was sufficiently large to make necessary some regulation of the future conditions of their servitude by law. The first General Assembly of Virginia held in that year gave legal sanction and recognition to the servitude by the passage of special enactments providing for the recording and strict performance of all contracts between master and servant. The right of free marriage was limited in the case of female servants, and servants in general were prohibited from trade with the Indians. Corporal punishment was provided as a penalty in cases where a free man suffered fine unless the master remitted the fine, and a general discretionary power was given to the Governor and Council for regulation of other cases. [95]

The main principles on which the institution of servitude was based were by this time clearly developed, and its growth henceforth consisted in the gradual addition of incidents originating in customs peculiar to colonial conditions, which, recognized by judicial decisions, became fixed in local customary law, or by the enactment of special statutes were established as a part of the statutory law.

AN INDENTURE WITH CERTIFICATE FOR LEAVING ENGLAND

INDENTED SERVITUDE

Or White Slavery

In the policy of the London Company towards its colonists during the first twelve years we have seen the beginning and gradual development of an idea which, adopted and amplified by the later government of the Company and in the administration of Virginia as a Royal Colony, grew into the system here called Indented Servitude, which throughout the colonial period was widely extended in all the American colonies and became an important factor in their economic and social development. Gradually, and not always consciously, it was formed into a hard and fixed system, in some respects analogous to the later institution of slavery, from which, however, it was always broadly distinguished both in social custom and in law.

The servitude thus developed was limited and conditional. With respect to its origin it was of two kinds, resting on distinct principles:[96]

First. Voluntary Servitude, based on free contract with the London Company or with private persons for definite terms of service, in consideration of the servant's transportation and maintenance during servitude.

Second. Involuntary Servitude, where legal authority condemned a person to a term of servitude judged necessary for his reformation or prevention from an idle course of life, or as a reprieve from other punishment for misdemeanors already committed.

Though involuntary on the part of the servant, this kind involved a contract between the authority imposing the sentence and the person that undertook the transportation of the offender, [97] and the master's right to service resting upon the terms of this contract made or assigned to him was practically on the same footing as involuntary servitude.

However, let us define Slavery: What exactly is slavery?

In recent years, there has been such an outcry that 'servitude' is not slavery. Let us take a brief moment to explore that.

Clearly to understand what ***slavery*** is in general, or ***white slavery*** in particular, we must in the first clearly understand what its opposite ***freedom*** is.

FREEDOM consists in the full possession and perfect security of those natural and divinely bestowed privileges called RIGHTS.

These may be included under three distinct heads.

1st. The right to life and to soundness and safety of body.

2nd- The right to exercise all those faculties of body and mind by which the true ends of existence are attained.

3rd- The right to property, or the avails of honest industry.

It follows, of course, that SLAVERY consists in the deprivation of these rights.

So many today still say, it was not slavery. It is not the same, it does not compare to that the African Americans suffered.

Let us use some common sense here. Two women are brutally raped, and both suffered greatly. One woman was abducted, and raped by multiple men for days. The other was raped after leaving a study hall on her college campus. Both women are hospitalized and later join a recovery group. While the one woman's attack was obviously worse, do you really think that the people in the group are going to discredit the other victims rape because it did not 'compare' to the others? Of course not, rape is rape, and slavery is slavery, neither are comparable and the victims both suffer. However, by calling the Irish a myth, based on the grounds that as a whole, they did not suffer as long or in the population as African Slavery is an injustice to their sufferings and memory.

As you have read earlier: *Out of the first 295 settlers, according to The Virginia Company records; 104 of them were Gentleman. This gave the Colony a population of gentlemen that was six times greater than that in England. "Gentleman" in the early 1600s, by definition, had no manual skills, and neither did the majority of their servants. According to Smith, (Travels and Works, Vol i, Vol ii) He went on to say " 100 good laborers would have done more than a 1000 of those who went.*

In order for the corporation of Virginia to survive, Virginia needed workers. More workers and less 'genlte' men. It is evident from the previous chapter that the Company had sent 'foreign' workers, specifically those with a special trade. Irishmen and of course English laborors had been supplied. Although we know documentation on this transportation is scarce, we know they were there. Virginia needed to plant corn to sustain, plant tobacco to export, build towns and roads.

This is when the Virginia Company began to *market* the New World. Unfortunately, when word got back that the 'Adventure' was not all that it was cracked up to be, many died, suffered or were killed, the Virginia company had a great decline in volunteers. This is when Virginia took it upon themselves to give incentive. They created the 'headrights', essentially they offered anyone who volunteered or "offered a body,' into the service of the Colony, 50 acres of land.

The headright land was rewarded in very few documented cases, those promises never fulfilled. It did give incentive for many, this is when flesh became a commodity, people were sending servants to Virginia against their will. Children were being kidnapped of the streets. Victims were being absconded from taverns, or tricked, and thrown onto ships headed for Virginia.

King James, through the company's request, sent hundreds of Irish boys and girls to Virginia, "those vagrants and orphans." The Virginia company then appealed to the mayor of London to rid the city of its "swarme of unnecessary inmates" by sending to Virginia 'any who were destitute and lying in the streets." They were taken against their will, forced onto ships, chained, whipped for disobedience, sold and forced to serve a master.

They were termed servants, given a number of years to serve contract forced into servitude. Years of service was constantly added to the Indentured Servants contract for the slightest offenses. Very few servants actually survived to the end of their contracts. Contract times were continually added to in the early colonial years.

Many people state that the difference between the African slaves and the white slaves was that the Africans were considered 'sub-human' whereas the white slaves were not. That is actually false. The Irish were Catholic, they were not considered 'Christian', they were in the same sub human boat as the Africans, and the Heathen Indians.

Another false statement the Anti Irish Mythers say is that a child of an Indentured Servant was not born into slavery, that is also false. Any child born in the colony took on 'mothers status' if the mother was free so was the child. If the mother was a servant, she was punished- usually whipped and additional years were added onto her contract, and the child became a servant until they became 'of age'. That goes way beyond the maximum sentence or contract term. There are so many accounts in the Court Records of Virgina, I have listed a few here and also dedicated a chapter to other instances that give true light to the condition these 'servants' faced.

Anne Usher was an 8 year old girl who lived on Shirly Plantation. She and three other girls were raped by another servant. She was convicted for her crime of being raped and sentenced to sixty lashes, she died. Her Mother was also convicted and sentenced to thirty lashes for 'interfering'.

Elizabeth Abbott was a servant who was 'rebellious'. She was whipped on several occasions. Thomas Gates testified in court that he examined the body of said servant, that was whipped by a boy named Will, who was ordered by his master, Mr. Prodor to give the girl 500 lashes, which said examiner did examine." She was transported against her will and tried several times to escape. She suffered multiple beatings, once with 'fishhooks', and died. This was not uncommon among the white servants.

When I began my research for my novel 'Jayes', I had absolutely no idea of the extent of the horrors these people endured. They were called 'servants' or 'indentured servants', not slaves. I always believed that slavery in America was always, and only, the African Americans. That is not the truth. Yet, while the population of the African Americans outweighs that of the white slaves, they were not the only ones.

King James' Proclamation provided the Colonies the much- needed labor it needed to farm the tobacco fields, build the roads, fell the trees and build the towns. This Proclamation actually paid Englishmen to turn over subjects for transportation to the Colonies.

And be ... it enacted ... that it shall and may be lawful to and for any justice of peace, to whom any rogue, vagabond, or sturdy beggars … shall be brought, to reward any person or persons that shall apprehend any rogue, vagabond, or sturdy beggar, by granting unto such person or persons an order or warrant under his hand and seal to the constable, headborough, or tithingman of such parish where such rogue, vagabond, or sturdy beggar passed through unapprehended, requiring him to pay such person or persons the sum of 2s. for every rogue, vagabond, or sturdy beggar which shall be so apprehended….

Provided always, and be it enacted … that it shall and may be lawful for the justices of peace in any of the counties of England and Wales, in their quarter sessions assembled … , to transport or cause to be transported such rogues, vagabonds, and sturdy beggars as shall be duly convicted and adjudged to be incorrigible to any of the English plantations beyond the seas….

Not all Englishmen agreed with the ill treatment 'enslavement' of their Kinsman, even if this treatment benefitted the Purse of England. That England "carrieth away daily men" and "sold our own Countrymen' is very disheartening, yet to think with as much documentation of this kind available, we never read about this in our history books.

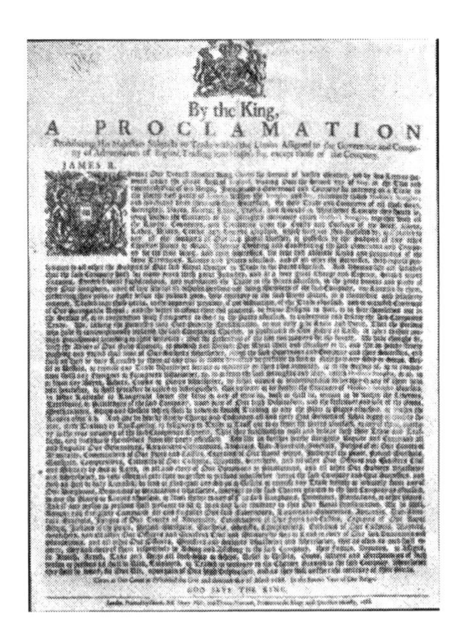
By the King,
A PROCLAMATION
JAMES R.
GOD SAVE THE KING.

Dedicated to the most honorable Sir Henry Vane,

The trade of America is prejudicial, very dishonest, and highly dishonorable to our Nation. It is prejudicial, in that it carrieth away daily such men as might serve their Country, either in fighting to defend it at home, or else abroad.

'Tis dishonorable, in that we are upbraided by all other Nations that know that trade for selling our own Countrymen for the Commodities of those places. And, I affirm, that I have been told by the Dutch and others, that we English were worse than the Turks, for that they sold strangers only, and we sold our own Countrymen. And it is well known, that people in authority, and some that profess much to Christianity of those parts, will hang a man for selling or taking away an Indian that worshiped the Devil, when at the same time they allow others, and will themselves buy of their own Nation. which have most barbarously been stolen out of their Country.

And 'tis dishonest, if murder be so, for when they have by Spirits or lying tales, forced them aboard the ships, in their transportation only, there is yearly many starved to death, those that remain are sold to those that will give most for them; some for fourteen years, others for ten, and less, but the least four: and it were better for them to serve fourteen years with the Turks, then four in the Plantations with most of the Masters in those places, especially in Virginia, for besides, their being back-beaten and belly-beaten, it is three to one if they live out their servitude, by reason of the unwholesomeness of the Country.

In which disasters that happen to our Nation, I cannot but condole their misfortunes, as if we of all Europe were of the seed of Cham, when the Spaniard at the same time managed their businesses so well, that scarcely will one of them serve in the Indies, except it be the Viceroy, or some great Personage, and I know that Nation in nothing exceeds us, but in their keeping together as one people.

Gardyner, George. 1651

Hammond writes of a massacre, which more likely is the massacre of 1644 rather than the more publicized massacre of 1622. John Hammond died in 1707 in England having lived in Virginia and Maryland for over 20 years.

At the first settling and many years after, it deserved most of those aspersions (nor were they then aspersions but truths) it was not settled at the public charge; but when found out, challenged, and maintained by Adventurers, whose avarice and inhumanity, brought in these inconveniences, which to this day brands Virginia.

Then were jails emptied, youth seduced, infamous women drilled in, the provisions all brought out of England, and that embezzled by the Trustees (for they durst neither hunt fowl, nor Fish, for fear of the Indian, which they stood in awe of, their labor was almost perpetual, their allowance of victual small, feto plant corn for their food, to range the wood for flesh, the rivers for fowl and fish, to find out somewhat staple for supply of clothing, to continue a commerce, to purchase and breed cattle, &c. but the bud of this growing happiness was again nipt by a cruel Massacre committed by the Natives, which again pulled them back and kept them under, enforcing them to get into Forts (such as the infancy of those times afforded: they were taken off from planting; their provisions destroyed, their Cattle, Hogs, Horses, & killed up, and brought to such want and penury, that diseases grew rife, mortality exceeded; but receiving a supply of men, ammunition and victuals out of England, they again gathered heart, pursued their enemies, and so often worsted them, that the Indians were glad to sue for peace, and they desirous of a cessation consented to it.w or no cattle, no use of horses nor oxen to draw or carry, (which labors men supplied themselves) all which caused a mortality; no civil courts of justice but under a Marshall law, no redress of grievances, complaints were repaid with stripes, moneys with scoffs, tortures made delights, and in a word all and the worst that tyranny could inflict or act, which when complained of in England-

John Hammond

These people were 'deplorables' of the early 1600s. There may have been some actual criminals in Virginia, they did sentence people to transportation for crimes. Keep in mind, many were kidnapped, 'spirited or tricked', and literally kidnapped off the streets to be sold. Children, Women and Men, no one was spared. There was a time people were terrified of being taken, parents would not let their children out to play in fear of 'kidnabbing'. This was so horrible in England that on May 9, 1645 Parliament issued an Ordinance 'against stealing children.'

Children actually were valuable, there time of 'service' was generally more than 7 years, until they became of age. And also, they were assumed easier to control. Keep in mind, if they survived the passage, they very rarely survived servitude and never found freedom.

From 1625 to 1635 the population in Virginia near tripled! At least 75% of the population were servants. In 1635 the white labor was approximately 10:1 compared to the 'negro'. They worked and lived side by side, they were listed together in wills, and even laws stated 'servant or slave'.

"Servants and Slaves which such person is in possession and crops, at the time of his or her death shall continue to work on plantation…"

Lodge, in his discussion of the indented white servant: "As early as 1623 laws were framed to compel obedience to masters, and for the next three years there was much severe legislation to regulate servants. They were not allowed to marry, if they ran away additional service and severe punishment; and for a second offense they were branded on the cheek, while those who harbored them faced heavy penalties. Years of service was added for an assault on their masters (even verbal) engaging in trade, refusing to work (laziness) as well as running away. These provisions of the law enabled the masters to protract the period of servitude, and rendered the condition of the servants miserable in the seemed suspicious, a neighbor was to view the body. They were coarsely clothed, fed upon meal and water sweetened with molasses, and were frequently punished with great barbarity."

Early Colony Records, some of which you can access on microfilm through the Rockefeller Library, Williamsburg Virginia, lists hundreds of Indented 'prisoners'. These are State records that list those sent or sentenced to Virginia between 1623 and 1635. These include individuals from Ireland and England, including orphans and vagrants as well as criminals. They were all treated the same when they were sent to Virginia.

JOHN GIBBONS:

On February 27, 1619, John Gibbons, a boy from the streets of London, was among the youngsters rounded up so that they could be sent to Virginia.

John is one of the characters in *Jayes.* Although Virginia did not distinguish between 'criminals' and those poor should that were 'rounded up'. In the book John does, and he is also a protector of other children that suffered his fate.

RICHARD CLARKSON

On January 29, 1620, it was decided that Richard Clarkson, who was being detained at Bridewell Prison, would be sent to Virginia.

Sir John William, 1674:

"New England was kept full by a continual immigration of white servants from England, that is to say, of men, women and children, saved from the gallows, plucked naked and starving out of the gutter, trepanned by scoundrelly crimps, kidnapped bodily in the streets and spirited away across the Atlantic. From the earliest days of English colonization, the seeds to be sown in the Great Continent of the West had been gathered by the weeds that grow by the roadside. In 1610 three-hundred disorderly persons were sent to Virginia. In 1617 and 1618 a cargo of poor and impressed immigrants, in 1620 a parcel of poor and naughty children."

There are hundreds of entries that list those "Sent to Virginia". Whatever the reason they were sent, kidnapped or convicted, grown man or boy, they were all received and endured the same fate in the New World. They were called servants, yet they had the same rights as the first African Americans that landed in Virginia in 1618, and also those of the Indians that were either kidnapped or taken prisoner.

It has been taught that these people came "to work for passage and were then freed. Nearly 75% of those sent before 1649 never lived to see freedom, many were sent against their will.

A great body of servants in the late part of the 17th century was comprised mostly by voluntary servants. They were free persons, largely from England, Wales, Scotland, Ireland and Germany, who wished to go to the colony as settlers to better their condition, but were too poor to bear the charges of their transportation. [98]They consequently entered into a voluntary contract with any one that would assume these charges and their maintenance for such a term of years as would repay the outlay, placing themselves for this limited time at the disposal of the person for any reasonable service. The contract was made in Great Britain with resident planters or the agents of colonists, but more frequently with shipmasters who traded in Virginia and disposed of the servant on their arrival as they saw fit. The agreement was by deed indented, and hence arose the term "Indented" Servants. [99]This class of so-called "Kids" was supplemented by a smaller class of persons who went on agreements for fixed wages for a definite time.

[100]The other large class was supplied chiefly from English paupers, vagrants and dissolute persons sent under the arbitrary exercise of royal prerogative or by court sentences, and later by the action of English penal statutes. In the earlier years it included a large number of poor children from the counties and towns of England, who were sent to apprenticeship on easy conditions. [101]The penal regulations of the colony up to the year 1642 tended also to recruit this class. A very large number of the convicts sent to the American plantations were political and not social criminals.

Of the Scotch prisoners taken at the battle of Worcester sixteen hundred and ten were sent to Virginia in 1651. Two years later a hundred Irish Tories were sent, and in 1685 a number of the followers of Monmouth that had escaped the cruelties of Jeffrey's. Many of the Scotch prisoners of Dunbar and of the rebels of 1666 were sent to New England 5 and the other plantations. [102]

As early as 1611 Governor Dale, anxious to fill out the number of two thousand men for establishing military posts along James river, had recommended that all convicts from the common jails be kept up for three years. They " are not always," he said, " the worst kind of men, either for birth, spirit, or body and would be glad to escape a just sentence and make this their new country, and plant therein with all diligence, cheerfulness and comfort."

This request passed unheeded, and the earliest introduction of any of the criminal class seems to have been in 1618, when a man convicted of manslaughter and sentenced to be hanged was reprieved, " because he was a carpenter and the plantation needed carpenters." [103] In the early years of the seventeenth century England suffered, particularly in her border counties, from a number of malefactors whom it was impossible to bring to justice. Magistrates and most of the gentlemen of the counties countenanced them, and even had them in their employ for private ends.

Many schemes were proposed to the king for remedying the evil and compelling the justices and officers to perform their duty.

Transportation had been made use of before, and the king now proposed to send the offenders to Virginia. [104]From 1618 to 1622 a number came, but the large increase was in the latter half of the century. In 1653 an order of the Council of State appointed a committee concerning the transportation of vagrants to the foreign plantations. In 1661 another committee was appointed to further the sending of people, and power was given to Justices of the Peace to transport felons, beggars and disorderly persons.[105]

Sufficient numbers had been sent under this power, and by the transportation of political offenders, to furnish ringleaders for an attempt to subvert the government in 1663. In consequence of this and the danger of the continued importation of " great numbers " of these "wicked villains," the General Court, upon the petition of the counties of Gloucester and Middlesex, issued an order prohibiting any further importation of them after the twentieth of January, 1671.[106]

Through the influence of Lord Arlington this order was confirmed in England and was made to apply to the other American colonies as well as to Virginia. A strict system of search was applied to every ship that entered Virginia ports, and for the next half-century the colony had a respite from this class of " Newgaters " and " Jail Birds." [107]

Their transportation was now diverted to the West Indies, but this proved so ineffectual in putting a stop to petty felonies that in the 4th year of George I. (1717) Parliament passed a statute over the most vigorous protests from the Virginia merchants in London, making the American colonies practically a reformatory and a dumping-ground for the felons of England. In 1766 the benefits of this act were extended to include Scotland, though Benjamin Franklin, on the part of Pennsylvania, memorialized Parliament against it, and in 1768 the speedier transportation of felons was ordered.[108] The practice was only stopped by the War of the Revolution. The preamble of the act of 1779 significantly remarks that "whereas the transportation of felons to His Majesty's American Colonies is attended with many difficulties," they are now to be sent to " other parts beyond the sea, whether situate in America or not." [109] They were finally disposed of in convict galleys or sent to the new penal colonies in New South Wales or at Botany Bay.[110]

Virginia, contrary to some of the colonies, never favored the importation of this class. They were seldom reformed, and their " room " was held much more desirable than their " company," says

Jones.[111] Many attempts were made to prevent their coming by the imposition of heavy duties, but they were not finally and effectually prohibited until I788. [112]The ability given the States to lay a tax of $10 on all persons imported was incorporated into the Constitution of the United States, mainly through the efforts of George Mason of Virginia, and was partly designed to keep out convicts. [113]From this attitude of the colony it probably received a much smaller number than some of the other colonies. [114]

Another important source of involuntary servitude was found in the practice of " spiriting," which grew up in the reign of Charles I. and continued throughout the Commonwealth period and the reign of Charles II. It was an organized system of kidnapping persons, young and old, usually of the laboring classes, and transporting them to the plantations to be sold for the benefit of the kidnapper or shipmaster to whom they were assigned. [115]It became widely extended in England, but Bristol and London were the centers of the traffic. Throughout London and the parishes of Middlesex county its agents, called " spirits/' were distributed; men and women, yeomen, tradesmen, doctors and a class of rogues and idlers who earned a livelihood by this means. [116]The ladies of the court, and even the mayor of Bristol, were not beneath the suspicion of profiting by this lucrative business. All manner of pretenses were used to decoy the victims aboard ships lying in the Thames or to places where they could be assaulted and forcibly conveyed on board, to be disposed of to the ship's company or to merchants.

The practice first arose in connection with the West India plantations.[117] Barbados and other island plantations probably received a much greater number than the American colonies. [118]We find a case belonging to Virginia as early as 1644. [119]In 1664 the abuse had grown so bad that tumults were frequently raised in the streets of London. It was only necessary to point the finger at a woman and call her a " common spirit " to raise a " riot " against her. The Lord Mayor and aldermen of London, and a number of merchants, planters and shipmasters, sent petitions urging the establishment of a registry office to put an end to the practice. [120]The office was established in September of that year, and was to register all covenants and issue certificates to the merchants. [121]The penalty for not registering any person who was to be transported as a servant was 20, and the consent of friends or relatives in person at the office was necessary for the transportation of any one under twelve years of age, and good reasons had to be shown for such transportation. Even these strict regulations failed to stop the practice, and in 1670 it was necessary to resort to Parliament to prevent the abuse by imposing as a penalty death without benefit of clergy.[122]

Further technical distinctions arose in law determined by the title under which servitude was due. Thus, where verbal contracts alone existed, or where it was specially stipulated for, "Servitude according to the Custom" took place, and the servant was held for the customary term, whatever it might be, unless a contract was proved. After the statute of 1643, which set a definite term for all servants brought in without indentures, this became known as servitude by act of Assembly. Spirited servants, as a rule, came under this act. The servitude of felons and convicts, after the penal statutes, was known as servitude by act of Parliament, and that of offenders sentenced in Virginia as servitude by order of court. These distinctions were of little practical importance, however, as all servants except convicts met with the same treatment both in social custom and in law.

The servants in Virginia were usually English, Scotch or Irish, but there were also a few Dutch, French, Portuguese and Polish. [123]They were usually transported persons, but residents in the colony also sold themselves into servitude for various reasons. The demand for servants before the rise of slavery was always very great in the American colonies and was further enhanced by that of the island plantations. It was the impossibility of supplying this by the regular means that furnished the justification professed in the English penal statutes and gave encouragement to the illicit practice of spiriting.[124] In the early years before these means were resorted to, dealing in servants had become a very profitable business.

The London merchants were not slow to see the advantages of such a trade; a servant might be transported at a cost of from 6 to 8 and sold for 40 or 60, and a systematic speculation in servants was begun both in England and in Virginia. [125]Regular agencies were established, and servants might be had by any one who wished to import them " at a day's warning." [126]Others were consigned to merchants in Virginia or sent with shiploads of goods on a venture. [127]The demand continued unabated till near the last quarter of the seventeenth century.

The numbers were so considerable in 1651 that the commissioners of the Commonwealth who were sent to demand the submission of Virginia were authorized, in case of resistance, to levy the servants for reducing the colony. [128]From this time to the beginning of the decline of the system the yearly importations were very large, the number imported from 1664 to 1671 averaging 1500 a year.

Several causes combined to fasten the system very early upon Virginia: the stimulus given to the acquisition of wealth resulting from the establishment of private property in land; the phenomenally rapid growth of tobacco culture, occasioned by the productiveness of labor employed in it, and the returns to be had[129]. in ready money from its sale;[130] the increasing cost of hired labor; the "head right" of fifty acres which was received for every person transported; 3 but particularly the unfortunate condition of the laboring classes in England, whose real wages (owing to the great rise in prices in the latter part of the sixteenth century) were exceedingly low and gave rise to a large class of unemployed.

Legal Status of the Servant. The history of the legal development of the institution properly begins with 1619 and falls broadly into three general periods:

First, 1619-1642, characterized by the development of certain incidents of servitude from practices originating in the first twelve years of the Company's government. These gradually become fixed during this period chiefly in Customary Law.

Second, 1642-1726, in which the incidents of the former period are extended and further established by Statute Law, and the system reduced to legal uniformity in contrast to the somewhat varying practices of the courts in the former period. The institution reaches also in this period its highest practical development.

Third, 1726-1788, the period of decline of the system in consequence of the rising institution of negro slavery.

First Period, 1619-1642

After the Assembly of 1619, until near the middle of the century, very little direct legislation appears in regard to servants, but in this interim there grew up many customs recognized by the tribunals which affected very seriously the personal rights of servants. One of the earliest and most important customs was the right assumed by the master to assign his servant's contract whether he gave his consent or not. This originated in the practice with the Company of disposing of apprentices and servants to planters on their agreeing to reimburse the Company for the expenses of the servant's transportation, and in the custom with officers of the government of renting their tenants and apprentices to planters in order to insure an easier or more certain support. The depressed condition of the colony following the Indian massacre of 1622 made the sale of servants a very common practice among both officers and planters. [131]In 1623 George Sandys, the treasurer of Virginia, was forced to sell the only remaining eleven servants of the Company for mere lack of provisions to support them, and a planter sold the seven men on his plantation for a hundred and fifty pounds of tobacco. The practice was loudly condemned in England and bitterly resented on the part of servants, but the planters found their justification in the exigencies of the occasion, and their legal right to make the sale seems never to have been actually called into question.

Assignments of contracts for the whole or the unexpired portion of the servant's term became from this time forward very common. As a result, the idea of the contract and of the legal personality of the servant was gradually lost sight of in the disposition to regard him as a chattel and a part of the personal estate of his master, which might be treated and disposed of very much in the same way as the rest of the estate. He became thus rated in inventories of estates, and was disposed of both by will and by deed along with the rest of the property.[132]

But aside from these incidents of property which attached to the condition of the servant, his position before the law was very little different from that of the freemen of the colony. His personality was recognized by the enactment of special laws for his protection and in his being subjected, with the rest of the colonists, to the payment of a 1 poll tax for the support of the government and of tithes to the minister. In the early period, like a freeman, he was liable to military service in behalf of the state. He enjoyed rights of trade, except with the Indians, and could acquire property. His testimony was always received in court, unless he was a convict, and he was a valid witness to contracts. [133]His religious instruction was provided for in the same manner as that of freemen. The courts carefully guarded his contract and effected speedy redress of his grievances. He might sue and be sued, and had the right of appeal to the supreme judiciary of the colony, and throughout this period he enjoyed the important political right of the suffrage on an equality with freemen, a right which in most cases had not been exercised before. [134]In penal legislation, however, the distinction was generally made between the servant and the freeman in the servant's liability to corporal punishment for offenses for which a freeman was punished by fine or imprisonment. A law of 1619 provided that " if a servant willfully neglect his master's commands he shall suffer bodily punishment," but the right of the master to regulate his servant's conduct in this way was of slow growth and had no legislative sanction before 1662. During this period correction remained in the hands of the Assembly and of the courts. [135]

When Wyatt came as Governor in 1621 he was instructed to see that all servants fared alike in the colony and that punishment for their offenses should be service to the colony in 1 public works, and by a law of 1619 servitude for wages was /provided as a penalty for all " idlers and renegades." 3 That such provisions should be realized it was necessary for the servant to perform service in addition to the term of his contract. In this we have the germ of additions of time, a practice which later became the occasion of a very serious abuse of the servant's rights by the addition of terms altogether incommensurate with the offenses for which they were imposed. It became a means with the courts of enforcing specific performance of the servant's contract, and was so applied contrary to the common-law doctrine relating to contracts, which only provided for damages in cases of breach of contract and not for specific performance.

The common law of England had the character of national law in the colony, and accompanied the colonists as a personal law having territorial extent. Although the relation of master and servant in the case of apprenticeship as an extension of the relation of parent and child, guardian and ward, was an effect of the common law having personal extent, yet the relation of master and servant in indented servitude was unknown to that law, and could neither be derived from nor regulated by its principles. It had to depend entirely for its sanction on special local statutes, or on the action of tribunals which had no precedents before them and acted as the necessities of the occasion demanded, with little regard to established doctrines of the common law. The growth of the institution is thus marked by the development of local customary and statute law, and only very gradually assumed a fixed shape as this development proceeded.[136]

The master's title to service rested on the provisions of the contract. These were very varied, sometimes specifying, besides the ordinary conditions, treatment of a special nature, sometimes stipulating for a trusteeship of such property as the servant possessed, and sometimes for gifts of land or of apparel and corn sufficient to set the servant up as a freeman when his term had expired. [137]Such provisions were recognized by the courts in their strict enforcement of the contract, and led to the establishment of customary rights such as additions of time and freedom dues. A servant might claim on the expiration of his term freedom dues in apparel and corn whether stipulated for or not. Their amount was at first customary and determined where sued for by appointees of the court, but finally they became fixed in statutory law.[138]

Monthly courts were held as early as 1622, and by virtue of their general jurisdiction over all cases not involving more than a hundred pounds of tobacco (which was later extended to 5 and 10 causes and to those of less than 1600 pounds of tobacco) they had jurisdiction over disputes between master and servant within this limit, and the Commissioners as conservators of the peace had power to regulate the conduct of the servant whenever necessary. Before this the Governor and Council or the General Assembly had had sole jurisdiction of all causes. After quarter courts were established in 1632 appeals lay to it, as before to the Governor and Council, and to the Assembly as the supreme appellate court in the colony. The servant by his right of suit in these courts and of appeal had a speedy and effective remedy for his grievances, and the rulings of the justices established many precedents which greatly mitigated the conditions of his servitude. [139]

In 1640 a master who had bought a maid-servant, " with intent to marry her," was ordered by the General Court to do so within ten days or to free her on the payment of 500 Ibs. of tobacco. And where insufficient food and clothing were provided servants were taken away until the master corrected the fault. [140]When the record of his contract was not sufficient to protect the servant on the expiration of his term from the greed of his master, he might make it appear upon testimony in the County Court that the conditions of the contract had been fulfilled and receive a certificate of the fact, which thus became indisputable evidence of his right to freedom. The courts also recognized the servant's right to acquire and hold property.[141]

In 1643 the ten monthly courts were reduced to six County Courts, with jurisdiction over Cases above 20 shillings, or 200 Ibs. of tobacco. Cases of less amount could be decided in the discretion of any commissioner. The inconvenience of resorting to the general court at Jamestown caused a grant in 1645 of general jurisdiction of all cases in law and equity to the county courts. Two years later the jurisdiction of the General Court was limited to cases of 1600 Ibs. of tobacco in value or over. In 1662 there were 17 county courts having jurisdiction in all cases " of what value or nature whatsoever not touching life or member," and the name Commissioner was changed to Justice of the Peace. The Quarter Courts now became the General Court, held twice a year, and appeals lay to it as formerly, and from it to the Assembly. In 1659 appeal to the Assembly had been limited to cases involving more than 2500 Ibs. of tobacco. This limitation was removed in 1661, and justice facilitated by a reference of all cases except those of the winter term to itinerant chancellors.

In the practices of the courts regulating the punishment of servants, we see the way prepared for later provisions of the statute law not so favorable to them. By virtue of the power of the courts to regulate the private as well as the public conduct of servants, and by the discretionary power given by enactments to the Governor and Council, they might be subjected to indignities of punishment not worthy of a freeman. In but few cases did the courts permit servants' offenses to be punished by fine; the usual penalty was whipping or additional servitude to the master or to the colony.

This probably would not have been the case if the servant had generally had anything wherewith to discharge a fine, but as he had not, some other means of satisfaction was found necessary. Penal legislation regarding servants did not differ greatly in severity, however, from that applied to freemen, except in the case of absconding servants, where very severe punishment was early inflicted, designed by its severity to prevent recurrence of the offense.[142] Towards the end of the period the servant's great abuse of his rights of trade, by allowing himself to be tempted by loose persons to embezzle and sell his master's goods, made necessary some restriction. The Assembly of 1639 conditioned this right henceforth on the master's consent, imposing severe penalties upon persons who should induce any servant to trade secretly, and the courts seem to have rigidly enforced the provisions of this act.

Before the close of the first half of the century, then, we have seen the growth, mainly through judicial decisions, of certain customary rights on the part both of the servant-and of the master as recognized incidents of the condition of servitude. These were on the part of the servant the right to a certificate of freedom, to freedom dues and to the possession of property; on the part of the master, to the free assignment of the servant's contract by deed or will, to; additions of time in lieu of damages for breach of contract, and the right of forbidding the servant to engage in trade. Corporal punishment and additions of time have also become the ordinary modes of regulating the servant's conduct and punishing his offenses.

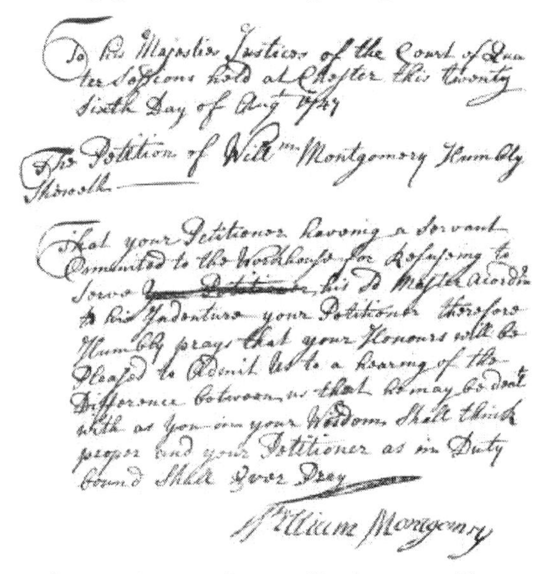
To his Majesties Justices of the Court of Quar
ter Sessions held at Chester this twenty
sixth Day of Aug^t [illegible]

The Petition of Willm Montgomery Humbly
Sheweth ——

That your Petitioner having a Servant
Committed to the Workhouse for Refusing to
Serve [illegible] his sd Master Accordi
to his Indenture your Petitioner therefore
Humbly prays that your Honours will be
Pleased to Admit us to a hearing of the
Difference between us that he may be dealt
with as you in your Wisdom shall think
proper and your Petitioner as in Duty
bound shall Ever Pray

William Montgomery

PETITION AGAINST A SERVANT WHO REFUSED TO WORK

Second Period, 1642-1726

From the year 1642 the statute books begin to fill with legislation concerning servants, mainly confirming or modifying such rights as had been already developed and subjecting the system of servitude to more uniform regulation. Until 1643 no definite term had been fixed by law for the duration of servitude when not expressed in indentures. The terms specified in the indentures varied from two to eight years, the usual one being from four to five years, but until this time custom had regulated the servitude of such persons as came in without indentures, and what was known as servitude "according to the custom of the country" had begun to grow up. Where no contract but a verbal one existed, there was always room for controversy between master and servant, each trying to prove an agreement that would be to his advantage. To put a stop to such controversies the Assembly passed a law definitely fixing the term in all cases where servants were imported "having no indentures or covenants," according to the age of the servant. The master was at first the judge of the servant's age, but as this naturally worked to the servant's disadvantage, the judgment of ages was put in the hands of the county courts after 1657. Unless the master produced his servant in court for this purpose within four months after arrival he could only claim the least term allowed by the law, and after 1705 the servant had two months allowed in which to prove an alleged indenture for a less time.[143]

By the beginning of the period several abuses had grown up that prevented or seriously interfered with the master's realization of his right to service. Hitherto there had been no legal restriction to prevent a man-servant from marrying, though by an act of 1619 a female servant could not marry without the consent either of her parents or of her master, or of both the magistrate and minister of the place, upon pain of severe censure by the Governor and Council. The right of free marriage was one which for very obvious reasons would work to the disadvantage and inconvenience of the master, particularly if the marriage was made without his knowledge, and in 1643 a law was passed providing "that what man servant so ever hath since January 1640 or here-after shall secretly marry with any maid or woman servant without the consent of her master he or they so offending shall in the first place serve out his or their time or times with his or their masters and after serve his master one complete year more for such offence committed," and the maid " shall for her offence double the time of service with her master or mistress." When the offender was a free man he had to pay double the value of the maid's service to her master and a fine of 500 Ibs. of tobacco to the parish. For the offense of fornication with a maid-servant the guilty man was required to give her master a year's service for the loss of her time, or, if a freeman, he might make a money satisfaction. In 1662 the master's losses from neglect of work or stolen goods and provisions were sufficient to make necessary a further restriction upon the secret marriage of servants. The act provided that "no minister either publish the banns or celebrate the contract of marriage between any servants unless he have from both their masters a certificate that it is done with their consent," under penalty of the heavy fine of ten thousand pounds of tobacco. Servants, whether male or female, guilty of marriage contrary to the act, with each other or with free persons, suffered the addition of a year's time to their servitude, and the guilty free person was condemned to a like term of service or the payment of 1500 Ibs. of tobacco to the master.[144]

Another great abuse was the practice which greedy and wealthy planters had of covenanting with runaway servants as hirelings or sharers on remote plantations, thus encouraging them by more favorable terms to desert their proper service. This had been anticipated by an enactment of the Assembly of 1619, which provided "that no crafty or advantageous be suffered to be put in practice for enticing away tenants or servants of any particular plantation from the place where they are. seated," and that it should be the " duty of the Governor and Counsel of Estate most severely to punish both the seducers and the seduced and to return them to their former places." But by 1643 the practice on the part of these planters had become so flagrant that complaints of it were made at every quarter court, and the Assembly enacted that any person so contracting with a servant and entertaining him for a whole year, without a certificate of the freedom of the servant from the commander or commissioner of the place, should forfeit to the master twenty pounds of tobacco for every night the servant was entertained, while the servant was to be punished at the discretion of the Governor and Council.[145]

But more than anything else the habit on the part of servants themselves of absconding from their masters' service, stealing their masters' goods and enticing others to go with them, worked to the detriment of the masters and the peril of the colony. The courts had attempted by the most severe punishments to put a stop to the practice. Whipping, additions of time from one to seven years, branding, and even servitude in irons, proved ineffectual. The possibility of entire escape from servitude or of service on better terms proved too great a temptation, and with an unruly class of servants such attempts became habitual. Statute after statute was passed regulating the punishment and providing for the pursuit and recapture of runaways; but although laws gradually became severer and finally made no distinction in treatment between runaway servants and slaves, it was impossible to entirely put a stop to the habit so long as the system itself lasted.

The loss to the master was often serious even if he recovered the servant. A loss of time from several months to a year or more, and the expense of recapture, which at first fell upon him, made the pursuit of the servant often not worthwhile for the remaining time for which he was entitled to his service. [146]The rise of this practice was not due to the severity of the service to which the servant was subjected. The courts, we have seen, provided a speedy remedy for any misusage, and by an act of 1642 it was provided that " where any servants shall have just cause of complaint against their masters or mistresses by harsh or unchristian like usage or otherwise for want of diet, or convenient necessaries that then it shall be lawful for any such servant or servants to repair to the next commissioner to make his or their complaint." The commissioner was then required to summon the master or mistress before the county court which had discretion to settle the matter, taking care "that no such servant or servants be misused by their masters or mistresses where they shall find the cause of the complaint to be just." Runaways began to increase with the importation of an undesirable class of servants, a few of whom were present in the colony from the earliest days, and who during this period were largely recruited by the addition of felons and "spirited " persons. They were the common offenders, and by their habits corrupted the better class of servants.[147]

When this class grew more numerous in the latter half of the seventeenth century servants became so demoralized that they would run away in "troops," enticing the negro slaves to go with them. In counties, whose situation made escape peculiarly easy the abuse was very great. In 1661 it had become so bad in Gloucester that the

Assembly authorized that county to make whatsoever laws it saw fit to meet the case of such runaways.[148] Servants would plot how they might run away even before they landed in Virginia, and under the liberty given them on the plantations, and with an accessible back country, it was not a difficult matter to accomplish. They frequently made their escape to the adjoining provinces of Maryland and North Carolina, where their condition being unknown they might enjoy their freedom, or if discovered their recovery was attended with such difficulties as to insure their safety.

The right of the master to claim his servant in another jurisdiction was one not always recognized, even though the institution existed there, as it depended on colonial legislation having an intercolonial application. In the absence of statutes providing for the return of fugitive servants from one jurisdiction to another, the justices refused to take the responsibility of acting, and so frequently much injustice and inconvenience resulted. The only redress left to the master was the power to levy on goods in Virginia belonging to inhabitants of the province in question.

North Carolina became such an asylum for absconding servants and slaves that it was popularly known in Virginia as the " Refuge of Runaways." [149]The Eastern Shores of Virginia and Maryland were also favorite resorts. Servants frequently escaped to the Dutch plantations and sometimes even to New England. To restrict the practice and to prevent absconding debtors, a pass was required for any person leaving the colony, and masters of ships were put under severe penalties not to transport any servant or slave without such a pass or license from his master. [150]Certificates of freedom were also required to be given in due form to every servant on the expiration of his term, and under the power given by the statutes any person travelling in the colony, if not able to give an intelligent account of himself or to show his certificate, might be taken up as a runaway. The law for the capture of runaways was at first very inefficient, and went through a number of experimental changes before one that was effective was discovered. In the first acts relating to runaways no means of discovery and no method of pursuit and return to the master were prescribed. The pursuit seems at first to have devolved upon the master, but the loss resulting from this caused the General Court in 1640 to direct pursuit to be made by the sheriff and his posse at the expense of the county from which the fugitive escaped.[151] Pursuit by hue and cry, adopted from the English custom, seems also to have been in use, but by 1658 it had been so much neglected that a special act for its enforcement was necessary. Constables also pursued under search-warrants, but they neglected their duty, and in 1661 the Assembly had to promise them rewards of 200 Ibs. of tobacco from the master. This proved insufficient and had to be increased and even paid out of the public revenues, to be reimbursed by the master. Additional rewards from 3 to 10, according to the value of the servant and his distance from home, were offered by masters. In 1669 the practice was so bad that any one was permitted to take up a runaway and receive a reward of 1000 Ibs. of tobacco from the public, to be reimbursed by the servitude of the offender "to the country when free of his master."

In consequence of the growth of these abuses, and designed as a corrective of them, we find a great extension of the principles of additions of time and of corporal punishment, to such a degree in fact as to prove often a source of great injustice to the servant. The principle of additions of time, we have seen, was early extended by the action of the courts beyond its application as a punishment merely, and became the ultimate resort of the master in his legal claim of damages for breaches of contract by the servant; [152] but some confusion seems to have existed in the minds of the judges and the framers of the later statute law as to the exact theory on which the principle should be applied.

Though continued as a punishment until the abolition in 1643 of servitude to the colony for offenses, it seemed in the case of several kinds of offenses, both before and after that time, to partake of the nature of damages to the master for loss resulting from the offense, as well as of a penalty for the offense itself. In other cases it was clearly viewed in the light of damages alone. It was of the former character generally in such offenses as secret marriage and fornication, and of the latter for unlawful absence from his master's service or for acts of violence toward his master or overseer.

The term of servitude that was imposed was determined by the offense or the damage sustained, and was, except in a few offenses, not excessive, varying from one to two years.

In such cases as fornication or having a bastard the addition might be considerable. (This was an offense even if the woman was raped.) A woman-servant, for having a bastard, served her master from one and a half to two and a half years, and if the bastard were by a negro or a mulatto she might be sold to additional service for five years for the benefit of the public. Besides the master's claim on the female servant he might claim also a year's service from the guilty man, but in both cases the servant was given liberty to discharge this claim by a money satisfaction as in the case of free persons.[153]

The greatest abuse of additions, however, arose in connection with runaway servants. Before terms were definitely specified by statutes they were capable of very arbitrary assessment at the hands of the courts. The length of the term was sometimes left to the discretion of the master or was adjudged more than he himself cared to exact. Additional terms from two to seven years, served in irons, to the public, were prescribed in extreme cases.[154] The additions possible under the statutes were also very great, as ultimate recourse was had on the servant for all the expenses of his capture and return to his master. These expenses included rewards, sheriff's fees and jail fees. These latter were not fixed until 1726, and were a source of great abuse. When the master refused to pay these expenses, or could not be found, the servant was publicly sold or rented for such a time as would repay the public disbursements, and was then returned to his master to serve the remainder of his time and that due by addition. [155]

The act of 1643 provided that runaways from their " master's service shall be liable to make satisfaction by service at the end of their times by indenture, double the time of service so neglected, and in some cases more if the commissioners find it requisite and convenient," and subsequent acts allowed the master to recompense himself by service for all expenses to which he had been put in recovering his servant. The rate at which he could do this was fixed by the act of 1705 at one year's service for every 800 Ibs. of tobacco, or a month and a half for a hundred pounds. [156]

The servant, however, might commute this penalty by giving security for the payment of these expenses within six months, and the master was forced to accept security or payment when offered. The servant was also protected from injustice by the necessity imposed upon the master of presenting his claim in the next county court after the return of the runaway, or becoming liable to the loss of it altogether.[157] Where the master's goods had been stolen, or negroes enticed to accompany the runaway, the addition of time sufficient for compensation might be large.

The servant was required to serve for the lost time of the negro as for his own, since the negro was held by a statute of 1661 to be "incapable of making satisfaction by addition of time." [158]Additions thus frequently amounted to as much as four or five years, or even seven in some cases, and were often more than the original term of servitude. [159]

Corporal punishment as a common mode of regulating the servant's conduct was acquired by the master as a legal right during this period, and when retained in the hands of the local magistrate or other officers it became, under the power given by the statutes, readily susceptible of abuse. The extension of this important power beyond the administration of the courts was largely a result of the necessity of providing some severe correction in the case of runaways.

The servant had generally no means wherewith to remit a fine, and so in penal offenses, where free persons were fined, we have seen that the servant was whipped, unless his master discharged the fine. In many cases, also it was a general punishment both under the laws of England and under those of the colony, so that a law of 1662 provided for the erecting of a whipping-post in every county; but even before this time the master had assumed the right of administering corporal punishment to his servant.

In this year it became a right recognized by law, but when a master received an addition of time for his servant's offense it remained doubtful whether corporal punishment could also be administered. This question was settled by the Assembly in 1668. It was declared that " moderate corporal punishment " might be given to runaways either by the master or by a magistrate, and that it should "not deprive the master of the satisfaction allowed by law, the one being as necessary to reclaim them from perishing in that idle course as the other is just to repair the damages sustained by the master."[160]

The power thus given was doubtless abused, for in 1705 an act was passed restraining masters from giving "immoderate correction," and requiring an order from a justice of the peace for the whipping of " a Christian white servant naked under penalty of a forfeit of forty shillings to the party injured. The act is significant as showing also the master's right to employ corporal punishment as a regulation of the conduct of servants in general. [161]

Slaves were for the first time included in the act against runaways in 1670, and it was provided, *"that every constable into whose hands the said fugitive shall by any commissioner's warrant be first committed shall be and hereby is enjoyed by virtue of this act (though omitted in the warrant) to whip them severely and convey him to the next constable (toward his master's home) who is to give him the like correction and soe every constable through whose precinctshe passeth to doe the like."* [162]

In 1705, the severity of this act was somewhat mitigated by requiring justices who made the commitment to the constable to specify in their warrants the number of lashes to be given the runaway, "not exceeding the number thirty-nine." Corporal punishment was also extended in offenses committed against the master solely.

In 1673, the General Court ordered that a servant " for scandalous false and abusive language against his master have thirty-nine lashes publicly and well laid on in James City and that he appear at Middlesex County Court next and there openly upon his knees in the said court ask forgiveness which being done is to take of any further punishment allotted him." [163]

Besides the power to regulate his servant's conduct and enforce the performance of his duties, the master acquired a sort of general control over his servant's person and liberty of action. By custom the servant enjoyed frequent respites from service and might freely employ this time as he saw fit. In consequence of an abuse of this privilege, however, it became necessary to restrict it upon the consent of his master.

The plot of certain servants in Gloucester county in 1663 to rise against their masters and subvert the government caused great alarm throughout the colony, and led to a strict regulation of the liberty previously allowed servants of leaving their masters' plantations and assembling together. To suppress " unlawful meetings of servants," an act directed "that all masters of families be enjoined to take especial care that their servants do not depart from their houses on Sundays or any other days without particular license from them," and the different counties also were empowered to make by-laws for preventing unlawful meetings and for punishing offenders.

Though the servant's right to the personal enjoyment of his property was recognized when protected by the terms of his contract or by the courts, his disposal of it became conditioned on his master's consent by the acts against dealing with servants, and the right of trade was practically taken away. [164]The habit had also grown up on the part of masters of converting to their own use goods brought in by their servants or afterwards consigned to them.

In 1662 an act was passed to restrain this, providing that all servants " shall have the propriety in their owne goods and by permission of their master dispose of the same to their future advantage." The revisal of 1705 confirmed the right of servants to goods and money acquired "by gift or any other lawful ways or means/' with " the sole use and benefit thereof to themselves," making no reference to the necessity of the master's consent for a disposal of them.

The continuation of the act against dealing with servants was a practical limitation, however, of any rights they may have had. [165]'The servant's right to the possession of his personal estate now rested on statute and not on the occasional action of the courts or the will of his master; but he could not during servitude acquire a freehold interest in land, and tenancy of small tracts with the permission of the master was exceptional.[166]

Other important rights became fixed or limited by the statute law of the period and certain new rights were developed. The servant's claim to freedom dues recognized by the custom of the country and enforced by the courts was at first only a general one and not specific, the amount granted varying according to the will of the master or of the court in which it was sued for, unless it had been specified in the contract.

A clause was inserted in the act of 1705 confirming this right and making it thereafter certain in amount. Every male servant was to receive upon his freedom "ten bushels of indian corn, thirty shillings in money or the value thereof in goods and one well fixed musket or fuzee of the value of twenty shillings at least"; a woman-servant fifteen bushels of Indian corn and forty shillings in money or value. In later times these dues were discharged by a money equivalent and gifts of apparel.[167]

The freedom of a servant could be proved either by reference to the registry of his contract or to a court record, if he did not himself have a certificate of the fact from the county court or commissioner or from his master. In 1662, to facilitate the discovery of runaways and to protect innocent persons from arrest as such, or from penalties for entertaining suspected runaways, the clerk of the county court was directed to issue a certificate of freedom to every servant who produced proof before the court of the expiration of his term.[168]

Though designed as much for the protection of the master as of the servant, it became of great importance to the latter as his title to liberty and a guarantee that his rights as a free man would be fully respected. The necessity of such a guarantee appears not only from the restrictive nature of the legislation of this period, but from the records of the old General Court. Meager as they are, they present a number of instances of servants suing for their freedom who were either held or sold for periods longer than their lawful time.

The right was much abused, however, on the part of the servant. Heavy penalties had continually to be inflicted to prevent the theft of certificates or the use of forged or counterfeit ones. Stringent regulations had to be put on the granting and re-issuing of them, and where the servant made a fresh contract for service the certificate was to remain in the hands of the master till the contract expired.

The servant was further protected from an involuntary extension of his contract with his master by any intimidation or pressure brought to bear upon him by reason of his unequal position. After 1677 'no contracts for further service or for freedom dues could be made by a master with his servant during servitude except with the approbation of one or more justices of the peace, [169] under penalty of having to free his servant.'

By 1705 any contract for "further service or any other matter relating to liberty or personal profit " between master and servant had to be made in the presence and with the approbation of the court of the county. A practical limitation was also put upon the master's absolute right of assignment of his servant's contract. As the white servant was considered a Christian, as originally from a Christian land, the principle was established that he could only be held in servitude by Christians or those who were sure to give him " Christian care and usage." Thus, free negroes, mulattoes or Indians, although Christians, were incapacitated from holding white servants, and so also were all infidels, such as "Jews, Moors and Mohometans." Where any white servant was sold to them, or his owner had intermarried with them, the servant became " ipso facto " free.

An important right acquired by the servant during this period was the power given him to bring his complaint into court by petition " without the formal process of an action." This right, confirmed by the act of 1705, proved a great boon to the servant in case of unjust usage.

The county court had full discretion in such a case and might free or sell the servant away from his master. The right was extended to complaints of every character affecting the servant's rights. He could in this way sue for his freedom dues, his property or wages, or for damages for unlawful whipping. Another right granted by the act was that of commutation by a money satisfaction of corporal punishment for breach of the penal laws, and of additions of time for the expenses of capture in the case of runaways. [170]A right which was implied, if not expressly stipulated for in the contract, was that of a sick or disabled servant to claim support and medical attention at his master's charge during servitude, without any reciprocal right on the part of the master to further service therefor. The master was prevented by the liability of his goods and chattels to seizure from avoiding this obligation by freeing his servant and throwing him upon the parish.

Such rigor as is perceptible in the legislation of this period, and in general regarding the servant, we have seen appears particularly in the case of runaways, and is to be traced to the influence of the developing institution of slavery. Little practical distinction was made in the treatment of runaway servants and slaves where the practice was habitual, and the servant by his association with the negro fugitive became subjected to indignities that would not otherwise have been inflicted. [171]

The influence of slavery is also to be traced in the disposition to regard the servant as property and subject to the same property rights as the rest of the personal estate. As an important part of his master's estate he had become liable to the satisfaction of his debts and could be levied on equally with the goods and chattels.[172]

The conception of the servant as a portion of the personal estate is shown to be fully developed by an act of 1711, which directed that servants and slaves should be continued on the plantation of a person who died intestate, or who did not otherwise direct in his will, to finish the crop, upon which they were to remain in the hands of the executors or administrators ; while the slaves were then to pass to the heirs at law, as by the act of 1705 they had been declared to be real estate.[173]

The period is thus characterized by a twofold development: first, on the part of the master, from a conception of his right to the service guaranteed by the contract and to such incidents as enabled him to realize this right, to a conception of property in the servant himself which he would employ to the utmost advantage allowed him by the law; and on the part of the servant, from a desire to fulfil the conditions of his contract to a desire in general to escape from servitude whether based on lawful contract or on the exaction of his master: secondly, a reduction of the relation of master and servant to fixity and uniformity throughout the colony by the action of statute law in ascertaining their respective rights and duties.

Third Period, 1726-1788

During this period the institution of white servitude gradually declined before the growing institution of negro slavery, which proved economically far superior to it. We find the development of no new rights on the part of the master, and on the part of the servant only that of assent to the assignment of his contract.

This was not granted until 1785, when the system itself was practically at an end. The contract could now be assigned only on the free consent of the servant, attested in writing by a justice of the peace.

The various modifications introduced affecting rights already established were generally in mitigation of the servant's condition, and point to a very rapid decline of indented servitude after the middle of the century. This is indicated by a reduction of penalties for such abuses as harboring runaways or dealing with servants, and by the repeal in 1763 of former acts providing for the servitude of persons who came in without indentures, while making no provision to regulate it in future. In 1765 the practice of binding the bastard children of a white woman-servant or free woman for thirty-one years was declared by the Assembly to be "an unreasonable severity to such children," and the term was limited to twenty-one years for males and eighteen for females.

This does however show us that the indentured servitude did pass from generation to generation. It was unlawful for an indented servant to marry during the term of their contract. Therefor, when a child was born, they entered a service for 18-31 years. The parent was usually given 'correction,' and years added to their contract.

By the act of 1769 they were to be treated as apprentices, to be instructed, and to claim all the rights of other apprentices. [174]Unimportant changes were introduced in the law relating to runaways, designed to facilitate their recovery with least expense to the master, and consequently with least injustice to the servant. In earlier years, severe punishment was given often to a runaway servant.[175]Freedom dues were fixed with a money equivalent, and were the same for both men and women. Injury to a servant might be redressed by "immediate discharge" from service by order of a court. Much had improved for the white servants in the mid to late 1700s.

The legislation as a whole was not important and developed no new principles. The legal fixity of the conception of the servant as a piece of property is apparent, and becomes further developed through the influence of slavery and as a result of the long terms. An average servant term was from seven to fourteen years, most of which at this time were the English felons were transported to the colony.[176]

The act of 1785 legally defines servants as, "all white perons not being citizens of any of the confederated states of America who shall come into this commonwealth under contract to serve another in any trade or occupation." This definition excluded black slaves, hirelings who were citizens of any of the confederated states, but included convicts (whose importation was not finally prohibited until 1788) and apprentices from abroad. The term of servitude was limited to a period not exceeding seven years, except in the case of infants under fourteen who might be bound by their guardians until the age of twenty-one, and all servants, the act declares, "shall be compellable to perform such contract specifically during the term thereof."

Corporal punishment by order of a justice was the power in a master's hands of enforcing such performance, and the benefit of the servant's contract was to pass to "the executors, administrators, and legatees of the master."[177]

We have seen that the relation between a master and a servant was at first a relation between legal persons, based on contract, and that such property right as existed, consisted in the master's right to the labor and services of his servant, while the servant enjoyed a reciprocal right to support and, to some extent, to protection and instruction from his master. Gradually the conception of property grew at the expense of that of personality, and that with a limited class of servants personal liberty became so restricted that they stood in respect to their masters in a position somewhat analogous to that of slaves. The broadest practical and legal distinction was made, however, between the servant in general and the slave, and the institution of white servitude differed widely from that of slavery, both in nature and in origin. It rested for its sanction on national or municipal law alone, while slavery was based upon international as well as municipal law.

The extent servitude was of limited duration, while slavery was for life. (Although the Indented Servant contracts were continually extended for slight offenses, they were termed 'for a period of time'.) The personality of the servant was always recognized and his status could not descend to his offspring, unless the child was born illegally a bastard durng the servants termed contract, unlike the case with the slave's, nor did the master at any time have absolute control over the personal liberty of his servant as of his slave. The servant in the 1700s, had rights which his master was bound to respect, and besides the guarantee of personal security, enjoyed a limited right to private property. The conception of the servant himself, as a piece of property, did not go beyond that of personality, while the slave did not remain as personal estate, but came to be regarded as a chattel real or as real estate. The mutual effects of the institutions upon each other are shown, however, in the growth of this conception of property, and particularly also in the legislation respecting runaways, unlawful assemblies, or absence from the master's plantation. *Servitude may thus be regarded as preparing the way both legally and practically for the institution of slavery as it existed in Virginia.*[178]

Social Status of the Servant. The actual condition of the servant improved, though in great measure determined by his legal status and by certain social laws, was also largely influenced by many customs that had no sanction in law, and the distinction between servant and slave became as clearly denned under the action of these and the practical working of the law as in the letter of the law.

In regard to employment a marked distinction was frequently made between the servant and the slave. The industry of the colony was chiefly agricultural, its staple throughout the seventeenth century being tobacco. Where the servant was engaged in field labor he was worked side by side with the negro slave, under the direction of overseers who were frequently the best of his own class. This was not in itself a hardship, as the work was the same as that of the planters themselves and of every common freeman, and the servant was not required to do more in a day than was done by his overseer.

As the number of negroes began to increase, the more difficult and greater part of the work was put upon them, and the servant, was reserved for lighter and finer tasks. Though associated with the negro, he was no longer compelled to live with him in "gangs" and "quarters," and, unlike him, could make complaint if insufficient clothing or lodging were provided. [179]Women-servants were now commonly employed as domestics, as by an act of 1662 they became "tythable" and their master subject to the payment of levies for them if they were put "to work in the ground", the negress, however, had no such exemption in her favor, and was frequently employed in field labor with the men. With regard to their labor, the slave, Beverley says, was better off than the husbandmen and day-laborers of England, and the servant's lot was still easier.[180]

Very large numbers of the servants were also artisans and skilled workmen and were employed in building and other trades. Almost every profession was represented, and on the large plantations, which provided mostly their own necessities, there was a great demand for such servants and for industrial apprentices. Many servants were thus taken into the families of their masters in various capacities, and were treated with as much consideration as if working under a free contract for wages. Considerable domestic manufacturing was of necessity carried on at all times, and after the introduction of large numbers of slaves for the field labor, white servants were generally utilized for that purpose. They were thus better housed, clothed and fed than the negro, as a result of the position they occupied toward their master as well as from the protection afforded them by the law.[181]

Besides a general social obligation of protection and defense recognized by most masters toward their servants as dependents, the law only held a servant responsible for his own free acts and not for those performed under the orders of his master. [182]Where the servants were apprentices a high personal trust was involved, and the master, besides occupying the position of guardian, was bound to render religious and secular as well as mechanical instruction.

Not only was attendance at church required by law, but all servants and apprentices were to be instructed together with their masters' children every Sunday, just before evening prayer by the minister of the parish. When such obligations were recognized, the great distinction between the positions of a servant and a slave is at once manifest. [183]Where these obligations rested upon the provisions of the contract they seem to have been carefully guarded by the courts.

A servant complained in a general court of 1640 of her "master's ill usage by putting her to beat at the mortar for all his house-hold, when he had promised to use her more like his child than a servant, and to teach her to read and instruct her in religion. The court considering the "grievous and tyrannical usage" of her master, ordered her to be freed, though she had yet a year to serve, and to receive her freedom dues.[184] Up until this point, many servants had been given severe penalties for issuing grievances against their masters.

Frequent respites from service were also granted in the 1700s. It was not only the custom to allow servants Saturday afternoons as well as the Sabbath for free disposal, but all the old holidays were rigidly observed. An industrious servant was thus given an opportunity to lay up a competence for his start in the world as a free man. Tenure of small tracts of land was sometimes permitted by masters, and with the live stock given him he might raise cattle, hogs and tobacco and so become possessed of considerable property.

The evolution from the days of the London Company of an aristocracy of wealth rather than of blood was a somewhat slow process, so that there was nothing in the servant's position itself (except that it debarred him from the possession of landed property and consequently of certain civic rights) to condemn him to a very inferior social position. No odium attached to his condition or person as to the slave's, and where he proved worthy of consideration he might enjoy many of the social privileges that would have been accorded him as a free man.[185]

The servant himself was disposed to regard his condition as only that of a free man rendering services for a sort of wages advanced to him in his transportation and maintenance, and his legal disabilities as only a temporary suspension of his rights necessary to insure a more complete realization by his master of the right to service. Constantly looking forward to his full freedom, he considered his position as analogous to apprenticeship, or to that of the ordinary hired laborer rather than to that of the slave.

The natural pride of the free man sustained by this feeling, together with the strong race prejudice that has ever separated the Englishman from an inferior and dependent race, and his religious sentiment as a Christian, or at least of Christian origin, sufficed to make a very great practical distinction between his social position and that of the negro and Indian, slave or free. These sentiments were effective with the better class of servants in keeping them aloof from association with such inferiors.

With convicts and the lower classes, where such considerations were not always sufficient, the law took precaution by the most stringent measures to uphold them and to prevent race contamination. Freemen and servants alike were subjected to severe penalties for intercourse with negroes, mulattoes and Indians, and inter marriage with them or with infidels was prohibited by many statutes prescribing the punishment both of the offender and of the minister who performed the ceremony. [186]

[187]The Governor and Council in court in 1630 ordered " Hugh Davis to be soundly whipped before an assembly of negroes and others for abusing himself to the dishonor of God and shame of a Christian by defiling his body in lying with a negro which fault he is to acknowledge next sabbath day." A similar case came before the court the next year. Very few negroes, however, were brought to Virginia before the latter half of the century, but the records of the general court during the period (1670-76) of increased importations of negroes under the African Company, having no reference to the recurrence of the offence, points to a disposition on the part of the whites in general to avoid race contamination.[188]

The growth of a considerable class of mulattoes, particularly mulattoes by negroes, is appreciable towards the end of the century, however, and is shown by the passing of several acts to restrict it. The first statute on the subject, that of 1662, imposed double fines for fornication with a negro, but no occasion for restricting intermarriage seems to have arisen till 1691, when an act was passed *for prevention of that abominable mixture and spurious issue which hereafter may increase in this dominion as well by negroes, mulattoes and Indians intermarrying with English or other white women as by their unlawful accompanying with one another*, and punished the intermarriage of a free white man or woman with a negro, mulatto or Indian, bond or free, with banishment forever from the colony within three months after the marriage, and the justices of the county were "to make it their perticular care that this act be put into effectual execution."

The revisal limitation of servants' marriages upon the master's consent was a sufficient safeguard in their case, and but little responsibility may be regarded as attaching to them for the growth of the mulatto class. As was natural between two dependent classes whose conditions were different and widely in favor of one class, race prejudice and pride were at their strongest and developed jealousies which did not exist between the master and his dependent or the freeman and the slave. A disposition on the part of servants to keep themselves free from all association with negroes is very perceptible.

The presence in the latter part of the seventeenth century of quite a number of the English lower classes and criminals, together with a greater development of the aristocratic sentiment from the influx of a considerable number of gentlemen just after the civil war in England. [189]Statues of 1705 altered this penalty to the imprisonment of the offender six months and a fine of ten pounds Virginia currency, the person who performed the marriage forfeiting ten thousand Ibs. of tobacco.

When a woman-servant was guilty of having a mulatto or negro bastard she was, as a free woman, sold for five years as a punishment, or subjected to a fine of fifteen pounds, while the necessity of the master's license barred the unlawful intermarriage of servants. Where the offense occurred, then it was more likely to do so in the case of a free person than of a servant, as the master would not be likely to give his consent to any such marriage, having much to lose and nothing to gain from the service of the issue which might be sold away from him by the churchwardens of the parish.

In one instance a girl was given her freedom because her master had consented to such a marriage, and such rulings of the courts probably checked exceptional cases. The practical distinction to be made between servants as whites, and negroes and Indians was one constantly recognized by the courts and the Assembly. The consideration of racial distinction alone seems to have led the Assembly in 1670, when the question of the legal power of the free Christian Indian or negro to hold a servant came up, to declare in the negative.

The real condition of the servant in the American colonies was much better than has generally been supposed, and was decidedly better in Virginia than in some of the other colonies. Though what was practically white slavery seems to have existed in some of the island plantations of England, there is no instance, so far as I have been able to discover, of a white person sold into slavery in Virginia.

How far the general character of white servitude progressively changed and differed from slavery has been sufficiently shown, and in considering the apparent barbarities to which a servant was subjected we should remember that neither in England nor on the Continent was the condition of the dependent classes any better. The doctrine of the rights of man had not yet arisen in the seventeenth century, nor was it until the latter part of the next century that its practical fruits began to appear. "During the civil war several gentlemen of quality fled hither and others of good parts but they are all dead, and I hope in God there never will be such a cause to make any come in again." Beverley, who was opposed to Nicholson and his government, confirms this view.

Not until the late years of the eighteenth century was feudal serfdom generally abolished on the continent of Europe, and as late as 1835, the prison and the flogging board still constituted a part of the equipment of every Hungarian manor. [190]In England villeinage passed away comparatively early as a result of the social disturbances of the fourteenth century, though a case was pleaded in the courts as late as 1618. Its extinction was thus gradual without any legislative abolition, and it was many years before the principle of free contract labor was fully worked out.

The tendency of the agrarian reforms of England, in contrast to those of some continental countries, was to develop a class of landless freemen whose position was worse than if they had possessed land on semiservile conditions. The small farmer gradually gave way before the capitalist farmer, and the large laboring class that was formed was stripped of all interest in the soil. These laborers were compelled to work by the various statutes regulating labor and apprenticeship under some master, and had to do so generally on long terms, with fixed wages and hours of labor, and restrictions were placed on departure or dismissal from service under severe penalties.

The system introduced by the final statute of laborers, the so-called Statute of Apprentices of 1563, embodying the results of many previous measures, had the effect of checking migration of servants and in general of lengthening the period of servitude, and remained effective until the industrial revolution which followed the introduction of machinery.[191]

Some improvement in the economic condition of English servants is discernible during the latter part of the seventeenth century, but not much can be said as to the betterment of the social condition. Where they were in their master's household, and received rations and apparel in part payment of wages, they were not generally as well fed and clothed as the indented servants in Virginia. Their labor was more burdensome and the arbitrary treatment to which they were subjected was frequently more severe. Corporal punishment was a common mode of regulating their conduct, and shackles were used to prevent their running away.

For extreme maltreatment on the part of the master the only redress was discharge from service, or in some cases a paltry forfeit of less than a pound to the servant. They were frequently discharged from their service contrary to the statute, and besides maltreatment their wages and apparel were often withheld. The condition of the English servant was thus sufficiently bad to make numbers of them migrate to Virginia in the hope of bettering it.[192]

The Middlesex records and sessions rolls give a number of interesting cases that throw light on the condition of the English servant. For an assault upon his master, an offense which would have been punished in Virginia by whipping or addition of time, a servant was in 1618 adjudged " to be imprisoned for a year, to be flogged on two market days at Brainford, to be put one day in the stock at Acton and on his knees in the open church to ask forgiveness of his master and afterwards to be reimprisoned."

Unruly and disorderly servants and apprentices were sent to houses of correction, when they became effective after 1609, "to labour hardly e as the quality of their offence requireth." In 1652 a servant on covenant for a year's service complained of her mistress, and the sessions found "that the said lady did violently beat her servant with a great stick and offered to strike her with a hammer and that the said lady doth retain the wages due," and ordered dismissal and payment.

In another case a master confesses "that he hath most uncivilly and inhumanly beaten a female servant with great knotted whipcord so that the poor servant is a lamentable spectacle to behold." Another master was held to answer " for giving his servant immoderate correction by beating him with three roddes one after the other." A case which must be regarded as very exceptional occurred in 1655. An apprentice complained that his master made him work on Sunday and further misused him " by fastening a lock with a chain to it and tying and fettering him to the shoppe and that said master, his wife and mother did most cruelly and inhumanly beat his said apprentice and also whipped him till he was very bloody and his flesh rawe over a great part of his body, and then salted him and held him naked to the fire being so salted to add to his pain."[193]

That the servant sometimes met with very harsh treatment cannot be denied, however. In a case of judicial punishment by a commissioner of a county court, before the punishment had been regulated by statute, a servant was whipped almost to death, and the passing of an act by the Assembly in 1662 prohibiting private burial of servants or others, because of the occasion thus given for "much scandall against divers persons and sometimes not undeservedly of being guilty of their deaths," shows that sometimes the master abused his right of corporal punishment in an extreme degree. [194]The cruelty of some masters was sufficient towards the middle of the seventeenth century to interfere seriously with the importation of servants, and the Assembly in 1662 attempted to put a stop to it by giving the servant an easy remedy upon complaint to the commissioners for all his grievances. From this time forward harsh treatment may generally be considered as exceptional.

Beverley says of the treatment of servants, "The cruelties and severities imputed to that country are an unjust reflection, no people more abhor the thought of such usage than the Virginians nor try more to prevent it now whatever it was in former days."

This statement seems to be borne out by other contemporary authorities and by the records of the courts, which show that every safeguard was thrown around the servant, and that wherever the slightest pretext for freeing him appeared it was taken advantage of. Justice was readily accessible. Every few miles a justice might be found to whom complaint could be made, and the county courts, which met in the early times as often as necessity required, and later every month, redressed servants' grievances in a "summary" manner.[195]

A servant could legally sue for his freedom on retention in service after his contract had expired, or for his master's violation of the act of 1676 by attempting to make any contract with him to his damage, or upon purchase by negroes, mulattoes, Indians or infidels, or upon the intermarriage of any such person with his owner; but the courts going beyond this in the discretionary power granted them by law, would free a servant for breach of the terms of indenture by the master, for breach of a contract to marry, for a second complaint of ill-usage, and sometimes even upon a first complaint where no fault of the servant appeared.

The number of such suits occurring both in the General and the county courts, and the fraudulent concealment of indentures, show a continual disposition on the part of the master to extend the servitude, though unjustly, for as long a period as possible. [196]By the acts giving the master additions of time for the birth of a bastard child to his servant, a premium was actually put upon immorality, and there appear to have been masters base enough to take advantage of it. This was restrained by an act of 1662, which provided that the maid-servant should be sold away from her master in such cases and no compensation allowed him for the loss of her time. Complete freedom would probably have been granted but for the harmful effect on the servant herself.[197]

The speedy rendering of justice to the servant through the special procedure provided in his case, and the unrestricted right of appeal to the higher courts, placed him in an exceptional position. The fact that the law was interpreted in the most favorable light possible for the servant, and that no fear was ever entertained of a servile insurrection, except in the single case of the Gloucester plot of 1663, which was due to political rather than social reasons, may be regarded as confirming the positive statements of contemporary writers as to the comparatively easy conditions of servitude during the period of indented service.

We may conclude that where the servant showed himself at all deserving his lot was in general very easy and frequently much better than he had ever before enjoyed.[198]

We have seen that by provisions of the statutes and tinder the practice of the courts a servant might legally obtain his freedom in several ways; the ordinary mode, however, was on the expiration of the term of his contract. He might then claim a certificate of freedom, and with his title to liberty resting on this or on the records of a court, all his legal disabilities were at once removed and he became "as free in all respects and as much entitled to the liberties and privileges of the country as any of the inhabitants or natives."[199]

To determine the place and influence of the servant as a freedman in the very complex social and economic development of the colony is by no means an easy matter. Merged as he was in the general class of free men, such effects as were due to his presence were not easily distinguishable. The process itself was largely unconscious on the part of the people and but barely recorded in contemporary history.

Little historic material has thus survived on which to base satisfactory conclusions. Enough remains, however, to give decisive proof of a very rapid evolution of servants when free, and to show that they did not continue as a class at all, and so could not have formed, as has been mistakenly supposed, the lowest stratum of Virginia society in the eighteenth century.

The various classes that made up the society of colonial Virginia were separated from each other only by the broadest and most general distinctions, and graded almost imperceptibly into one another. The law recognized no distinction whatever except in the case of the twelve councillors. The class which stood at the head of the social order and formed a kind of aristocracy was mainly an outgrowth of the official class and of landed proprietors, who, having acquired wealth or large estates, had been able to preserve them in their families for several generations through the action of the law of entails.

A number of wealthy would-be aristocrats, without real culture and refinement, together with the poor but proud younger sons of the aristocrats, hung on to and aped the manners of the class above them; but the solid middle class of independent yeomanry, with plain and unpretentious manners, was far more numerous, and even in the latter part of the eighteenth century formed nearly half the population of the colony. The lowest class of all is described by a contemporary as "a seculum of beings called overseers, the most abject, degraded, unprincipled race."[200]

The freed servants may in all justice be said to have recruited all these classes at different periods during the continuance of indented servitude, but toward the beginning and in the first years of the eighteenth century probably more largely that of the small independent planters or laborers and the class of overseers.

Though pride and wealth generally acted to make the upper classes hold themselves aloof from the lower, the good-will and generous hospitality characteristic of all classes gave them all more or less of a common life and freedom of association with each other, and where those elements were present in any man that would merit his rise he was not likely to be kept down by any false ideas due to caste sentiment.

The rapidity with which some freedmen rose to positions of trust and distinction is bundant proof of the opportunity which lay open to all that possessed true desert. Many servants were besides this of better origin and education than the generality of the freemen, and were frequently employed in such responsible positions as teachers, and many ministers were imported on conditions almost parallel to those of indented ' servants.[201]

In the first half of the seventeenth century their rise to prominence was often very rapid. Several members of the Assembly of 1654 were men who had been servants, and in 1662 we are told that "the Burgesses which represent the people . . . are usually such as went over servants thither," who "by time and industry . . . have acquired competent estates." [202]

Intermarriage of free persons and servants was very common. Masters sometimes bought female servants for their wives, and it was not uncommon for men-servants to marry into their masters' families when they gained their freedom.[203] No impassible social barrier thus seems to have existed, nor were opportunities lacking for the material improvement of the servant. To better his fortune when out of indenture at least two courses were open to him. He might remain with his master or some other person as a hired man or tenant upon his lands, or he might become an independent planter by taking up whatever unoccupied land in the community had proved too barren to be already patented by freemen, or by moving to the frontier where abundance of good land was to be had on the easiest terms.

There was a constant demand for labor, both agricultural and mechanical, throughout the colonial period, a demand satisfied neither by the indented servants nor by the large importations of slaves. The wages of hired labor were consequently always high, particularly those of artisans or tradesmen of the slightest capacity.

Freedmen who were content to become members of the laboring class had abundant opportunity and inducement to do so. Until domestic manufacturers were checked by the repressive measures of the English Board of Trade, considerable encouragement was given to skilled workmen to exercise their crafts or to establish themselves in an independent position.

When the profits of tobacco-planting increased, however, this industry probably absorbed a large number of freedmen, as very favorable conditions of tenantship were offered on the great estates, where men usually held on what constituted practically a life tenure. The disposition to become a freeholder, however, particularly after the servant enjoyed a claim to land in his own right, was most marked of all. [204]In the earlier times, though the person importing him could claim fifty acres for his importation, the servant does not appear to have been legally entitled to any grant of land from the government. A grant was frequently stipulated in the contract with a master, and became also in some places a custom, which like freedom dues was recognized by the courts.

In 1690 the instructions to Governor Howard directed that every servant receive a patent of fifty acres in fee on attaining his freedom, and it is probable that henceforth he was regarded as having a legal claim to such a grant. Before this the rules for leasing or patenting lands in many cases allowed him to acquire the tenancy of small tracts at a nominal rent, and lands were also left with other bequests to servants in their masters' wills. [205]

The practice of the sale of rights to land due for the importation of people, to the colony, both by the holders of them and by the secretary, for the small sum of four or five shillings, and the modes of granting out lapsed and unseated lands, made it a very easy matter in later times for the servant to become the proprietor of landed property in the old settled communities, and when good land could not be obtained in this way there was always room for him on the frontier. Though much of the frontier land was patented out in large tracts, to lie unsettled for a time, it was gradually broken up into small ones and disposed of by the owners to squatters and settlers, so that the Piedmont and western parts of Virginia became characterized by farms of moderate extent rather than by large plantations as in Eastern Virginia.[206]

Titles to land in the first instance rested on patents granted for special services, for consideration, or for the importation of persons to the colony as settlers. A condition of ceding the land within a limited period after the patent's issue accompanied such grants comparatively early. Where this condition was not fulfilled the land lapsed and a new patent might be issued to any one petitioning the General Court and the Governor, on similar terms, the theory being that land grants were made to encourage settlers only.

Seating involved considerable expense for improvements, the building of a house, clearing and planting three acres of every fifty, and a full stocking of the land. All this was more than the patentee to large tracts could undertake. It was not an uncommon thing for the right to land to lapse several times over, unless it could be disposed of by sale. The sale of rights became thus as general as the sale of the land itself, and they were readily purchasable for very small sums. After 1705, fifty-acre rights, according to the Royal Instructions, could be bought at five shillings per right.

Unseated lands also, where the escheat was not traversed and no equitable right was shown to the lands, could be easily obtained on petition to the Governor by payment into the treasury of a composition of two pounds of tobacco for each acre. In the early years, however, no time limit was imposed upon the seating of lands, and the abuse of land-grabbing, which had begun almost immediately on the general introduction of property in the soil in 1619, had had sunacient time to result in the concentration of all the best lands along the river-courses in the hands of comparatively few persons. This was facilitated by the ownership or the buying up of large numbers of fifty- acre claims, called "head rights," for the importation of settlers.

Claims were admitted for the members of a man's family, himself as well as his wife, children, and all servants imported at his charge, and even for the negroes brought in (this latter kind was soon denied). Corrupt practices prevailed also in the offices issuing the grants, head rights were used many times over, and rights could be purchased of the secretary at three to four shillings, or even a half-crown. In this way, large tracts came into the possession of a few men, to lie mostly barren and uncultivated unless tenanted. Tracts of 20,000, 30,000 and 50,000 acres existed of which not fifty were under cultivation. When the two new counties of Spottsylvania and Brunswick were set apart during Spottswood's government, with an exemption from quit-rents for several years, Spottswood himself was accused of taking 40,000 acres.

The growth of this class of small farmers was effective in developing over a large portion of the State a very strong type of peasant proprietorship, and sufficiently shows that the servant was under no necessity of becoming either a pauper or a criminal. That he did to some extent fit within these classes is what might naturally be expected from the introduction of English convicts as servants, and after they came in some numbers we have indications that they were responsible for much of the crime committed, but pauperism in Virginia before the first quarter of the eighteenth century was almost unknown.

Under the stimulus of regained freedom and the abundant opportunity afforded for individual endeavor, the freed servant may in general be regarded as growing up with the country, as becoming an independent and often valued citizen, and materially aiding in the development of the resources of the colony. Trained by his long apprenticeship in the best practices of agriculture or of his trade, and thoroughly acclimated, he was better able than a new-comer to take a place profitably both to himself and to the public in the social and political order.

From what has been said the importance of the system of white servitude in colonial development is apparent. Such effects as were due to it were to some extent obscured by the institution of slavery, which, existing for some time alongside the earlier system and finally supplanting it, either greatly counteracted or enhanced its influence. Yet it is possible to make some general deductions as to the social and economic results which followed its introduction into the American colonies.

Its superiority to a system of perfectly free labor under colonial conditions could not be doubted if it were certain to lead to the development of a class of independent freeholders. The benefit to production to be derived from long and certain terms of service with contract labor was sufficiently shown in the experience of contemporary England. We can see how advantageously such an extension of the time and certainty of labor supply as was involved in indented servitude, together with the power of control by the master and the economy of providing for large numbers of servants together, would work in a new and sparsely settled country whose industry was chiefly agricultural and dependent for success on a foreign trade and consequently on the efficient management of large landed estates by a capitalist class. [207]Some form of cheap labor was a necessity; the slavery of Christians and white men was naturally abhorrent, that of Indians impracticable on a large scale, and negro slavery was comparatively slow in becoming an object of desire to the Virginia planters.

The gradual and tentative development in practice of indented servitude from what at first was theoretically but a modification of free contract slavery clearly shows its recognized economic superiority to such a system as existed in England. Designed not only as a labor supply, but as an immigration agency. Later as laws developed, it had generally the effect of a trial apprenticeship, greatly strengthening the position of the capitalist employer and developing a class of industrially efficient free men. It supplied the entire force of skilled and domestic labor of the colony for more than half a century, and continued, after slavery as a general labor supply had supplanted it, to be the source of all high-grade labor well into the eighteenth century. It provided for the growth of a strong yeomanry during the seventeenth and eighteenth centuries, preventing a complete absorption of the land into large estates; and in furnishing a great number of independent settlers and citizens, particularly for the back territory, it had a most marked effect on the political as well as the economic development of the country.

The moral influence of the system cannot in general be said to have been good. The tendency was to harden the master's feeling towards servitude and to prepare him for a readier adoption of slavery, and the introduction of undesirable classes into a society already lax in habit was not likely to improve the moral tone or the social welfare of the colony

By the temporary disfranchisement of the servant during his term, common after the middle of the seventeenth century, a serious public danger was avoided. There could be no guarantee of the judicious exercise of the suffrage with this class who, for the most part, had never enjoyed the privilege before. Their servitude may be regarded as preparing them for a proper appreciation of suffrage when obtained, and the duties of citizenship. In the later days of public improvement and town-building, the imported craftsmen were a valuable class.

In comparison with the institution of negro slavery, the superiority of white servitude for social and moral considerations seems to have been recognized by the Virginia planters, but from a purely economic point of view its inferiority was fully apparent, and from the first considerable importation of negro slaves the ultimate destruction of the system was easily foreseen. The slowness with which negro slavery was adopted shows a conscious effort on the part of Virginia, so long as it was permitted to act freely, to resist the encroachment upon servitude.[208] At the same time that English policy was forcing slavery upon the colony it cut off the supply of indented servants, and the decline of the system after the last quarter of the seventeenth century was very rapid.

The final extinction of indented servitude in Virginia did not take place till some time after the close of the Revolutionary War; as late as 1774 there was still some demand for servants, and the importation of convicts was not finally prohibited until 1788. [209]The real efficiency of the system, however, had ceased long before. Even in the late years of the seventeenth century negro slaves were more in demand for supplying old plantations or beginning new ones than servants, and where a demand existed for white servants it was for artisans and apprentices, and large prices had to be paid to get good ones. [210]White servitude survived after the downfall of the system in an apprenticeship of domestic growth, originating in the binding of poor or bastard children for a term of years for their instruction and to save the parish the expense of their support; but this had no historic connection with the apprenticeship which constituted a part of indented servitude, and itself finally passed away under the regime of perfectly free labor.

The experience of Virginia was largely repeated in the other colonies, and the general effects of the system were much the same in all. The influence on internal development was even more clearly marked in Maryland and Pennsylvania than in Virginia. In Pennsylvania, the large number of German settlers who came in this way, driven from home by religious or political persecution, became the most valued of citizens. [211]The rise and influence of the freedman in Maryland was as perceptible as in Virginia. Though that colony was unfortunate in receiving a larger number of the convict class, very few of them seem to have remained in the country on attaining their freedom, but returned to Europe or migrated to distant settlements.[212] In the other southern and middle colonies and in New England servants were not numerically so large a class., and their rise and absorption into the higher classes became from social and political reasons even more easy than in Virginia and Maryland.[213]

The actual conditions of servitude varied somewhat in the different colonies, assuming in some respects a harsher, in others a milder character than we have seen in Virginia. In Massachusetts, the elective franchise seems to have been exercised by servants only up to the year 1636, and the qualification of church membership was required of all voters to 1664. In Virginia, the "inhabitants" voted for burgesses until 1646, and until 1670 the freed servant enjoyed the suffrage along with other free men, there being no property or other qualification. [214]

The terms of servitude also in many of the colonies were longer than in Virginia. In Maryland, the common term seems to have been five years. Seven-year terms were frequent in Massachusetts, and in Rhode Island even ten. Provision was taken for the strict enforcement of the full term, and enfranchisement was not encouraged. Additions of time, corporal punishment, limitation of the rights of trade and free marriage, and provisions for the capture and return of runaways, were much the same.[215]

Greater numbers of Indian and mulatto servants seem to have been made use of in New England than in the other colonies, though the importation of white servants was specially encouraged by the enactments against Indian slave-trading. Georgia and the Carolinas also encouraged the importation of servants of the better class, while the colonies in general made an attempt to protect themselves against convicts and servants of undesirable classes, as Irish Papists and aliens.[216]

The wide prevalence of the system, not only in the American but in the island plantations of England, had -a most important bearing on the social economy of Great Britain and of other European countries, similar in a less degree to the effect of the large European emigration of the present day. Not only were many of the evils of a congested population lessened, but elements of the greatest social and political danger were effectively gotten rid of by forced transportation. [217]The effect on England of the removal of large numbers of political and social offenders was wholly beneficial; and though many of the emigrants from the Continent were religious or political refugees, a great number were also from the poorer classes, and their withdrawal was a considerable economic relief.[218]

In conclusion, an important political effect on the American colonies should be noted. The infusion of such large numbers of the lower and middle classes into colonial society could only result in a marked increase of democratic sentiment, which, together with a spirit of rebellion against the unjust importation of convicts and slaves, increased under British tyranny the growing restlessness which finally led to the separation of the colonies from the mother country.[219]

Documents

Letters Patent to Sir Humfrey Gylberte June 11, 1578.

Elizabeth by the grace of God Queene of England, &c. To all people to whom these presents shall come, greeting.

Know ye that of our especiall grace, certaine science and meere motion, we have given and granted, and by these presents for us, our heires and successours, doe give and graunt to our trustie and welbeloved servaunt Sir Humphrey Gilbert of Compton, in our castle of Devonshire Knight, and to his heires and assignee for ever, free libertie and licence from time to time, and at all times for ever hereafter, to discover, finde, search out, and view such remote, heathen and barbarous lands, countreys and territories not actually possessed of any Christian prince or people, as to him, his heirs & assignee, and to every or any of them, shall seeme good: and the fame to have, hold, occupie and enjoy to him, his heires and assignee for ever, with all commodities, jurisdictions, and royalties both by sea and land; and the said sir Humfrev and all such as from time to time by licence of us, our heiress and successours, shall goe and travell thither, to inhabits or romaine there, to build and fortifie at the discretion of the sayde Sir Humfrey, and of his heires and assignee, the statutes or actes of Parliament made against Fugitives, or against such as shall depart, romaine or continue out of our Realme of England without licence, or any other acte, statute, lawe or matter whatsoever to the contrary in any wise notwithstanding. And wee doe likewise by these presents, for US, our heires and successours, give full authoritie and power to the saide Sir Humfrey, his heires and assignee, and every of them, that tree and they, and every of any of them, shall and may at all and every time and times hereafter, have, take and lead in the same voyages, to travell thitherward, and to inhabits there with him, and every or any of them, such and so many of our subjects as shall willingly accompany him and them, and every or any of them, with sufficient shipping and furniture for their transportations, so that none of the same persons, nor any of them be such as hereafter shall be specially restrained by us, our heires and successors. And further, that he the said Humfrey, his heires and assignee, and every or any of them shall have, hold, occupy and enjoy to him, his heires and assignee, and every of them for ever, all the soyle of all such lands. countries, & territories so to be discovered or possessed as aforesaid, and of all Cities, Castles, Townes and Villages, and places in the same, with the rites, royalties and jurisdictions, as well marine as other, within sayd lands or countreys of the seas thereunto adjovning, to be had or used with ful power to dispose thereof, & of every part thereof in fee simple or otherwise, according to the order of the laws of England, as near as the same conveniently may be, at his, and their will & pleasure, to any person then being, or that shall romaine within the allegiance of us, our heires and successours, paying unto us for all services, dueties and demaunds, the fift part of all the oare of gold and silver, that from time to time, and at all times after such discoverie, subduing and possessing shall be there gotten: all which hands, countreys and territories, shall for ever bee holden by the said Sir Humfrey, his heires and assignee of us, our heires and successors by homage, and by the sayd payment of the sayd fift part before reserved onely for all services.

And moreover, we doe by these presents for us, our heires and successours, give and graunt licence to the sayde Sir Humfray Gilbert, his heires or assignee, and to every of them, that tree and they, and every or any of them shall, and may from time to time, and all times for ever hereafter, for his and their defence, encounter, expulse, repell and resift, as well by Sea as by land, and by all other wayes whatsoever, all and every such person and persons whatsoever, as without the special licence and liking of the sayd Sir Humfrey, and of his heires and assignee, shall attempt to inhabits within the sayd countreys, or any of them, or within the space of two hundreth leagues nerre to the place or places within such countreys as aforesayd, if they shall not bee before planted or inhabited within the limiter aforesayd, with the subjects of any Christian prince, being amitie with her-Majesty, where the said sir Humfrey, his heires or assignee, or any of them, or his, or their or any of their associates or companies, shall within sixe yeeres next ensuing, make their dwellings and abidings, or that shall enterprise or attempt at any time hereafter unlawfully to annoy either by Sea or land, the said sir Humfrey, his heires or assignee, or any of them, or his, or their, or any of their companies: giving and graunting by these presents, further power and authorite to the sayd sir Humfrey, his heires and assignee, and every of them from time to time, and at all times for ever hereafter to take and surprise by all maner of meanes whatsoever all and every person and persons, with their shipper, vessels, and other goods and furniture, which without the licence of the sayd sir Humfrey, or his heires or assignee as aforesayd, shall bee found traffiquing into any harborough or harboroughs creeke or creekes within the limites aforesayde, the subjects of our Realmes and dominions, and all other persons in amitie with us, being driven by force of tempest or shipwracke onely excepted, and those persons and every of them with their ships, vessels, goods, and furniture, to detaine and possesse, as of good and lawful prize, according to the discretion of him the sayd sir Humfrey, his heires and assignee, and of every or any of them. And for uniting in more perfect league and amitie of such countreys, lances and territories so to bee possessed and inhabited as aforesayde, with our Realmes of England and Ireland, and for the better encouragement of men to this enterprise: wee doe by these presents graunt, and declare, that all such countreys so hereafter to bee possessed and inhabited as aforesayd, from thencefoorth shall bee of the allegiance of us' our heiress and successours. And wee doe graunt to the sayd sir Humfrey, his heires and assignee, and to all and every of them, and to all and every other person and persons, being of our allegiance, whose names shall be noted or entred in some of our courts of Record, within this our Realme of England, and that with the assent of the said sir Humfrey, his heires or assignee, shall nowe in this journey for discoverie, or in the second journey for conquest hereafter, travel to such lands, countries and territories as aforesaid, and to their and every of their heires: that they and every or any of them being either borne within our sayd Realmes of England or Ireland, or within any other place within our allegiance, and which hereafter shall be inhabiting within any the lands, countreys and territories, with such licence as aforesayd, shall and may have, and enjoy all the priveleges of free denizens and persons native of England, and within our allegiance: any law, custome, or usage to the contrary notwithstanding

And forasmuch, as upon the finding out, discovering and inhabiting of such remote lands, countreys and territories, as aforesayd, it shall be neeessarie for the safetie of all men that shall adventure themselves in those journeys or voiages, to determine to live together In Christian peace and civil quietnesse each with other, whereby every one may with more pleasure and profit, enjoy that whereunto they shall attaine with great Paine and perill: wee for us, our heires and successours are likewise pleased and contented, and by these presents doe give and graunt to the sayd sir Humfrey and his heires and assignee for ever, that he and they, and every or any of them, shall and may, from time to time, for ever hereafter within the sayd mentioned remote lands and countreys, and in the way by the Seas thither, and from thence, have full and meere power and authoritie to correct, punish, pardon, governe and rule by their, and every or any of their good discretions and policies, as well in causes capitall or criminall, as chill, both marine and other, all such our subjects and others, as shall from time to time hereafter adventure themselves in the sayd journeys or voyages habitative or possessive, or that shall at any time hereafter inhabite any such lands, countreys or territories as aforesayd, or that shall abide within two hundred leagues of any sayd place or places, where the sayd sir Humfrey or his heires, or assignee, or any of them, or any of his, or their associate or companies, shall inhabite within sixe yeers next ensuing the date hereof, according to such statutes, lawes and ordinances, as shall be by him the said sir Humfrey, his heires and assignee, or every, or any of them, devised or established for the better governement of the said people as aforesayd: so alwayes that the sayd statutes, lawes and ordinances may be as neere as conveniently may, agreeable to the forme of the lawes & pollicy of England: and also, that they be not against the true Christian faith or religion now professed in the Church of England, nor in any wise to withdraw any of the subjects or people of those lands or places from the allegiance of us, our heires or successours, as their immediate Soveraignes under God. And further we do by these presents for us, our heires and successours, give and graunt full power and authority to our trustie and well-beloved counsellor, sir William Cecill Knight, lord Burleigh, our high treasurer of England, and to the.lord treasurer of England of us, for the time being and to the privie counsel! of us, our heires and successours, or any fours of them, for the time being that he, they, or any foure of them, shall, and may from time to time, and at all times hereafter, under his or their handes or scales by vertue of these presents, authorize and licence the sayd sir Humfrey Gilbert, his heires and assignee, and every or any of them by him and themselves, or by their or any of their sufficient attorneys, deputies, officers, ministers, factors and servants, to imbarke and transport out of our Realmes of England and Ireland, all, or any of his or their goods, and all or any of the Roods or his or their associates and companies, and every or any of them, with such other necessaries and commodities of any of our Realmes, as to the said lord treasurer or foure of the privie counsel! of us, our heires, or successours for the time being, as aforesayd, shall be from time to time by his or their wisedoms or discretions thought meete and convenient for the better reliefe and supportation of him the sayd sir Humfrey, his heires and assignee, and every or any of them, and his and their, and every or any of their said associates and companies, any act, statute, lawe, or other thing to the contrary in any wise notwithstanding.

Provided alwayes, and our will and pleasure is, and wee doe hereby declare to all Christian Kings, princes and states, that if the said sir Humfrey, his heires or assignee, or any of them, or any other by their licence or appointment, shall at any time or times hereafter robbe or spoile by Sea or by land, or doe any act of unjust and unlawful! hostilitie to any of the Subjects of us, our heires, or successours, or any of the Subjects of any King, prince, ruler, governour or state being then in perfect league and amitie with us, our heires or successours: and that upon such injurie, or upon just complaint of any such prince, ruler, governour or state, or their subjects, wee, our heires or successours shall make open proclamation within any of the portes of our Realme of England commodious, that the said Sir Humfrey, his heires or assignee or any other to whom these our Letters patents may extend, shall within the terme to be limited by such proclamations, make such restitution and satisfaction of all such injuries done, so as both we and the said Princes, or others so complayning, may horde us and themselves fully contented: And if the saide Sir Humfrey, his heires and assignee, shall not make or cause to bee made satisfaction accordingly, within such time so to be limited; that then it shall be lawfull to us, our heires and successours, to put the said Sir Humfrey, his heires and assignee, and adherents, and all the inhabitants of the said places to be discovered as is aforesaide, or any of them out of our allegiance and protection, and that from and after such time of putting out of protection the saide Sir Humfrey, and his heires, assignes, adherents and others so to be put out, and the said places within their habitation, possession and rule, shall be out of our protection and allegiance, and free for all princes and others to pursue with hostilitie as being not our Subjects, nor by us any way to be advowed, maintained or defended, nor to be holden as any of ours, nor to our protection, dominion or allegiance any way belonging, for that expresse mention, &c. In witnesse whereof, &c. Witnesse ourselfe at Westminster the 11, day of June, the twentieth yeere of our raigne. Anno Dom 1578.

The First Virginia Charter: April 10, 1606

James, by the grace of God [King of England, Scotland, France, and Ireland, Defender of the Faith], etc. Whereas our loving and weldisposed subjects, Sir Thomas Gates and Sir George Somers, Knightes; Richarde Hackluit, Clarke, Prebendarie of Westminster; and Edwarde Maria Winghfeilde, Thomas Hannam and Raleighe Gilberde, Esquiers; William Parker and George Popham, Gentlemen; and divers others of our loving subjects, have been humble sutors unto us that wee woulde vouchsafe unto them our licence to make habitacion, plantacion and to deduce a colonie of sondrie of our people into that parte of America commonly called Virginia, and other parts and territories in America either appartaining unto us or which are not nowe actuallie possessed by anie Christian prince or people, scituate, lying and being all along the sea coastes between fower and thirtie degrees of northerly latitude from the equinoctiall line and five and fortie degrees of the same latitude and in the maine lande betweene the same fower and thirtie and five and fourtie degrees, and the ilandes thereunto adjacente or within one hundred miles of the coaste thereof;

And to that ende, and for the more speedy accomplishemente of theire saide intended plantacion and habitacion there, are desirous to devide themselves into two severall colonies and companies, the one consisting of certaine Knightes, gentlemen, marchanntes and other adventurers of our cittie of London, and elsewhere, which are and from time to time shalbe joined unto them which doe desire to begin theire plantacions and habitacions in some fitt and conveniente place between fower and thirtie and one and fortie degrees of the said latitude all alongest the coaste of Virginia and coastes of America aforesaid and the other consisting of sondrie Knightes, gentlemen, merchanntes, and other adventurers of our citties of Bristoll and Exeter, and of our towne of Plymouthe, and of other places which doe joine themselves unto that colonie which doe desire to beginn theire plantacions and habitacions in some fitt and convenient place betweene eighte and thirtie degrees and five and fortie degrees of the saide latitude all alongst the saide coaste of Virginia and America as that coaste lieth;

Wee, greately commending and graciously accepting of theire desires to the furtherance of soe noble a worke which may, by the providence of Almightie God, hereafter tende to the glorie of His Divine Majestie in propagating of Christian religion to suche people as yet live in darkenesse and miserable ignorance of the true knoweledge and worshippe of God and may in tyme bring the infidels and salvages living in those parts to humane civilitie and to a setled and quiet govermente, doe by theise our lettres patents graciously accepte of and agree to theire humble and well intended desires;

And doe, therefore, for us, our heires and successors, grannte and agree that the saide Sir Thomas Gates, Sir George Sumers, Richarde Hackluit and Edwarde Maria Winghfeilde, adventurers of and for our cittie of London, and all suche others as are or shalbe joined unto them of that Colonie, shalbe called the Firste Colonie, and they shall and may beginne theire saide firste plantacion and seate of theire firste aboade and habitacion at anie place upon the saide coaste of Virginia or America where they shall thincke fitt and conveniente betweene the saide fower and thirtie and one and fortie degrees of the saide latitude; and that they shall have all the landes, woods, soile, groundes, havens, ports, rivers, mines, mineralls, marshes, waters, fishinges, commodities and hereditamentes whatsoever, from the said first seate of theire plantacion and habitacion by the space of fiftie miles of Englishe statute measure all alongest the saide coaste of Virginia and America towardes the weste and southe weste as the coaste lieth, with all the islandes within one hundred miles directlie over againste the same sea coaste; and alsoe all the landes, soile, groundes havens, ports, rivers, mines, mineralls, woods, marrishes [marshes], waters, fishinges, commodities and hereditamentes whatsoever, from the saide place of theire firste plantacion and habitacion for the space of fiftie like Englishe miles, all alongest the saide coaste of Virginia and America towardes the easte and northeaste [or toward the north] as the coaste lieth, together with all the islandes within one hundred miles directlie over againste the same sea coaste; and alsoe all the landes, woodes, soile, groundes, havens, portes, rivers, mines, mineralls, marrishes, waters, fishinges, commodities and hereditamentes whatsoever, from the same fiftie miles everie waie on the sea coaste directly into the maine lande by the space of one hundred like Englishe miles; and shall and may inhabit and remaine there; and shall and may alsoe builde and fortifie within anie the same for theire better safegarde and defence, according to theire best discrecions and the direction of the Counsell of that Colonie; and that noe other of our subjectes shalbe permitted or suffered to plante or inhabit behinde or on the backside of them towardes the maine lande, without the expresse licence or consente of the Counsell of that Colonie thereunto in writing firste had or obtained.

And wee doe likewise for us, our heires and successors, by theise presentes grannte and agree that the saide Thomas Hannam and Raleighe Gilberde, William Parker and George Popham, and all others of the towne of Plymouthe in the countie of Devon, or elsewhere, which are or shalbe joined unto them of that Colonie, shalbe called the Seconde Colonie; and that they shall and may beginne theire saide firste plantacion and seate of theire first aboade and habitacion at anie place upon the saide coaste of Virginia and America, where they shall thincke fitt and conveniente, betweene eighte and thirtie degrees of the saide latitude and five and fortie degrees of the same latitude; and that they shall have all the landes, soile, groundes, havens, ports, rivers, mines, mineralls, woods, marishes, waters, fishinges, commodities and hereditaments whatsoever, from the firste seate of theire plantacion and habitacion by the space of fiftie like Englishe miles, as is aforesaide, all alongeste the saide coaste of Virginia and America towardes the weste and southwest, or towardes the southe, as the coaste lieth, and all the islandes within one hundred miles directlie over againste the saide sea coaste; and alsoe all the landes, soile, groundes, havens, portes, rivers, mines, mineralls, woods, marishes, waters, fishinges, commodities and hereditamentes whatsoever, from the saide place of theire firste plantacion and habitacion for the space of fiftie like miles all alongest the saide coaste of Virginia and America towardes the easte and northeaste or towardes the northe, as the coaste liethe, and all the islandes alsoe within one hundred miles directly over againste the same sea coaste; and alsoe all the landes, soile, groundes, havens, ports, rivers, woodes, mines, mineralls, marishes, waters, fishings, commodities and hereditaments whatsoever, from the same fiftie miles everie waie on the sea coaste, directlie into the maine lande by the space of one hundred like Englishe miles; and shall and may inhabit and remaine there; and shall and may alsoe builde and fortifie within anie the same for theire better saufegarde according to theire beste discrecions and the direction of the Counsell of that Colonie; and that none of our subjectes shalbe permitted or suffered to plante or inhabit behinde or on the backe of them towardes the maine lande without the expresse licence or consente of the Counsell of that Colonie, in writing thereunto, firste had and obtained.

Provided alwaies, and our will and pleasure herein is, that the plantacion and habitacion of suche of the saide Colonies as shall laste plante themselves, as aforesaid, shall not be made within one hundred like Englishe miles of the other of them that firste beganne to make theire plantacion, as aforesaide.

And wee doe alsoe ordaine, establishe and agree for [us], our heires and successors, that eache of the saide Colonies shall have a Counsell which shall governe and order all matters and causes which shall arise, growe, or happen to or within the same severall Colonies, according to such lawes, ordinannces and instructions as shalbe in that behalfe, given and signed with our hande or signe manuell and passe under the Privie Seale of our realme of Englande; eache of which Counsells shall consist of thirteene parsons and to be ordained, made and removed from time to time according as shalbe directed and comprised in the same instructions; and shall have a severall seale for all matters that shall passe or concerne the same severall Counsells, eache of which seales shall have the Kinges armes engraven on the one side there of and his pourtraiture on the other; and that the seale for the Counsell of the saide Firste Colonie shall have engraven rounde about on the one side theise wordes: Sigillum Regis Magne Britanie, Francie [et] Hibernie; on the other side this inscripture rounde about: Pro Consillio Prime Colonie Virginie. And the seale for the Counsell of the saide Seconde Colonie shall alsoe have engraven rounde about the one side thereof the foresaide wordes: Sigillum Regis Magne Britanie, Francie [et] Hibernie; and on the other side: Pro Consilio Secunde Colonie Virginie.

And that alsoe ther shalbe a Counsell established here in Englande which shall in like manner consist of thirteen parsons to be, for that purpose, appointed by us, our heires and successors, which shalbe called our Counsell of Virginia; and shall from time to time have the superior managing and direction onelie of and for all matters that shall or may concerne the govermente, as well of the said severall Colonies as of and for anie other parte or place within the aforesaide precinctes of fower and thirtie and five and fortie degrees abovementioned; which Counsell shal in like manner have a seale for matters concerning the Counsell [or Colonies] with the like armes and purtraiture as aforesaide, with this inscription engraven rounde about the one side: Sigillum Regis Magne Britanie, Francie [et] Hibernie; and rounde about the other side: Pro Consilio Suo Virginie.

And more over wee doe grannte and agree for us, our heires and successors, that the saide severall Counsells of and for the saide severall Colonies shall and lawfully may by vertue hereof, from time to time, without interuption of us, our heires or successors, give and take order to digg, mine and searche for all manner of mines of goulde, silver and copper, as well within anie parte of theire saide severall Colonies as of the saide maine landes on the backside of the same Colonies; and to have and enjoy the goulde, silver and copper to be gotten there of to the use and behoofe of the same Colonies and the plantacions thereof; yeilding therefore yerelie to us, our heires and successors, the fifte parte onelie of all the same goulde and silver and the fifteenth parte of all the same copper soe to be gotten or had, as is aforesaid, and without anie other manner of profitt or accompte to be given or yeilded to us, our heires or successors, for or in respecte of the same.

And that they shall or lawfullie may establishe and cawse to be made a coine, to passe currant there betwene the people of those severall Colonies for the more ease of trafiique and bargaining betweene and amongest them and the natives there, of such mettall and in such manner and forme as the same severall Counsells there shall limitt and appointe. And wee doe likewise for us, our heires and successors, by theise presents give full power and auctoritie to the said Sir Thomas Gates, Sir George Sumers, Richarde Hackluit, Edwarde Maria Winghfeilde, Thomas Hannam, Raleighe Gilberde, William Parker and George Popham, and to everie of them, and to the saide severall Companies, plantacions and Colonies, that they and everie of them shall and may at all and everie time and times hereafter have, take and leade in the saide voyage, and for and towardes the saide severall plantacions and Colonies, and to travell thitherwarde and to abide and inhabit there in everie of the saide Colonies and plantacions, such and somanie of our subjectes as shall willinglie accompanie them, or anie of them, in the saide voyages and plantacions, with sufficiente shipping and furniture of armour, weapon, ordonnance, powder, victall, and all other thinges necessarie for the saide plantacions and for theire use and defence there: provided alwaies that none of the said parsons be such as hereafter shalbe speciallie restrained by us, our heires or successors.

Moreover, wee doe by theise presents, for us, our heires and successors, give and grannte licence unto the said Sir Thomas Gates, Sir

George Sumers, Richarde Hackluite, Edwarde Maria Winghfeilde, Thomas Hannam, Raleighe Gilberde, William Parker and George Popham, and to everie of the said Colinies, that they and everie of them shall and may, from time to time and at all times for ever hereafter, for theire severall defences, incounter or expulse, repell and resist, aswell by sea as by lande, by all waies and meanes whatsoever, all and everie suche parson and parsons as without espiciall licence of the said severall Colonies and plantacions shall attempte to inhabit within the saide severall precincts and limitts of the saide severall Colonies and plantacions, or anie of them, or that shall enterprise or attempt at anie time hereafter the hurte, detrimente or annoyance of the saide severall Colonies or plantacions.

Giving and grannting by theise presents unto the saide Sir Thomas Gates, Sir George Somers, Richarde Hackluite, and Edwarde Maria Winghfeilde, and theire associates of the said Firste Colonie, and unto the said Thomas Hannam, Raleighe Gilberde, William Parker and George Popham, and theire associates of the saide Second Colonie, and to everie of them from time to time and at all times for ever hereafter, power and auctoritie to take and surprize by all waies and meanes whatsoever all and everie parson and parsons with theire shipps, vessels, goods and other furniture, which shalbe founde traffiqueing into anie harbor or harbors, creeke, creekes or place within the limitts or precincts of the saide severall Colonies and plantacions, not being of the same Colonie, untill such time as they, being of anie realmes or dominions under our obedience, shall paie or agree to paie to the handes of the Tresorer of the Colonie, within whose limitts and precincts theie shall soe traffique, twoe and a halfe upon anie hundred of anie thing soe by them traffiqued, boughte or soulde; and being stranngers and not subjects under our obeysannce, untill they shall paie five upon everie hundred of suche wares and commoditie as theie shall traffique, buy or sell within the precincts of the saide severall Colonies wherein theie shall soe traffique, buy or sell, as aforesaide; which sommes of money or benefitt, as aforesaide, for and during the space of one and twentie yeres nexte ensuing the date hereof shalbe whollie imploied to the use, benefitt and behoofe of the saide severall plantacions where such trafficque shalbe made; and after the saide one and twentie yeres ended the same shalbe taken to the use of us, our heires and successors by such officer and minister as by us, our heires and successors shalbe thereunto assigned or appointed.

And wee doe further, by theise presentes, for us, our heires and successors, give and grannte unto the saide Sir Thomas Gates, Sir George Sumers, Richarde Hackluit, and Edwarde Maria Winghfeilde, and to theire associates of the saide Firste Colonie and plantacion, and to the saide Thomas Hannam, Raleighe Gilberde, William Parker and George Popham, and theire associates of the saide Seconde Colonie and plantacion, that theie and everie of them by theire deputies, ministers and factors may transport the goods, chattells, armor, munition and furniture, needfull to be used by them for theire saide apparrell, defence or otherwise in respecte of the saide plantacions, out of our realmes of Englande and Irelande and all other our dominions from time to time, for and during the time of seaven yeres nexte ensuing the date hereof for the better releife of the said severall Colonies and plantacions, without anie custome, subsidie or other dutie unto us, our heires or successors to be yeilded or paide for the same.

Alsoe wee doe, for us, our heires and successors, declare by theise presentes that all and everie the parsons being our subjects which shall dwell and inhabit within everie or anie of the saide severall Colonies and plantacions and everie of theire children which shall happen to be borne within the limitts and precincts of the said severall Colonies and plantacions shall have and enjoy all liberties, franchises and immunites within anie of our other dominions to all intents and purposes as if they had been abiding and borne within this our realme of Englande or anie other of our saide dominions.

Moreover our gracious will and pleasure is, and wee doe by theise presents, for us, our heires and successors, declare and sett forthe, that if anie parson or parsons which shalbe of anie of the said Colonies and plantacions or anie other, which shall trafficque to the saide Colonies and plantacions or anie of them, shall at anie time or times hereafter transporte anie wares, marchandize or commodities out of [any] our dominions with a pretence and purpose to lande, sell or otherwise dispose the same within anie the limitts and precincts of anie of the saide Colonies and plantacions, and yet nevertheles being at the sea or after he hath landed the same within anie of the said Colonies and plantacions, shall carrie the same into any other forraine countrie with a purpose there to sell or dispose of the same without the licence of us, our heires or successors in that behalfe first had or obtained, that then all the goods and chattels of the saide parson or parsons soe offending and transporting, together with the said shippe or vessell wherein suche transportacion was made, shall be forfeited to us, our heires and successors.

Provided alwaies, and our will and pleasure is and wee doe hereby declare to all Christian kinges, princes and estates, that if anie parson or parsons which shall hereafter be of anie of the said severall Colonies and plantacions, or anie other, by his, theire, or anie of theire licence or appointment, shall at anie time or times hereafter robb or spoile by sea or by lande or doe anie acte of unjust and unlawfull hostilitie to anie the subjects of us, our heires or successors, or anie of the subjects of anie king, prince, ruler, governor or state being then in league or amitie with us, our heires or successors, and that upon suche injurie or upon juste complainte of such prince, ruler, governor or state or their subjects, wee, our heires or successors, shall make open proclamation within anie the ports of our realme of Englande, commodious for that purpose, that the saide parson or parsons having committed anie such robberie or spoile shall, within the terme to be limitted by suche proclamations, make full restitucion or satisfaction of all suche injuries done, soe as the saide princes or others soe complained may houlde themselves fully satisfied and contented; and that if the saide parson or parsons having committed such robberie or spoile shall not make or cause to be made satisfaction accordingly with[in] such time soe to be limitted, that then it shalbe lawfull to us, our heires and successors to put the saide parson or parsons having committed such robberie or spoile and theire procurers, abbettors or comfortors out of our allegeannce and protection; and that it shalbe lawefull and free for all princes and others to pursue with hostilitie the saide offenders and everie of them and theire and everie of theire procurors, aiders, abbettors and comforters in that behalfe.

And finallie wee doe, for us, our heires and successors, grannte and agree, to and with the saide Sir Thomas Gates, Sir George Sumers, Richarde Hackluit and Edwarde Maria Winghfeilde, and all other of the saide Firste Colonie, that wee, our heires or successors, upon peticion in that behalfe to be made, shall, by lettres patents under the Greate [Seale] of Englande, give and grannte unto such parsons, theire heires and assignees, as the Counsell of that Colonie or the most part of them shall for that purpose nomminate and assigne, all the landes, tenements and hereditaments which shalbe within the precincts limitted for that Colonie, as is aforesaid, to be houlden of us, our heires and successors as of our mannor of Eastgreenwiche in the countie of Kente, in free and common soccage onelie and not in capite.

And doe, in like manner, grannte and agree, for us, our heires and successors, to and with the saide Thomas Hannam, Raleighe Gilberd, William Parker and George Popham, and all others of the saide Seconde Colonie, that wee, our heires [and] successors, upon petition in that behalfe to be made, shall, by lettres patentes under the Great Seale of Englande, give and grannte unto such parsons, theire heires and assignees, as the Counsell of that Colonie or the most parte of them shall for that purpose nomminate and assigne, all the landes, tenementes and hereditaments which shalbe within the precinctes limited for that Colonie as is afore said, to be houlden of us, our heires and successors as of our mannor of Eastgreenwich in the countie of Kente, in free and common soccage onelie and not in capite.

All which landes, tenements and hereditaments soe to be passed by the saide severall lettres patents, shalbe, by sufficient assurances from the same patentees, soe distributed and devided amongest the undertakers for the plantacion of the said severall Colonies, and such as shall make theire plantacion in either of the said severall Colonies, in such manner and forme and for such estates as shall [be] ordered and sett [downe] by the Counsell of the same Colonie, or the most part of them, respectively, within which the same lands, tenements and hereditaments shall ly or be. Although express mention [of the true yearly value or certainty of the premises, or any of them, or of any other gifts or grants, by us or any our progenitors or predecessors, to the aforesaid Sir Thomas Gates, Knt. Sir George Somers, Knt. Richard Hakluyt, Edward-Maria Wingfield, Thomas Hanham, Raleigh Gilbert, William Parker, and George Popham, or any of them, heretofore made, in these presents, is not made; or any statute, act, ordnance, or provision, proclamation, or restraint, to the contrary hereof had, made, ordained, or any other thing, cause, or matter whatsoever, in any wise notwithstanding.] In witnesses whereof [we have caused these our letters to be made patents;] witnesses our self at Westminster the 10th day of April [1606, in the fourth year of our reign of England, France, and Ireland, and of Scotland

List of the First Settlers: Arrived April 26, 1607
Ships: Susan Constant, Godspeed and Discovery

105 Men and Boys (Some names are not mentioned)

Mr. Edward Maria Wingfield.
Captain Bartholomew Gosnoll.
Cap. John Smyth.
Cap. John Ratliffe.
Cap. John Martin.
Cap. George Kendall.
Mr. Robert Hunt Preacher.
Mr. George Percy.
Anthony Gosnoll.
Cap. Gabriell Archer.
Rob. Ford.
William Bruster.
Dru Pickhouse.
John Brookes.
Thomas Sands.
John Robinson.
Ustis Clovill.
Kellam Throgmorton.
Nathaniell Powell.
Robert Behethland.
Jeremy Alicock.
Thomas Studley.
Richard Crofts.
Nicholas Houlgraue.
Thomas Webbe:
John Waler.
William Tankard.
Francis Snarsbrough.
Edward Brookes.
Richard Dixon.
John Martin.
George Martin.
Anthony Gosnold:
Thomas Wotton.
Thomas Gore.
Anthony Gosnold:
Thomas Wotton.
Thomas Gore.
Francis Midwinter.
William Laxon.
Edward Pising.
Thomas Emry.
Rob. Small.
Anas Todkill. Iohn Capper.
James Read, Blacksmith.
Jonas Profit, Sailer.
Tho. Couper, Barber.
John Herd, Brick layer.
William Garret, Bricklayer
Edward Brinto, Mason.
William Love, Taylor.
Nic. Skot, Drum.
John Laydon.
William Cassen.
George Cassen.
Tho. Cassen.
William Rods.
William White.
Ould Edward.
Henry Tauin.
George Golding.
John Dods.
William Iohnson.
Will. Vnger.
Will. Wilkinson. Surgeon
Labourers.
Samuell Collier.
Nat. Pecock.
James Brumfield.
Rich. Mutton.

List of Ancient Planters in Virginia:

The term "Ancient Planter" is applied to those persons who arrived in Virginia before 1616, remained for a period of three years, and paid their passage. They received the first patents of land in the new world as authorized by Sir Thomas Dale in 1618 for their personal adventure.

Giles Allington
William Andrews
William Askew
Henry Bagwell
Thomas Bagwell
William Baker
John Barnum
William Bayley
Thomas Baywell
Mary Beheathland
Robert Beheathland
Theophilus Beriston
Richard Biggs
Richard Birchett
John Blore (Blower)
Reynold Booth
Mary Bouldin(g)
Thomas Bouldinge
William Bouldin
Richard Boulton
John Boxe
Cheney Boyse
Richard Brewster
John Brewer
Rev. Richard Buck
William Burditt
John Burrows - see Ancient Planters: John Burras/Burris/Burroughs Family Project
William Capps
John Gundry
Mary Gundry
Edward Gurgany - father or son?
Adria Harris
Thomas Harris
John Hatton
Walter Heyley
Nicholas Hodgskines
Bartholomew Hospkins
Oliver Jenkines
John Johnson
Elizabeth Joones
Samuel Jordan - see Ancient Planters: Jordan Family project
William Julian
Martha Key(Keie)
Thomas Key(Keie)
Richard Kingsmill
Thomas Lane
William Lansden
Anne Burras Laydon
John Laydon
John Lightfoote
Albiano Lupo - see Ancient Planters: Lupo Family Project
Elizabeth Lupo (married John Chandler secondly)
Francis Mason
Cornelius Maye
William Morgan
Susan Old

Thomas Carter
Nathaniel Cawsey
Thomasine Cawsey
Isack Chaplaine
Frances Chapman
William Claiborne
John Chandler
Edward Clarke
Pettiplace Clause
Ann Clay(e)
John Clay(e)
Joseph Cobb
Francis Cole
Susan Collins
Henry Coltman
William Coxe
Captain Raleigh Croshaw
Capt. James Davis - see Ancient Planters: Captain
Rachel Davis
Henry Dawkes
Adam Dixon
John Dods
John Downeman
Thomas Dowse
Elizabeth Dunthorne
Clement Evand
Margery Fairfax
William Fairefax
Thomas Farmer
Cecily Jordan Farrar
Robert Fisher
Mary Beheathland Flinton
Joanne Flinton
John Flood
William Gany
Thomas Garnett
Sir Thomas Gates
Thomas Godby
Thomas Graves
Isabella Pace
Richard Pace
William Parker
Robert Partin
Francis Paul
William Perry
William Pierce
Abraham Piersey
John Poole
Robert Poole, Sr.
Robert Poole, Jr.
John Powell
William Powell
John Price
Miles Prickett
John Proctor
William Sparkes
William Spencer
Thomas Spilman
Thomas Stepney
Thomas Sully
Robert Sweet
John Taylor
Richard Taylor
Thomas Thornbury
Henry Tucker
William Tucker
Henry Turner
Thomas Turner
John Ward
Edward Waters
William Waters
Ameyle Wayne (Waine)
Francis West
Temperance Flowerdew Yardley West
Henry Williams
Thomas Willoughby
John Woodliffe
Robert Wright

Thomas Gray
Robert Greenleaf
Susan Greenleaf
Edward Grendon
Christopher Safford
Robert Salford
Joane Salford
Thomas Savage
Sameul Sharpe
William Sharpe
John Sleight
John Smith
Sir George Yeardley
Richard Yonge

On the Misfortune of Indentured Servants

Gottlieb Mittelberger:

Indentured, or bonded, servants were an important source of labor in seventeenth- and eighteenth-century America. The term generally refers to immigrants who, in return for passage from Europe to America, had bound themselves to work in America for a number of years, after which time they would become completely free. The practice was closely related to the tradition of apprenticeship, in which a youth was assigned to work for a master in a certain trade and in return was taught the skills of the trade.

Convicts were another important source of colonial labor; thousands of English criminals were sentenced to labor in the colonies for a specified period, after which time they were freed.

Gottlieb Mittelberger came to Pennsylvania from Germany in 1750. He returned to Europe four years later. Mittelberger's own fortunes were not so bleak as those of his shipmates. Mittelberger served as a schoolmaster and organist in Philadelphia for three years. He returned to Germany in 1754.

Both in Rotterdam and in Amsterdam the people are packed densely, like herrings so to say, in the large sea-vessels. One person receives a place of scarcely 2 feet width and 6 feet length in the bedstead, while many a ship carries four to six hundred souls; not to mention the innumerable implements, tools, provisions, water-barrels and other things which likewise occupy much space.

On account of contrary winds, it takes the ships sometimes 2, 3 and 4 weeks to make the trip from Holland to. England. But when the wind is good, they get there in 8 days or even sooner. Everything is examined there and the custom-duties paid, whence it comes that the ships ride there 8, 10 to 14 days and even longer at anchor, till they have taken in their full cargoes. During that time, every one is compelled to spend his last remaining money and to consume his little stock of provisions which had been reserved for the sea; so, that most passengers, finding themselves on the ocean where they would be in greater need of them, must greatly suffer from hunger and want. Many suffer want already on the water between Holland and Old England.

When the ships have for the last time weighed their anchors near the city of Kaupp [Cowes] in Old England, the real misery begins with the long voyage. For from there the ships, unless they have good wind, must often sail 8, 9, 10 to 12 weeks before they reach Philadelphia. But even with the best wind the voyage lasts 7 weeks.

But during the voyage there is on board these ships terrible misery, stench, fumes, horror, vomiting, many kinds of sea-sickness, fever, dysentery, headache, heat, constipation, boils, scurvy, cancer, mouth-rot, and the like, all of which come from old and sharply salted food and meat, also from very bad and foul water, so that many die miserably.

Add to this want of provisions, hunger, thirst, frost, heat, dampness, anxiety, want, afflictions and lamentations, together with other trouble, as . . . the lice abound so frightfully, especially on sick people, that they can be scraped off the body. The misery reaches the climax when a gale rages for 2 or 3 nights and days, so that everyone believes that the ship will go to the bottom with all human beings on board. In such a visitation, the people cry and pray most piteously.

When in such a gale the sea rages and surges, so that the waves rise often like high mountains one above the other, and often tumble over the ship, so that one fears to go down with the ship; when the ship is constantly tossed from side to side by the storm and waves, so that no one can either walk, or sit, or lie, and the closely packed people in the berths are thereby tumbled over each other, both the sick and the well - it will be readily understood that many of these people, none of whom had been prepared for hardships, suffer so terribly from them that they do not survive it.

I myself had to pass through a severe illness at sea, and I best know how I felt at the time. These poor people often long for consolation, and I often entertained and comforted them with singing, praying and exhorting; and whenever it was possible and the winds and waves permitted it, I kept daily prayer-meetings with them on deck. Besides, I baptized five children in distress, because we had no ordained minister on board. I also held divine service every Sunday by reading sermons to the people; and when the dead were sunk in the water, I commended them and our souls to the mercy of God.

Among the healthy, impatience sometimes grows so great and cruel that one curses the other, or himself and the day of his birth, and sometimes come near killing each other. Misery and malice join each other, so that they cheat and rob one another. One always reproaches the other with having persuaded him to undertake the journey.

Frequently children cry out against their parents, husbands against their wives and wives against their husbands, brothers and sisters, friends and acquaintances against each other. But most against the soul-traffickers.

Many sigh and cry: *"Oh, that I were at home again, and if I had to lie in my pig-sty!"* Or they say: *"O God, if I only had a piece of good bread, or a good fresh drop of water."* Many people whimper, sigh and cry piteously for their homes; most of them get home-sick. Many hundred people necessarily die and perish in such misery, and must be cast into the sea, which drives their relatives, or those who persuaded them to undertake the journey, to such despair that it is almost impossible to pacify and console them.

No one can have an idea of the sufferings which women in confinement have to bear with their innocent children on board these ships. Few of this class escape with their lives; many a mother is cast into the water with her child as soon as she is dead. One day, just as we had a heavy gale, a woman in our ship, who was to give birth and could not give birth under the circumstances, was pushed through a loop-hole [port-hole] in the ship and dropped into the sea, because she was far in the rear of the ship and could not be brought forward.

Children from 1 to 7 years rarely survive the voyage. I witnessed misery in no less than 32 children in our ship, all of whom were thrown into the sea. The parents grieve all the more since their children find no resting-place in the earth, but are devoured by the monsters of the sea.

That most of the people get sick is not surprising, because, in addition to all other trials and hardships, warm food is served only three times a week, the rations being very poor and very little. Such meals can hardly be eaten, on account of being so unclean. The water which is served out on the ships is often very black, thick and full of worms, so that one cannot drink it without loathing, even with the greatest thirst. Toward the end, we were compelled to eat the ship's biscuit which had been spoiled long ago; though in a whole biscuit there was scarcely a, piece the size of a dollar that had not been full of red worms and spider's nests.

At length, when, after a long and tedious voyage, the ships come in sight of land, so that the promontories can be seen, which the people were so eager and anxious to see, all creep from below on deck to see the land from afar, and they weep for joy, and pray and sing, thanking and praising God. The sight of the land makes the people on board the ship, especially the sick and the half dead, alive again, so that their hearts leap within them; they shout and rejoice, and are content to bear their misery in patience, in the hope that they may soon reach the land in safety. But alas!

When the ships have landed at Philadelphia after their long voyage, no one is permitted to leave them except those who pay for their passage or can give good security; the others, who cannot pay, must remain on board the ships till they are purchased, and are released from the ships by their purchasers. The sick always fare the worst, for the healthy are naturally preferred and purchased first; and so the sick and wretched must often remain on board in front of the city for 2 or 3 weeks, and frequently die, whereas many a one, if he could pay his debt and were permitted to leave the ship immediately, might recover and remain alive.

The sale of human beings in the market on board the ship is carried on thus: Every day Englishmen, Dutchmen and High-German people come from the city of Philadelphia and other places, in part from a great distance, say 20, 30, or 40 hours away, and go on board the newly arrived ship that has brought and offers for sale passengers from Europe, and select among the healthy persons such as they deem suitable for their business, and bargain with them how long they will serve for their passage money, which most of them are stiffly in debt for. When they have come to an agreement, it happens that adult persons bind themselves in writing to serve 3, 4, 5 or 6 years for the amount due by them, according to their age and strength. But very young people, from 10 to 15 years, must serve till they are 21 years old.

Many parents must sell and trade away their children like so many head of cattle; for if their children take the debt upon themselves, the parents can leave the ship free and unrestrained; but as the parents often do not know where and to what people their children are going, it often happens that such parents and children, after leaving the ship, do not see each other again for many years, perhaps no more in all their lives.

It often happens that whole families, husband, wife, and children, are separated by being sold to different purchasers, especially when they have not paid any part of their passage money.

When a husband or wife has died at sea, when the ship has made more than half of her trip, the survivor must pay or serve not only for himself or herself, but also for the deceased.

When both parents have died over half-way at sea, their children, especially when they are young and have nothing to pawn or to pay, must stand for their own and their parents' passage, and serve until they are 21 years old. When one has served his or her term, he or she is entitled to a new suit of clothes at parting; and if it has been so stipulated, a man gets in addition a horse, a woman, a cow.

When a serf has an opportunity to marry in this country, he or she must pay for each year which he or she would have yet to serve, 5 to 6 pounds. But many a one who has thus purchased and paid for his bride, has subsequently repented his bargain, so that he would gladly have returned his exorbitantly dear ware, and lost the money besides.

If someone in this country runs away from his master, who has treated him harshly, he cannot get far. Good provision has been made for such cases, so that a runaway is soon recovered. He who detains or returns a deserter receives a good reward.

If such a runaway has been away from his master one day, he must serve for it as a punishment a week, for a week a month, and for a month half a year.

Charter to Sir Walter Raleigh: 1584

ELIZABETH by the Grace of God of England, France and Ireland Queen, defender of the faith, &c. To all people to whom these presents shall come, greeting.

Know yee that of our especial grace, certain science, and mere motion, we have given and granted, and by these presents for us, our heirs and successors, we give and grant to our trustee and well-beloved servant *Walter Raleigh*, Esquire, and to his heirs assignee forever, free liberty and license from time to time, and at all times for ever hereafter, to discover, search, find out, and view such remote, heathen and barbarous lands, countries, and territories, not actually possessed of any Christian Prince, nor inhabited by Christian People, as to him, his heirs and assignee, and to every or any of them shall seem good, and the same to have, horde, occupy and enjoy to him, his heirs and assignee forever, with all prerogatives, commodities, jurisdictions, royalties, privileges, franchises, and preeminence, thereto or thereabouts both by sea and land, whatsoever we by our letters patents may grant, and as we or any of our noble progenitors have heretofore granted to any person or persons, bodies political or corporate: and the said *Walter Raleigh*, his heirs and assignee, and all such as from time to time, by license of us, our heirs and successors, shall go or travail thither to inhabit or remain, there to build and fortify, at the discretion of the said *Walter Raleigh*, his heirs and assignee, the statutes or act of Parliament made against fugitives, or against such as shall depart, romaine or continue out of our Realm of England without license, or any other statute, act, law, or any ordinance whatsoever to the contrary in anywise notwithstanding.

And we do likewise by these presents, of our especial grace, mere motion, and certain knowledge, for us, our heirs and successors, give and grant full authority, liberty and power to the said Walter Salem, his heirs and assignee, and every of them, that he and they, and every or any of them, shall and may at all and every time, and times hereafter, have, take, and lead in the said voyage, and travail thitherward, or to inhabit there with him, or them, and every or any of them, such and so many of our subjects as shall willingly accompany him or them, and every or any of them to whom also we do by these presents, give full liberty and authority in that behalf, and also to hare, take, and employ, and use sufficient shipping and furniture for the Transportations and

Navigations in that behalf, so that none of the same persons or any of them, be such as hereafter shall be restrained by us, our heirs, or successors.

And further that the said *Walter Raleigh*, his heirs and assignee, and every of them, shall have hold, occupy, and enjoy to him, his heirs and assignee, and every of them forever, all the soil of all such lands, territories, and Countries, so to be discovered and possessed as aforesaid, and of all such Cities, castles, towns, villages, and places in the same, with the right, royalties, franchises, and jurisdictions, as well marine as other within the said lances, or Countries, or the seas thereunto adjoining, to be had, or used, with full power to dispose thereof, and of every part in fee-simple or otherwise, according to the order of the laws of England, as near as the same conveniently may be, at his, and their will and pleasure, to any persons then being, or that shall romaine within the allegiance of us, our heirs, and successors: resewing always to us our heirs, and successors, for all services, duties, and demands, the lift part of all the oar of gold and silver, that from time to time, and at all times after such discovery, subduing and possessing, shall be there gotten and obtained: All which lances, Countries, and territories, shall forever beholden of the said *Walter Raleigh*, his heirs and assignee, of us, our heirs and successors, by homage, and by the said payment of the said fist part, resewed only for all services.

And moreover, we doe by these presents, for us, our heirs and. successors, give and grant license to the said *Walter Raleigh*, his heirs, and assignee, and every of them, that he, and they, and every or any of them, shall and may from time to time, and at all times for ever hereafter, for his and their defense, encounter and expulse, repel and resist as well by sea as by lance, and by all other ways whatsoever, all, and every such person and persons whatsoever, as without the special liking and license of the said *Walter Raleigh*, and of his heirs and assignee, shall attempt to inhabit within the said Countries, or any of them, or within the space of two hundredth leagues near to the place or places within such Countries as aforesaid (if they shall not be before planted or inhabited within the limits as aforesaid with the subjects of any Christian Prince being in amity with us) where the said *Walter Raleigh*, his heirs, or assignee, or any of them, or his, or their or any of their associates or company, shall within sine years (next ensuing) make their dwellings or abiding, or that shall enterprise or attempt at any time hereafter unlawfully to annoy, either by sea or lance, the said *Walter Raleigh*, his heirs or assignee. or any of them, or his or their, or any of his or their companies giving, and granting by these presents further power and authority, to the said *Walter Raleigh*, his heirs and assignee, and every of them from time to time, and at all times for ever hereafter, to take and surprise by all manner of means whatsoever, all and every those person or persons, with their shipper, vessels, and other goods and furniture, which without the license of the said *Walter Raleigh*, or his heirs, or assignee, as aforesaid, shall be found trafficking into any harbor or harbors, creek, or creeks, within the limits aforesaid, (the subjects of our Realms and Dominions, and all other persons in amity with us, trading to the Newfound land for fishing as heretofore they have commonly used, or being driven by force of a tempest, or shipwreck only excepted:) and those persons, and every of them, with their ships, vessels, goods and furniture to detain and possess as of good and lawful prize, according to the discretion of him the said *Walter Raleigh*, his heirs, and assignee, and every, or any of them. And for uniting in more perfect league and amity, of such Countries, lances, and territories so to bee possessed and inhabited as aforesaid with our Realms of England, and Ireland, and the better encouragement of men to these enterprises: we do by these presents, grant and declare that all such Countries, so hereafter to be possessed and inhabited as is aforesaid, from thenceforth shall bee of the allegiance of us. our heirs and successors. And wee doe grant to the said *Walter Raleigh*, his heirs, and assignee, and to all, and every of them, and to all and every other person, and persons being of our allegiance, whose names shall be noted or entered in some of our Courts of record within our Realm of England, that with the assent of the said *Walter Raleigh*, his heirs or assigns, shall in his journeys for discovery, or in the journeys for conquest, hereafter travel to such lands, countries and territories, as aforesaid, and to their, and to every of their heirs, that they, and every or any of them, being either borne within our said Realms of England, or Ireland or in any other place within our allegiance, and which hereafter shall be inhibiting within any the lands, Countries, and territories, with such license (as aforesaid) shall and may have all the privileges of free Denizens, and persons native of England, and within our allegiance in such like ample manor and forum, as if they were borne and personally resident within our said Realm of England, any law, custom, or usage to the contrary notwithstanding

And for as much as upon the finding out, discovering, or inhabiting of such remote lands, countries, and territories as aforesaid, it shall be necessary for the safety of all men, that shall adventure themselves in those marines or voyages, to determine to line together in Christian peace, and civil quietness each with other, whereby every one may with snore pleasure and profit enjoy that whereunto they shall attain with great Paine and peril, we for us. our heirs and successors, are likewise pleased and contented, and by these presents do give and grant to the said *Walter Raleigh*, his heirs and assignee forever, that tree and they, and every or any of them, shall and may from time to time for ever hereafter, within the said mentioned remote lances and Countries in the way by the seas thither, and from thence, inane full and mere power and authority to correct, punish, pardon, govern, and rule by their and every or any of their good discretions and policies, as well in causes capital, or criminal!, as civil, both marine and other all such our subjects as shall from time to time adventure themselves in the said journeys or voyages, or that shall at any time hereafter inhabit any such lances, countries, or territories as aforesaid, or shall abide within 200. leagues of any of the said place or places, where the said Walter Raleigh, his heirs or assignee, or any of them, or any of his or their associates or companies, shall inhabits within 6 years next ensuing the date hereof, according to such statutes, laws and ordinances, as shall bee by him the said Walter Raleigh his heirs and assignee, and every or any of them devised, or established, for the better government of the said people as aforesaid. So always as the said statutes, laws, and ordinances may be as near as conveniently may be, agreeable to the form of the laws, statutes, government, or policy of England, and also so as they be not against the true Christian faith, now professed in the Church of England, nor in any wise to withdraws any of the subjects or people of those lances or places from the allegiance of us. our heirs and successors, as their immediate Sovereign under God.

And further, wee doe be these presents for us. our heirs and successors, give and grant full power and authority to our trustee and well-beloved counselor sir *William Cecil* knight, Lorde *Burghley*, our high Treasurer of England, and to the Lorde Treasurer of England, for us. our heirs and successors for the time being, and to the privies Counsel, of us, our heirs and successors, or any four or more of them for the time being, that tree, they, or any four or more of them, shall and may from time to time, and at all times hereafter, under his or their hands or scales by virtue of these presents, authorize and license the said *Walter Raleigh*, his heirs and assignee. and every or any of them by him, and by themselves, or by their, of any of their sufficient Attorneys, deputies, officers, ministers, factors. and servants, to embark and transport out of our Realm of England and Ireland, and the Dominions thereof all, or any of his, or their goods, and all or any the goods of his and their associate and companies, and every or any of them, with such other necessaries and commodities of any our Realms, as to the said Lorde Treasurer, or four or more of the privies Counselee, of us. our heirs and successors for the time being (as aforesaid) shall be from time to time by his or their wisdoms, or discretions thought meet and convenient, for the better relief and suppuration of him the said *Walter Raleigh*, his heirs, and assignee, and every or any of them, and of his or their or any of their associate and companies, any act, statute, law, or other thing to the contrary in any wise notwithstanding.

Provided always, and our will and pleasure is, and we do hereby declare to all Christian kings, princes and states, that if the said *Walter Raleigh*, his heirs or assignee, or any of them, or any other lay their license or appointment, shall at any time or times hereafter. rob or spoil by sea or by lance, or do any act of unjust or unlawful hostility, to any of the subjects of us. our heirs or successors, or to any of the subjects of any the kings, princes, rulers, governors, or estates, being then in perfect league and amity with us, our heirs and successors, and that upon such injury, or upon lust complaint of any such prince, ruler, governor, or estate, or their subjects, wee, our heirs and successors, shall make open proclamation within any the Fortes of our Realm of England, that the said *Walter Raleigh*, his heirs and assignee, and adherents, or any to whom these our letters patents may extend, shall within the terms to be Emitted, by such proclamation, make full restitution, and satisfaction of all such injuries done, so as both we and the said princes, or other so complaining, may horde us and themselves fully contented. And that if the said *Walter Raleigh*, his heirs and assignee, shall not make or cause to be made satisfaction accordingly, within such time so to be limited, that then it shall be lawful to us our heirs and successors, to put the said *Walter Raleigh*, his heirs and assignee and adherents, and all the inhabitants of the said places to be discovered (as is aforesaid) or any of them out of our allegiance and protection, and that from and after such time of putting out of protection the said Walter Raleigh, his heirs, assignee and adherents, and others so to be put out, and the said places within their habitation, possession and rule, shall be out of our allegiance and protection, and free for all princes and others, to pursue with hostility, as being not our subjects, nor by us any way to be avouched, maintained or defended, nor to beholden as any of ours, nor to our protection or dominion, or allegiance any way belonging, for that express mention of the clear yearly value of tile certainty of the premises, or any part thereof, or of any other gift, or grant by us. or any our progenitors, or predecessors to the said Walter Raleigh, before this time made in these presents be not expressed, or any other grant, ordinance, provision, proclamation, or restraint to the contrary thereof, before this time given, ordained, or provided, or any other thing, cause, or matter whatsoever, in any wise notwithstanding. In witness, whereof, we have caused these our letters to be made patents. Witnesses ourselves, at *Westminster*, the 25. day of March, in the six and twentieth year of our Reign.

Source:

The Federal and State Constitutions Colonial Charters, and Other Organic Laws of the States, Territories, and Colonies Now or Heretofore Forming the United States of America Compiled and Edited Under the Act of Congress of June 30, 1906 by Francis Newton Thorpe, Washington, DC : Government Printing Office, 1909.

BIBLIOGRAPHY

Allen, William. North Carolina History, Vol 1, Parts 1-5

Anburey, T. Travels through America, 1776-81. 2 vols. London, 1789.

Anson, Sir Wm. R. The Principles of the English Law of Contract. 3d ed. Oxford, 1884.

Ashley, W. J. Introduction to English Economic History and Theory. 2d ed. London, 1893. 12mo.

Bacon, Sir Francis. Essays. 8vo. Boston, 1868.

Ballagh, James Curtis. White servitude in the colony of Virginia. 1895

Bancroft, George. History of the United States of America. 6 vols. 8vo. Rev. ed. N. Y. 1883.

Beverley, Robert. History of Virginia. Reprint from 2d London ed. Richmond, 1855.

Blackstone, Sir Wm. Commentaries on the Laws of England. 4 vols. N. Y. 1859-62.

Brackett, J. R. Negro in Maryland. J. H. U. Studies. Extra vol VI. Baltimore, 1889.

Brown, Alexander. The Genesis of the United States, 1605-1616. 2 vols. Boston, 1890.

Brown, Alexander, The First Republic in America, 1st ed., 1898

Bruce, John. Annals of the Honorable East India Company, 1600-1707-8. 3 vols. 4to. London, 1810.

Burk, John Daly. History of Virginia. 4 vols. 8vo. Petersburg, 1804-16.

Burke, Edmund. European Settlements in America. 2d ed. 2 vols. 8vo. London, 1758.

Byrd, Col. Wm. History of the Dividing Line and other Tracts (Westover MSS., vol. II.). Richmond, 1866. MS. Letters of, (1683-91). Va. Hist Soc., Richmond, Va.

Calendar of English State Papers. Colonial Series, 1513-1676. 6 vols. 8vo. Ed. by W. Noel Sainsbury. London, 1860, 1862, 1880. Domestic Series, 1581-1625, 1649-56, 1660-67. 27 vols. Ed. by Mary A. E. Green. 1625-41. 17 vols. Ed. Bruce and W. D. Hamilton.

Calendar of Virginia State Papers and other MSS., 1652-1793, preserved in the Capitol at Richmond. Ed. by Wm. P. Palmer. 6 vols. 4to. Richmond, 1875-86.

Campbell, Charles. History of the Colony and Dominion of Virginia. (Lippincott) Philadelphia, 1860.

Cambell, Wilson John. A history of Virginia from its Discovery until the year 1781; 1818

Chalmers, George. Political Annals of the Present United Colonies. 4 vols. London, 1780.

Cooke, John Esten. Virginia, a History of the People. Boston, 1884.

Cunningham, Wm. Growth of English Industry and Commerce in Modern Times. 8vo. Cambridge, 1892.

De Jarnette. MSS. relating to the Early History of Virginia, preserved in the State Capitol, Richmond. 2 vols. folio.

Doyle, J. A. English Colonies in America. 3 vols. N. Y. 1882.

Drake, Samual Adams. The Making of Virginia

Essex County Records, MS., 1683-86. (State Library, Richmond, Va.)

Eddis, Wm. Letters from America, historical and descriptive, 1769-77. London, 1792. 8vo.

Fitzhugh, Wm. MS. Letters of, 1679-99. Va. Hist. Soc., Richmond, Va.

Force, Peter. Tracts and other Papers relating to the Colonies in North America. 4 vols. 8vo. "Washington, 1836-46.

Franklin, Benjamin. Works; edited by J. B. Bigelow. 10 vols. N. Y. 1887.

Fyffe, C. A. History of Modern Europe. 3 vols. 8vo. N. Y. 1886-89.

General Court of Virginia, MS. Records of, 1670-76. Iv. folio. (Va. Hist. Soc., Richmond, Va.)

Hakluyt, Richard. Collection of Early Voyages, Travels and Discoveries of the English Nation. 5v. 4to. London, 1809-12

Hariot, Thomas. A Brief and True Report of the New-Found Land at Virginia. 1588

Hening, Wm. Waller. Statutes at Large of Virginia. 13 v. 8vo. Richmond, 1812. The New Virginia Justice. Richmond, 1799.

Henrico County Records, MS., 1686-99. 4 v. folio. (State Library, Richmond, Va.)

Howe, Henry. Historical Collections of Virginia. Charleston, S. C., 1852.

Hotten, J. C. Original Lists of Emigrants, 1600-1700. London, 1874.

Hurd, John C., LL. D. The Law of Freedom and Bondage in the United States. 2 v. 8vo. Boston, 1858-62.

Jefferson, Thomas. MSS. of, 1606-1711. 7 v. of. Letters, Patents, Proclamations, Correspondence, 1622, 1623, 1625; Orders, 1622-27, and Instructions to Governors; Council Book, 1679-1700; Laws, 1623-1711, with some omissions. Library of Congress, Law Dept, under title, cap. 19, 226; cap. 23, 199, 217, 218, 220, 221. Six vols. are largely contained in Hening and Burk. Writings; ed. H. A. Washington. 9 v. 8vo. N. Y. 1859. Writings; ed. P. L. Ford. 4 v. N. Y. 1892. Reports of Cases, General Ct. of Va., 1730-1740 and 1768-1792. 8vo. Charlottesville, 1829.

Jones, Rev. Hugh. Present State of Virginia. (Sabin, J., Reprints.) 8vo. N. Y. 1865.

Kalm, Peter. Travels into North America. 3 v. 8vo. London, 1771.

Land books of Virginia, MS., 1621 Land Office in the Capitol at Richmond.

Lecky, W. E. H. History of England in the 18th Century. 8 v. 8vo. London, 1878-82.

Lodge, Henry Cabot. A Short History of the English Colonies. Rev. ed. N. Y. 1881.

MacDonalcl, Col. Angus M. MSS. relating to the Early History of Virginia. 2 v. fo. (State Library, Richmond, Va.)

Madison, James. Papers of; ed. by H. D. Gilpin. 3 v. 8vo. N. Y. 1844.

Massachusetts Historical Society Collections. 4th Series. 6 v. 8vo. Boston, 1852-65.

Middlesex Co., England, Records. 4 v. 1888. Ed. by J. C. Jefferson.

Minor, John B., LL. D. Institutes of Common and Statute Law. 4 v. Richmond.

National Geographic News Article America's Lost Colony: Can New Dig Solve Mystery?
Willie Drye: March 2, 2004

Neill, E. D. History of the Virginia Company of London (1606-24). 4to. Albany, 1869. Virginia Carolorum (1625-85). Albany, 1869. The English Colonization of America. London,
1871. Virginia Vetusta, 1885.

Northampton (Accomac) County Records, MS. 2 v. folio. (State Library, Richmond, Va.) 1632.

Oldmixon, John. British Empire in America. 2 v. 12mo. London, 1708. Pennsylvania, Genl. Assembly Acts, 1700-97. 4v.

Prendergast, J. P. The Cromwellian Settlement in Ireland.
London, 1865.

Purchas, Samuel. His Pilgrimes. 5 v. fo. London, 1625-26.

Raleighs New Fort in Virginia, 1585, Edward Graham Daves

Reeves, J. History of the English Law. 5 v. (Finlason Ed.)
1880.

Richmond Standard. Richmond, Va. 1880.

Royal Commission on Historical Manuscripts, Reports of the. 8 v. London, 1870-81.

Smith, Capt. John. General History. 2 v. 8vo. Richmond,
1819. Works, 1608-31; ed. by Arber. 1 v. 8vo. Birmingham, 1884.

Spenser, Edmund. The Faerie Queene. London, 1590. N. pag. Early English Books Online: Text Creation Partnership. U of Michigan Library.

Spottswood, Gov. Alexander. Official Letters of. 2 v. Va. Hist.

Coll., N. S., ed. by R. A. Brock, 1882.

Statutes at Large of England and Great Britain. 20 v. London, 1811.

Statutes at Large of Virginia, 1792.

Stevens, Henry. Dawn of British Trade (Court Minutes of the East India Co., 1599-1603). 8vo. London, 1886.

Stith, Wm. History of the Discovery and Settlement of Virginia to 1624. (Sabin, J., Reprints.) N. Y. 1865.

Strachey, W. Historie of Travaile into Virginia Britannia. Ed. by Major. Hakluyt Society. Vol. 6. 1849. Lawes Divine, Morall and Martial, 1612. (Force, vol. HI.)

Surtees Society, Publications of the. 84 v. 8vo. London, 1835-89.

Taswell-Langmead, T. P. English Constitutional History. 4th ed. London, 1890.

Thurloe, John. Collections of State Papers; ed. by T. Birch. 7 v. London, 1742.

Tucker, St. George. Commentaries on Blackstone. 2 v.

Verney Family Papers; ed. by J. Bruce. No. 56 Camden Soc. Pub., 1866.

Virginia, Colonial Records of (1619-80). State Senate Doc. 4to.

Declaration of the State of the Colony of. London, 1620.

New Description of, 1649. (Force, II.)

Historical Magazine. 2 v. Ed. by P. A. Bruce. Richmond, 1893-4.

Historical Register; ed. by Wm. Maxwell. 6v. Richmond,

1848.

Historical Society, Collections of. 10 v. Ed. by R. A. Brock.

Richmond, 1882-91.

Present State, 1696. Blair, Chilton & Hartwell. London, 1727.

Virginia Company, MS. Records of the. (a) Collingwood MS.
2 v. fo. v. I. April 28, 1619-May 8, 1622; v. H. May 20, 1622-
June 7, 1624. (b) Randolph MS. 2v. fo. lUd. Iv. fo. Miscellaneous (1617).

Voyages of the English Nation, Richard Hakluyt, Vol 1.2 1889

Warder, Bill. "From Forraine Parts"; Non-English Europeons at Jamestown, 1607-1625

Washington, George. Writings of. Ed. by W. C. Ford. 9v. N.
Y. 1889.

Hid. Ed. by Jared Sparks. 12 v. Boston.

Whitaker, Alexander. Good Newes from Virginia. London, 1613.

Williams, E. Virginia Truly Valued. London, 1650.

Winder MS. 2v. fo. 1606-76. (State Library, Richmond, Va.)

Wirt, William. Life of Patrick Henry. Philadelphia, 1817.

The Letters of the British Spy. N. Y. 1832.

York County Records, MS., 1633-1709. 10 v. fo. State Library,
Richmond, Va.

Cabot, John, Cabot, Sebastian, 1474 (ca.)-1557, America -- Discovery and exploration British. 1898

Notes

[1] Stiths History pg.25
[2] Birth of a Nation; Jamestown 1607 Agnes Pryor
[3] Coke, 2 Inst. 729 and 734
[4] Ibid., p. 8 et seq
[5] Bancroft's "History of the United States," Vol. I, p. 122.
[6] Purchas's " His Pilgrimes," Vol. VIII, p. 469. The quotations from Purchas in this volume are from the Macmillan edition.
[7] Quoted by Campbell, p. 39, from Stith.
[8] "Site of Old Jamestown," by Samuel Yonge, p. 11.
[9] Stith's "History," p. 46.
[10] Purchases "His Pilgrimes," Vol. XVIII.
[11] Stephens, p. viii.; Bruce, I., 112, 136, 138, 154, 165; S. P. E. I., 10, 215; Cunningham, Growth of English Industry and Commerce, p. 268, cf. 125, 151, 267. Charter of 1606, Brown, p. 72.
[12] We have nothing extant to show the exact terms on which the colonists of 1606-7 as a whole, and the "supplies" until 1609, came to Virginia. When we come to the latter year we have in a pamphlet (Nova Britannia) and in a " broadside " of the Company, both issued to attract new adventurers and planters, a perfect outline of the Company's policy at that time. There is nothing, however, so far as I have been able to discover, that contradicts the view that the outline as we have it for 1609 was in its general character that of 1606, the chief difference being the length of the term, which was probably five years in 1606 instead of the seven years of 1609; on the contrary, all the evidence we have goes to substantiate this theory. In 1611, the instructions to Yeardley ordered that 100 acres of land be granted to each share owned by every planter, whether sent by the Company or transferred at his own charge before the coming away of Dale in 1616. This included some of the colonists of 1607. The patent of 1606 specially authorizes the council of the colony to pass lands, declaring all lands passed " by letters patent shall be sufficient assurance from the said patentees, so divided amongst the undertakers for the plantations of the said several colonies," and shows that a division of land was contemplated. (Brown, I., 63.)
[13] Nova Britannia, Force, I., 24, 28; Brown, Genesis of the"TJ. S., I., 228, 229; Charter of 1609; Va. Mag. of Hist and Biog., Oct., 1894, Vol. II., 156, 7, Instructions to yeardley: Decl. of Anct. Planters, Col. Rec. Va., 81.
[14] Of. Brown, II., 814; Neil, Va. Co., 257; Arber's Smith, 390; Burke, Vol. II., 332, 333, 334, under names Dodds, Simons, Martin. It is not to be supposed that mere adventure or gold- seeking would have constituted a sufficient motive to induce many persons to make such an experiment. A land grant of some kind

was undoubtedly promised before 1609 in addition to the proportional share of profits. This was in accordance with the policy under which earlier attempts at discovery or colonization had been made. Gilbert's Articles of Agreement with the Merchants Adventurers in 1582, under his patent of 1578, show the same general principle of Adventurers of the purse or person and of land grants, and Carlyle's project presents a scheme of " Adventurers " and " Enterprisers " who are to share equally in the lands, &c., discovered. Sainsbury MS., I., 32, 35; Haklyut, III., 234, 235; Va. Hist. Mag., Oct. '94, 186. Brown, I., 71, 72. Instructions, Nov. 20, 1606.
[15] Va. Co. Rec., I., 4, 64, 181. Va. Hist. Mag., Oct., 1893, 157. Of more than 800 colonists sent during the first three years, only about sixty survived; of a still larger number sent before 1619, but 400 were alive when Yeardley came, and half of these were unfit for work. Arber's Smith, Introd., cxxix.; Col. Rec. Va., 72
[16] J Va. Co. Rec., II., 94, 111. Stith, Append. 26. Later, when separate courts were established, subsequent to the charters of 1609 and 1612, for governing the Company, whenever members had a voice in these courts, the Virginia colonist enjoyed a like privilege, if he happened to be in England.
[17] The equivalent of 12 10s., or the expense of transportation. Brown, I., 252.
[18] Stith
[19] Nova Brit, Force, I., 24, 25. New Brit, Brown, L, 273, 274. The charter of 1609 empowered the appointment of such a commission
[20] Va. Mag. Hist and Biog., Oct., 1893, 158, 160, Discourse of the Old Company. Ibid., Oct, '94, 160, Instructions to Yeardley. MS. Rec. of Va. Co., III., 140; Robinson MS., 146; Winder MS., I., 16; Company's Register, 1615-23; Col. Rec. of Va., 20 et seq., Va. Co. Rec., I., 62, 65.
[21] Brown, IL, 777, 778, 779. "A Brief Declaration," 1616; Va. Hist Mag., Oct., 1893, 158. Discourse of the Old Company, 1625; Va. Co. Rec., IL, 196; Winder MS., L, 16. In justice to the Company, however, it should be said that its finances were in a very bad state. They had suffered greatly from traducers of the plantation both in England and Virginia. Many of the original subscribers became so disheartened by this or the mismanagement of the Company that they refused to pay up their subscriptions, and the Company was compelled to go into debt, relying upon the private purses of its warmest supporters. The state of affairs became so bad by 1612 that the Company took care to secure in its third charter the insertion of a special clause empowering them to collect subscriptions from its members. (Brown, II., 625.) In Nov. and Dec., 1610, on the report of Sir Thomas Gates of the imperative necessity of supplies, the Company determined that all adventurers, both those already free of the Company (i. e., who had paid up), and those who desired to be free, should subscribe at least the sum of 75, to be paid in three years, twenty-five each year, " towards a newe supply to be sent for the relief of the said colony in Virginia." Many members and other persons came to the relief of the Company, but a number of knights and gentlemen who subscribed refused to pay, and the Company was

forced in 1613 to petition for the King's writ to sue in the High Court of Chancery for the amounts due. Brown, II., 623-630, Brooke to Elsmere.
[22] I can find no authority whatever, except an erroneous reading of Stith (p. 139), for Chalmers' assertion that private property in land was instituted by Dale in Virginia in the year 1615 by a grant of 50 acres in fee to every free man in the colony. All the evidence we have proves conclusively that no such grant of lands was made, nor does Stith ascribe the change in the Company's policy at this time to Dale; it was the result, however, of the prosperous condition of the colony, which was largely the work of Dale. Dale was in England June 12, 1616, probably before the time of the issue of the Brief Declaration relating to the dividend of 50 acres, and it is possible if this were so that he was consulted in the matter. There is no authority, however, for the statement that it was due to his influence. From the " Declaration " itself it seems to have been dictated by other motives. Chalmers gives Stith as his authority on this point, and the mistake has crept into Virginia histories on the sole authority of Chalmers. He further errs in the date, while Stith gives it correctly. Stith, 139; Chalmers' Pol. Annals, 36; Campbell, 116; Cooke, 110; Burke, I., 177; Doyle, Va., Md. and the Carolinas, 152.
[23] Va. Co. Rec., I., 181; II., 83, 84, 251.
[24] Arber's Smith, 526; Va. Hist. Mag., Oct, '94, 156, 157; Va, Co. Rec., I., 14, 15; Stith, 139; Col. Rec. Va., Assembly of 1619.
[25] Stith, 131, 132; Chalmers, 34; Purehas, 1766 (Hamor).
[26] Decl. of Anc. Planters, Col. Rec. of Va., 75; Chalmers, 39; Stith, 132; Purehas, 1766.
[27] Va. Hist Reg., I., 107-110, Rolf's Relation, 1616; Purchas, Pilgrimes, 1766, Hamor's Narrative; Purchas, His Pilgrimage, 837; Va. Co. Rec., I., 65. The farms consisted of three acres, and the rental of a servant was two barrels and a half of corn.
[28] Smith, Hist, of Va., I., 241; Neil, London Co., 13, Early Settlement; Third Rept of Royal Comm. on Hist. MSS., Appd., 53; Arber's Smith, 107, 122, 448, 486, 487, cxxix.; MS. Rec. Va. Co., III., 142; Brown, II., 550.
[29] Col. Rec. Va., 68, 81.
[30] Stith, 132; Purchas, Pilgrimes, 1766; Ool. Rec. Va., 75, 76. " Having most of them served the colony six or seven years in that general slavery."
[31] Va. Hist Reg., I., 109, Rolf's Relation, 1616.
[32] Lord Delaware's Letter to the Patentees in England, July 7, 1610; Hist, of Travaile into Virginia Britannia, Introd., Hakluyt Soc., 34.
[33] ol. Rec. Va., 68, 69, 81; Force, III., 1647, Laws; Gal. State Papers, Col. 39. Dale's justification is to be found in the character of the colonists with whom he had to deal. Cf. Letter Dale to Salisbury, Brown, I., 506.
[34] Smith's "Works," p. 957
[35] John Smith, quoted in Campbell's " History," p. 382

---

[36] Cooke's "Virginia," p. 20
[37] Purchas, Samuel. His Pilgrimes. 5 v. fo. London, 1625-26: Purchas, Vol. XVIII, p. 477
[38] Spenser, Edmund. The Faerie Queene. London, 1590. N. pag. Early English Books Online: Text Creation Partnership. U of Michigan Library. Web. 5 November 2009. http://name.umdl.umich.edu/A12777.0001.001/.
[39] Smith's "Works," p. 436
[40] Purchases "His Pilgrimes," Vol. XVIII, p. 449 et seq
[41] Smith's " Works," p. 487
[42] Delaware's Report, in " Virginia Britannia," p. xxvi; Cook's "Virginia," p. 79.
[43] Smith's "Works," p. 635
[44] The First Republic," p. 128 et seq
[45] Virginia Britannia, p. xiii
[46] The First Republic," pp. 285, 329, 612
[47] "Report of Francis Maguel," in Brown, ed., Genesis, I, 393-399; and, Brown, First Republic, p. 125. See also, Francis Maguel, "Report of what Francisco Maguel, and Irishman, learned in the state of Virginia during his eight months that he was there, July 1, 1610," in Edward Wright Haile, ed., Jamestown Narratives: Eyewitness Accounts of the Virginia Colony, The First Decade: 1607-1617 (Champlain, Virginia: Roundhouse, 1998), pp.447-453.
[48] Brown, ed., Genesis, II, pp. 899-901, 1037, 10671068
[49] Susan Myra Kingsbury, ed., The Records of the Virginia Company of London, III (Washington, 1906-1935), 587.
[50] Brown, First Republic, p.58.
[51] Moryson to Salisbury, in Brown, ed., Genesis, I, 325.
[52] Kingsbury, Records, III, p.567. Francis was listed as being a resident of Mr. Richard Owen"s House near Westover Plantation, not as a resident of Elizabeth City, the site of Gookin"s residence.
[53] John Camden Hotten, ed., The Original Lists of Persons of Quality; ... 1600-1700, reprinted, 4th ed. (Baltimore: Genealogical Publishing Company, Inc. 1980), p.194.
[54] Kingsbury, Records, IV, 229
[55] Hotten, ed., Original Lists, pp. 194-195. Daniel Gookin left Virginia sometime in April or May 1622 on board
the Sea Flower and was the first to bring news to England of the March 22 attack. See Jester and Hiden, Adventurers, pp.182-183
[56] Brown, First Republic, p.461
[57] John Smith, "The General History of Virginia, New England, and the Summer Isles," in Haile, ed., Jamestown Narratives, p. 279
[58] Ibid., p.292; David F. Riggs, Embattled Shrine: Jamestown in the Civil War, (Shippensburg, Pennsylvania: White Mane Publishing Company, Inc., 1997), p.20. Thomas ap Richard is listed among the slain on March 22,

1622, as is "Henry a Welchman." See, Kingsbury, Records, III, 569-570. Also, John ap Roberts and Christopher Welchman are listed among the dead on 16 February 1623/24. See, Hotten, ed., Original Lists, pp. 190 and 195. In addition to a list of the dead another list entitled, "A List of Names; of the Living in Virginia, February the 16 [,] 1623[1624]" was compiled, and among the living are John and Lewis Welchman at Elizabeth City. Ibid., p. 183.

[59] Peter Winne, "Letter to Sir John Egerton, 26 November 1608," in Haile,ed., Jamestown Narratives, p.203. See also William Strachey, "The History of Travel into Virginia Britannia: The First Book of the First Decade," ibid., p. 577: "Lastly, the language of the Indians admitting much and many words, both of places and names of many creatures, which have the accents and Welch significations

[60] Brown, First Republic, p.71.

[61] Smith, "General History," ibid., p. 294. See also Smith"s description of how Winne naively gave weapons to the Germans at Jamestown, who then gave them to Chief Powhatan, and Winne"s failure to follow Smith"s orders when attacking the Paspahegh village near Jamestown. Ibid., pp. 304 and 316-317

[62] "We should never underestimate the importance of the accession of James VI of Scotland to the throne of England. Here was the first Scottish king to rule over both countries. For the first time a monarch would be styled, albeit at his own insistence, King of Great Britain." See, Christopher Lee, 1603: The Death of Queen Elizabeth I, the Return of the Black Plague, the Rise of Shakespeare, Piracy, Witchcraft, and the Birth of the Stuart Era, (New York: St. Martin"s Press, 2003), p.72. See also, ibid., p.124, for a discussion of the new king"s Scottish consorts and their ambitions for wealth and preferment once in power.

[63] Don Pedro de Zuñiga, "Letter of Don Pedro de Zuniga to the King of Spain," in Brown, ed., Genesis, I, 118119

[64] Smith, "General History," in Haile, ed., Jamestown Narratives, p.293. Smith"s "Dutchmen" were actually German glassmakers. (See below, footnote 22). In some cases, "Dutchman" derived from the German word, "Deutschmänner" or "Deutsch" meaning German. See, Hume, Virginia Adventure, p. 216.

[65] In the later Middle Ages, moreover, there was an influx of aliens" from northern Europe who established themselves outside the City of London"s jurisdiction in such places as Southwark; glaziers and goldsmiths were prominent among them." See, John Blair and Nigel Ramsay, eds. English Medieval Industries: Craftsmen, Techniques, Products, 2nd ed., (London: The Hambledon Press, 2001), p. xxiv; also see, ibid., pp. 214, 278-279, and 350-351. In addition, see, Elspeth M. Veale, "Craftsmen and the Economy of London in the Fourteenth Century," in A.E.J. Hollaender and William Kellaway, eds., Studies in London History, (Great Britain: Hodder and Stoughton Limited, 1969), pp. 133-151; and, Sylvia L. Thrupp, "Aliens in and Around London in the Fifteenth Century," ibid., pp. 251-272. Throughout the 16th and early 17th centuries, English scholars, explorers and politicians espoused colonization efforts for their country in order to achieve various goals.

One treatise, "Reasons for raising a fund for the support of a Colony at Virginia [1605?/1607?]," proclaimed: "That realme is most complete and wealthie which either hath sufficient to serve itselfe or can finde the meanes to exporte of naturall commodities then [if] it hath occasion necessarily to importe, consequently it muste insue that by a publique consent, a Collony transported into a good and plentiful climate able to furnish our wantes, our monies and wares that nowe run into the handes of our adversaries or [cold] frendes shall passé unto our frendes and naturall kinsmen and from them likewise we shall receive such things as shalbe most available to our necessaties, which intercourse of trade maye rather be called a home bread trafique than a forraigne exchange." Brown, Genesis, I, p. 39. See also, John Stepney, Lord De la Ware, Sir Thomas Smith, Sir Walter Cope, Master Waterson, "A True and sincere declaration of the purpose and ends of the Plantation begun in Virginia [...], (London 1610)," ibid., pp. 337-353; and Philip Alexander Bruce, Economic History of Virginia in the Seventeenth Century, reprinted (New York: Peter Smith, 1935), I, 1-70. As revealed by Carter C. Hudgins, Staff Archaeologists with Jamestown Rediscovery Project®, one stimulus for Jamestown"s establishment was an interest in the discovery of zinc ores required for brass production in England. Brass was used to make high quality cannons versus those made of iron. In early 17th century Europe, brass was created in a process known as cementation whereby copper was combined with a zinc carbonate referred to as calamine stone. England"s copper mines and copper products were controlled by two English monopolies called the Society of Mines Royal and the Society of Mineral and Battery Works; the latter monopoly responsible for producing brass. Unfortunately, English calamine stone was inadequate for industrial use. Through chemical analysis of a large sample of scrap copper pieces excavated at the James Fort archaeological site (c.1607-1610), Hudgins demonstrates that a large percentage of this copper originated from English mines and was intentionally sent to Jamestown by the copper monopolies to help find sources of calamine stone in Virginia. Complementing his scientific analysis, Hudgins, using documentary records of Jamestown residents, the Virginia Company of London, and the English copper monopolies, discovered that many of the copper monopolies" directors and shareholders were also organizers and investors in the Virginia Company. Hudgins" discoveries raise several important points. First, because many of the same directors and shareholders served in all three companies there was an attempt to assist English brass production through the Jamestown enterprise. Second, experimentation with brass production probably occurred at Jamestown as early as 1607 due to the presence there of Captain John Martin, son of Sir Richard Martin, the Lord Mayor of London, Master of the Mint, shareholder in the Society of Mineral and Battery Works, and lease holder for England"s brass production. Captain John Martin was knowledgeable in refining ores and involved in metal "tryalls" (experiments) at the fort. Third, both copper societies brought skilled European workmen into England to ensure success with their enterprises. The practice of using skilled labor from "forraine parts" was continued at Jamestown by the Virginia Company of London, and very early in the colony"s history. Carter C. Hudgins, "Articles of Exchange or Ingredients of New World Metallurgy? An Examination of the Industrial Origins and Metallurgical Functions of Scrap Copper at Early Jamestown (c. 1607-1617)", in press, Early American Studies, 2005.

[66] The latest scholarship identifies the glassblowers as being German based on a long tradition of glassmaking in certain areas of Germany. Grossalmerode, a town east of Kassel in the state of Hesse, and a site in the Spessart mountain range southeast of Frankfurt, was an important German glassmaking center. Also, Jamestown Rediscovery ® archaeologists have found at the 1607 fort site "industrial strength" crucibles, clay vessels of nearstoneware strength that could withstand high heat for melting raw materials. The interior of two of these crucibles contain molten glass, evidence of early glassmaking attempts at Jamestown, and a third bears the marks, PTV/GER, on its base. GER signifies the crucible was made in Grossalmerode, which had a 400-year history of crucible and glass production peaking in the early 17th century, and PTV identifies the maker as Peter Topfer, also from Grossalmerode. Beverly A. Straube, "Tinker, tailor, soldier, sailor ...," in William M. Kelso and Beverly A. Straube, Jamestown Rediscovery VI (Richmond, Virginia: The Association for the Preservation of Virginia Antiquities, 2000), pp. 62-66; William M. Kelso, Jamestown Rediscovery II (Richmond, Virginia: The Association for the Preservation of Virginia Antiquities, 1996), p. 40, Figure 43; and, Gary C. Grassl, unpublished letter to Jonathan McMahon, Department of History, College of William & Mary, May 19, 1999; Jonathan McMahon, "Non-English Migration to Seventeenth-Century Jamestown and Virginia," unpublished research paper as a JamestownYorktown Foundation Fellow, 1999. Many thanks to Nancy Egloff, Chief Historian at the Jamestown Settlement, for providing me a copy of Mr. McMahon"s paper as it is an excellent source of information about the multi-national population of 17th century colonial Virginia.

[67] Smith, "General History," in Haile, ed., Narratives, p. 287

[68] Ibid., pp. 294 and 304. Smith, just a little later in the same narrative, wrote he sent "four Dutchmen" to build Chief Powhatan"s house. Ibid., p. 296. This adds some confusion to the number of Germans versus Poles who arrived in 1608

[69] Grassl, unpublished letter

[70] Strachey, "The History of Travel," in Haile, Narratives, p. 635. Smith also described in 1609, "[...] the glasshouse, a place in the woods near a mile from James Town [...]." see Smith, "General History," ibid., p. 315.

[71] Kingsbury, Records, I, 493, 499-500, 510-515, 565-566; III, 494-495. Sir Robert Mansfield (or Mansell) was a Member of Parliament, treasurer of the

English Navy for life, served on the King"s Council for the Virginia Company of London, and had ties with the East India, Muscovy, North West Passage, and Somer Isles (Bermuda) companies, as well as other various trade ventures. He, with the Earl of Pembroke and other notables, acquired in 1618, "„[...] the sole patent of making all sorts of glass with pit-coal."" Sir Mansfield"s Virginia Company connections and glassmaking interests provide another possible example of a multi-company shareholder and director mating their financial interests with Jamestown"s, including the use of Continental European artisans. See, Brown, ed. Genesis, II, 941-942. The Earl of Pembroke, William Herbert, also served on the king"s council for the Virginia Company, patented 30,000 acres in the colony in 1620, and proposed sending settlers and cattle to Virginia. Ibid., II, 921. ;Ibid., I, 493; III, 495.
[72] Kingsbury, Records, IV, 23-24. Kingsbury, Records, IV, 108. "List of the Living," in Hotten, ed., Original Lists, p.180; and in the 1624/1625 Muster Vincentio, Bernardo, "his wife" and "a child" are listed as living at the plantation of George Sandys. Apparently, these four are the only Italians to survive into 1625. See, Jester and Hiden, eds., Adventurers, p.40. See also, C. E. Hatch, "Glassmaking in Virginia, 1607-1625," The William and Mary College Quarterly (1941): 130-138 and 227-229.
[73] Smith, "General History," in Haile, ed., Narratives, pp. 293 and 335
[74] See MS. Rec. Va. Co., III., 143, for a number of these edicts.
Two instances may serve to illustrate the policy of her government. Goods were to be sold to the colonists from the magazine at 25 per cent, profit, while the price of tobacco was fixed at 3 shillings. A violation of this edict was punished with three years' servitude to the colony. " Every person to go to church Sundays and holydays or lye neck and heel on the corps du guard the night following and be a slave the week following, second offence a month, third offence a year and a day."
[75] Col. Rec. Va., 77; MS. Rec. Va, Co., III., 142
[76] Col. Rec. Va., 75, 78, 81. "Good Newes from Virginia," 11, 21, 32
[77] Winder MSS., I., 47-52. Cf.
Ibid., 30, and MS. Rec. Va. Co., III., 168, 179, 180, 235. Cf.
" Good Newes from Virginia," II., 21, 32 sq.
[78] Va. Hist. Mag., Oct., 1894, 157

[79]Not till winter of 1616-17 was any freedom to return to England given to the Virginia colonists. Brown, II., 798.
[80] The charter of 1609, which gave the Company a more independent government, was of no advantage to the colonists, as the Governors appointed were given arbitrary powers. Col. Rec. of Va., 75, 76; Stith, 132, 147, 148; Arber's Smith, cxxix., 488; Force, III., 16.
[81] Va. Co. Rec., II., 32, 41, 42, 196.

---

[82] It is impossible to say just when the first actually " indented " servants were introduced into Virginia. They became a distinct class after 1619, and formal indentures were probably in use that year applying to servants sent to the planters. The Assembly of 1619 provided that all contracts of servants should be recorded and enforced. Whether indentures had been used by the Company or private persons previous to this is not clear. They seem to have been applied to the Company's tenants after 1619. The manuscript records of the Company contain a reference, under the date 1622, to a boy's indenture, and it is probable indentures were used in 1619. A registry was kept of persons transported in the Company's ships, but those sent otherwise by private persons were not included in it until 1622, when so much trouble had been occasioned by verbal contracts that the Company's bookkeeper was required henceforth to register all contracts for service. Col. Rec., 21, 28; Va. Co. Rec., II., 17, 23.

[83] 1 Instructions to Governor Yeardley, 1618; Va. Hist. Mag., Oct., 1894, 155, 156, 158, 159; MS., Libr. of Supreme Court, Wash. Va. Rec., cap. 23, 221, p. 72

[84] Va. Co. Rec., L, 22, 26; Stith, 163, 165; Force, III., No. 5, 10; IMd., 82; Collingwood MS., I., 30-35.

[85] Va. Co. Rec., 45, 59, 111, 119, 130-137, 151, 152. Ibid., MS. Rec., III., 123, 161, 170. The office of the marshal, vice-admiral and treasurer, when created, were to be so supported; the "physician general " had tenants, and the ministers also six apiece for their glebes. The support of the East India school, of the iron works and of a glass furnace was to be provided for on the same plan.

[86] Cal. S. P., Col. 19; Neill, London Co., 160, note, 161, 235; Cunningham, II., 42; Robinson MS., 68; MS. Rec. Va. Co., III., 162; Va. Co. Rec., I., 25, 36, 39, 40-42, 91, 97, 100, 124, 140, 169

[87] The Metayage system (French: métayage, Spanish: aparcería, Italian: mezzadria) is the cultivation of land for a proprietor by one who receives a proportion of the produce, as a kind of sharecropping. Another class of land tenancy in France is named fermage, whereby the rent is paid annually in banknotes.

[88] Va. Co. Rec., I., 117, 169, 173; Smith, II., 40, 106, 107; Va. Co. Rec. MS., III., 161, 163, 166, 170, July 5, 1621; Va. Hist. Reg., L, 159; Hen., I., 230; Appd. 8th Rept. Royal Com. on Hist. MSS,, pts. II. & III., 39-44. Geo. Sandys, March 30, 1623, writes to his brother, Sir Samuel Sandys: "The tenants sent on that so absurd condition of halves were neither able to sustain themselves nor to discharge their moiety, and so dejected with their scarce provisions and finding nothing to answer their expectations, that most of them gave themselves over and died of melancholy, the rest running so far in debt as left them still behind-hand and many (not seldom) losing their crops while they hunted for their belly." Cf. Nichols to Worsenholme, p. 41.

[89] Force, III., No. 5, 14, .15; Va. Co. Rec., I., 40-42; Hening, I., 230. Though the Company was forced by the city of London to grant exceptional terms to tenants

who had been formerly apprentices, by assigning them at the expiration of their tenantship a land grant of twenty-five acres in fee, yet it stipulated for the privilege of re-engaging them for further terms if the tenant freely consented.
[90] Va. Co. Rec., I., 87; MS., IMd., III., 171; Neill, London Co., 230; Force, III., 14. The average cost of a tenant was 16, of a servant 6 pounds
[91] Va. Co. Rec., I., 67, 83
[92] Stith, 165, 167, 368; Neill, London Co., 163; Va. Co. Rec., I., 25, 26, 33, 34. The Company was ordered to send the " men prest" in Nov., 1619, but it postponed doing so for nearly two months, in the hope of being relieved of the necessity. The importunity of the king, however, compelled it to yield. One hundred persons had been included in the first order, but it is probable that only half of these were sent to Virginia, and they were allowed to be selected. The Somers Island Company probably yielded to the request of the Virginia Company and took the rest. Collingwood MS., I., 47.
[93] Va. Hist. Mag., 160, 162, 164 (Oct., 1894); Col. Rec. Va,, 78, 81; Va. Co. Rec., I., 39; II., 124, 128, 196.
[94] IMd., I., 123, 137, 148, 153, 154, 161; II., 148, 150. In the four years 1619-23 forty-four patents were issued to as many different people for the transportation of a hundred persons each to Virginia; in the twelve years preceding only six patents had been granted.
[95] Col. Rec. Va,, 1, 21, 24, 25, 28; Laws, 1619
[96] The term Indented Servitude has been used as the one best characteristic of the system at large. Strictly indented servants not only formed the largest class, but gave legal definiteness to the system of white servitude.
[97] The right to the stipulated term of servitude was given to any one that would contract for the servant's transportation, and he seems to have had free disposal of this right when he reached Virginia. Va. Co. Rec., I., 91; II., 10, 11; Eng. Statutes at Large, 4 Geo., c. II.; Anson, 7, 43. This was probably in England a Contract of Record.
[98] 'Jefferson's Works, IX., 254 sq.; Jones, Present State, 53, 54.
[99] Neill, Va. Carolorum, 57, note. An indenture of 1628, made after assignments of contracts were recognized in Virginia, may be taken as typical of those generally in use. A husbandman of Surrey County, England, contracts and binds himself to a citizen and ironmonger of London " to continue the Obedient Servant of him, the said Edward hurd his heirs and assignes and so by him or them sente transported unto the countrey and land of Virginia in the parts beyond the seas to be by him or them employde upon his plantation there for and during the space of four yeares and will be tractable and obedient and a good and faithful servant onyst to be in all such things as Bhall be Commanded

him In consideration whereof the said Edward hurd doth covenant that he will transporte and furnishe to the said Logwood to and for Virginia aforesaid and allowe unto him sustenance meat and drink apparel and other necessaryes for his livelyhood and sustenance during the said service "sealed and delivered in the presence of two servants.

[100] Gal. State Papers, Domestic, 584; Stith, 168. Blackstone, I., 137, note; IV., 401 and note; Reeves, 598

[101] The servitude for offenses, early instituted by the governors and continued by the courts, can hardly be regarded as properly a part of the system, however. It was strict penal servitude in the interest of the commonweal. These convicts were not held by the colonists, but employed on public works as servants of the colony, or in service to the Governor in his official capacity, except in specific cases. Robinson MS., II., 12, 13, 65; Va. Go. MS. Rec., III., 215, 224. Cf. Hening, I., 351; II., 119, 441; III., 277.

[102] Mass. Hist. Coll., Vol. IX., 2, Dale to Salisbury

[103] Ibid., l^t; Middlesex Rec., II., 224. Others were granted reprieves earlier on condition of transportation, but it is probable that they went elsewhere than Virginia, Sir Thomas Smith was Governor of the East India Company at this time.

[104] Surtees Soc., Vol. 68, 419, 420, Appd.; Bacon, Essay on Plantations.

[105] Rec. Genl. Ct, 1670-2, 5, 52; Hening, II., 191; Rob. MS., 8, 67, 257, 261.

[106] Geo. I., c. 11, Statutes at Large; Va. MSS. fr. B. R. O., Vol. II., pt. 2,

[107] Cal. State Papers, Col. 28, 441; cf. Ashley, Economic Hist. Eng., 366

[108] Va. MSS. fr. B. R. O., Vol. II., Geo. III., c. 32; Ford, Works of Franklin, Vol. X., 120; Geo. III., c. 15.

[109] Geo. IH., c. 74

[110] Lecky, England in the Eighteenth Century, VI., 254

[111] Jones, Present State, 53, 54; Beverley, 233; " Va. Verges," 1622.

[112] Va. MSS. fr. B. R. O., 1697, p. 320; 1723, 1729, March 26; Hening, XII., 668. Cf. III., 251; V., 24, 546

[113] Madison Papers, Vol. III., 1430; Article I., sec. 9, Constitution of U. S.

[114] 'Lodge, Colonies, 242; Lecky, VI., 254 sq. Franklin's Works, X., 119.

[115] Middlesex Records, III., 38, 94, 245. The offense, when discovered, which was probably not true of one in twenty cases, was treated with remarkable leniency by the courts. Under the Civil Law it would have been punished with death, but we meet with petty fines of a few shillings, even when the " spirit " confessed the crime, and in one case only 12d.; a few hours in the pillory, or imprisonment till the fine was paid seems to have been considered by the judges a sufficient atonement. The Session Rolls of Middlesex show that a large number of the cases were not even brought to trial, though true bills had been brought against the offenders.

[116] Middlesex Rec., II., 306, 326, 335, 336; III., 100, 184, 229, 253, 257, 259, 271, 326, &c.; IV., 40, 70-87, 245; Cal. State Papers, Col. 411.
[117] IMd., 449; Va. MS. fr. B. R. (X, 1640-91, 170
[118] Middlesex Rec., Vol. III., 276; IV., 65, 69-73, 78, 79, 155, 196, 245.
[119] Va. MSS. fr. the British Record Office, Vol. I., 46. Of. State Papers (Calendar), 411, 457
[120] Gal. State Papers, Col. 220; Middlesex Rec., IV., 181.
[121] Cal. State Papers, Col. 221, 232. The office had been proposed in 1660
[122] This and the lessened demand for servants was sufficient to put an end to the abuse
[123] Jones, 54; Robinson MS., II., 255; Howe, Va., 207. Before the statute of 1661, which made negroes generally slaves, a number were held as servants for a term, and even afterward a few seem to have remained servants. Robinson MS., 10, 30, 250, 256; MS. Rec. Va, Co., III., 292; MS. Rec. Genl. Ct, 161, 218; 1673, 1675. From 1656-1676 and after 1691, Indian children sold by their parents, and captives, could legally be held only as servants; but the disposition was, when not restrained by law, to make them slaves. Acts of 1676 and 1682 legalized Indian slavery, but it was prohibited in 1670, and finally in 1691 by an act for free trade with all Indians, which the General Court construed as taking away all right to their slavery. Many were, however, unjustly reduced to slavery up to 1705, as the act was supposed to date from the revisal of 1705, and not from 1691. Hening, I., 396; II., 15, 143, 155, 283, 491, 562; III., 69 and note. Robinson MS., 256, 261, 262; MS. Rec. Genl. Ct, 29, 218. (Vld. Jeff. Cases in Genl. Court, p. 123; Robin et al. vs. Hardaway, 1772.) Mulatto bastards were also made servants; but the number from these sources was comparatively so insignificant that a consideration of them may be omitted. A proposition was even entertained of making servants of the women sent over for wives, whether they married or not.
[124] Hening, HI., 449; 4 Geo., c. 11, etc.
[125] Append, to Eighth Kept., etc., 41; Gal. State Papers, Col. 36, 76, 77, 100; Smith, II., 105; Purchas, His Pilgrimage, p. 1787
[126] 'Verney Papers, Camden Soc. Pub.; Neill, Virginia Carl. 109
[127] Cal. State Papers, Col. 36, 258, 268
[128] "New Description of Virginia," London, 1649; Thurloe State Papers, Vol. I., 198. The general muster of 1624 shows the number of servants then in Virginia as 378 in a population of 2500. They were well distributed, most of the planters having but one or two. Afterwards many planters brought in as many as 30, and in 1671 the servants were 6000, 15 per cent of the population. Hening, II., 515.
[129] Col. Rec, Va., Declaration, eto. The ancient planters regarded the massacre of 1622 as a judgment on their greed
[130] The tobacco culture was introduced into Virginia by Governor Yeardley in 1616, and even in this year restrictions had to be imposed to prevent the

planters from altogether neglecting corn. In 1619, Secretary John Pory tells us that their *' riches consist in Tobacco," and their " principall wealth " in servants, " but they are chargeable," he says, " to be furnished with armes, apparel and bedding and for their transportation and casuall both at sea and for their first yeare commonly at lande also, but if they escape they prove very hardy and sound able men." Purchas, His Pilgrimage, 837, Rolf's Relation; Campbell, 117; Pory to Carleton, Mass. Hist. Soc., IX., 4th, 9, 10. ;Smith, 165; Mass. Hist. Coll., Vol. IX., 4th sec., p. 10, note. See Pory to Carleton; Va. Co. of London, Va. Hist Coll., Vol. VII.; Vol. I., 14, 15. ;* Cunningham, 201, 422. Purchas, His Pilgrimage, p. 1821

[131] App. 8th Rep., I. and III., 39, 41-44; Smith, Hist, II., 40; Va. Hist. Mag., Oct., 1893, 162. The servants wrote indignant letters to their friends. One says he was " sold like a slave," but admits that his master's whole household " was like to be starved." Rolf says the " buying and selling of men and boys or to be set over from one to another for a yearly rent or that the tenants or lawful servants should be abridged their contracts " was held " a thing most intolerable in England."

[132] Accomac Rec. MS., 61, 82 (1635); Robinson MS., 9; York Co. Rec., 86.

[133] Hening, I., 123, 143, 144, 157, 196

[134] IW., 150, 157, 330, 333, 334, 403, 411, 412 (also 217); Ace. Rec. MS., 2, 24, 54, 76, 84; f Col. Rec. Va. Laws, 1619.

[135] Col. Rec. Va., 1619, 25, 28; Hening, I., 127, 130, 192. ; Col. Rec. Va., 12 et seq. Hening, I., 117. ; Robinson MS., 52.

[136] Hurd, Law of Freedom and Bondage, I., 116, 129, 139, 210, 220; Reeves, Eng. Law, II., 598; Anson, Law of Contract, 213 sq.

[137] Ace. Rec. MS., 88 (1637); Essex Rec. MS., 140 (1686

[138] Hening, I., 303, 319, 346; II., 66, 70. Rob. MS, 8; Ace. Rec. I., 10, 272, 273, 519; II., 58, 68; MS. Rec. Genl. Ct., 158; Col. Rec. Va., 81.

[139] Rob. MS., 8, 9, 27, 68, 243 sq.; Ace. Rec., 2, 39, 44, 58, 76, 35, 45, 85, 86, 91, 82. In 1637 a bad character, John Leech, threatened to have his master " up to James City to see if he could not get free of a year's service," alleging " that his master had not used him so well as he formerly had done," and that he would use against him speeches made by the master against the Governor and Council.

[140] Rob. MS., 8, 9, 68; Ace. Rec., 35, 76, 82.

[141] Robinson MS., 9-13, 27, 66, 69; Ace. Rec., 107. A number of servants, for a conspiracy "to run out of the colony and enticing divers others to be actors in the same conspiracy," were to be severely whipped and to serve the colony for a period of seven years in irons. This was in 1640. " Saml. Powell for purloining a pair of breeches and other things from the house of Capt. Jno. Howe deed, shall pay ffower dayes work to Elias Taylor with all charges of the court and the sheriff's ffees and to sit in the stockes on the next Sabbath day with a ribell his hatt from the beginning of morninge prayer until the end of the sermon with a

pair of breeches about his neck." Hening, I., 275, 445; Robinson MS., 10, 17 (1640).
[142] Rob. MS., 8, 9, 27, 68, 243 sq.; Ace. Rec., 2, 39, 44, 58, 76, 35, 45, 85, 86, 91, 82. In 1637 a bad character, John Leech, threatened to have his master " up to James City to see if he could not get free of a year's service," alleging " that his master had not used him so well as he formerly had done," and that he would use against him speeches made by the master against the Govenor and Council.
[143] Hening, I., 257, 411, 441; II., 169, 297, 447
[144] Rec.-Va.; 28; Hening,-!.; 253,- 438; -II.,- 114; -III.,' 444

[145] Col. Rec. Va., 22; Hening, I., 253, 254, 401
[146] MS. Rec. Genl. Ct, 201; Hening, III., 277, 452, 458
[147] MS. Rec. Va. Co., Library of Congress, II., 21; Westover MSS., II., 240. Cal. State Papers, Col. 19: Domestic, 447, 594, 1635, July 8, Dec. 5. Purchas, His Pilgrimage, 1809 (Virginia Verges); Neill, Lond. Co., 120, 160, note.
[148] Hening, I., 539; Northampton Bee., IL, 149; Hening, 1661, Drummond's servant. An interesting question might have arisen as to the master's claim had a runaway servant escaped to England or to a foreign country where the institution was not recognized. No such case seems to have occurred. A transported felon would probably have been seized and treated as an escaped convict in England, but what remedy the master could have had in this case, or when the fugitive was not a felon, is not clear.
[149] Hening, III., 271; IV., 173; IX., 187
[150] Hening, II., 21, 273; Va. Gazettes, 1736, Dec. 17, Feb. 25, Mar. 11. To facilitate discovery, habitual runaways had their hair cut " close above the ears," or were " branded in the cheek with the letter R." Hening, I., 254, 440, 517.
[151] Herring, I., 255, 401, 483, 539. Reeves, V., 355 (rev. ed.). The hue and cry was an ancient method of pursuing offenders in England, and rested on the statute of Winchester, 13 Edward I., 81, 82, c. I., and on 28 Ed. III., c. II. In Virginia a warrant was issued by the governor or some of the council, or a commissioner of the county, and masters of households were put under penalty of 100 Ibs. of tobacco for its speedy conveyance from house to house.
[152] MS. Rec. of Genl. Ct, 1640, 3, 8, 9, 10, 11, 12, 13, 16, 52, 53; Ace. Rec. MS., 1633, 10. The practice of the courts was not uniform, however. The General Court, on the 9th of July, 1640, ordered two runaway servants to be punished by whipping and " to serve out their time and add a year to their master to recompense his loss by their absence"; but a few months later a master was denied his claim to three months service due him by a servant's loss of time. At a court held the following week, the master of certain runaways is given a year's additional service, or " longer if said master shall see cause " for their loss of time, and for sheriff's fees paid by masters, " the servants shall make good the same at the expiration of their time by a year's service apiece to their said

masters." A maid-servant who was guilty of fornication was ordered to "serve her full time to her master as by covenant," and her husband to make satisfaction " for such further damages " as the master should make appear. The Accomac county court ordered a servant " to perform the full term of his indentures faithfully and truly " or to stand to the " censure " of the court. This was a case where recourse might have been had on the freedom dues as damages, but the court left these to the servant.

[153] Hening, I., 438; II., 114, 115, 168; III., 67, 140, 452. By an act or 1662 the father was liable to make satisfaction to the parish by additional service for the keeping of the child

[154] Robinson MS., 9-13; MS. Rec. Genl. Ct, 154, 161.

[155] Hening, L, 255, 539

[156] Hening, II., 458

[157] Ibid., III., 456, 458, 459; IV., 168, 171; XII., 191

[158] Ibid., II., 26. This is said to be the first statute sanctioning negro slavery in Virginia, but as early as 1625 the status of the negro, according to Jefferson, was determined by a case in the General Court. Jeff. Cases, Genl. Ct, 1720, etc., 119, note.

[159] MS. Rec. Genl. Ct, 1672, 3, 12, 15, 35, 44, 154, 158, 161, 188

[160] Hening, II., 75, 115, 118, 266, 448

[161] Hening, II., 195; cf. 171, 441; Neill, Va. Carolorum, 295, 296. Beverley, 55, 56. The attempt was made by a number of transported Oliverian criminals, who made use of the general political and religious discontent of the time. It was not a servile insurrection due to the harsh treatment of servants.

[162] Hening, II., 278. 2 MS. Rec. Genl. Ct, 44, 136

[163] Virginia Court Records

[164] Hening, I., 274, 445; II

[165] Hening, II., 165; HI., 450, 451; IV., 49. The servant frequently enjoyed the right of trade, however, with his master's consent, and many masters, besides paying wages or making gifts of money and stock, allowed servants the use of tracts of land. (Bullock, Account of Va., 1649, 52, 59.)

[166] Hening, IV., 46, 47, 49. An act of 1713 restrained a servant and overseer from keeping horses " without the license in writing of his master or mistress," nor could the master give license for the keeping of more than one, the reason "by the act alleged being that great numbers were kept by persons who had no interest in land, and were so " suffered to go at large on the lands of other persons," which was "prejudicial to the breed of horses" and "injurious to the stocks of cattle and sheep."

[167] Hening, III., 151. 3 Hening, I., 254; II., 116

[168] MS. Rec. Genl. Ct, 150, 156, 158, 161, 162, 166, 173, 204, 218 (1673-75).

[169] Hening, I., 254; II., 116; III., 454, 455. 'Hening, III., 450

[170] Hening, III., 448, 452, 453, 459. 2 Ibid., III., 449, 450

---

[171] Ibid., III., 456; IV., 170, 171
[172] Northampton Co. Rec., 147, 149; Fitzhugh's Letters, July 22, 1689. Fitzhugh writes to Mr. Michael Hayward that his debtor's estate is probably sufficient to save his debt, as he has "4 good slaves with some other English servants, and a large stock of tobacco"; York Co. Rec., 86
[173] Hening, IV., 284
[174] Hening, III., 445, 451; V., 552; VI., 359, 360; VIIL, 134, 135, 136, 337
[175] Hening, V., 552, 557; VI., 363; VIII., 135, 136
[176] Hening, XII., 150, 151, 191; 6 Geo. III., c. 32; 8 Geo. III., c. 15
[177] Hening, XII., 190, 191; IMd., Justice, 417, 418; Hening, XII.,
[178] Hurd, Law of Freedom and Bondage, I., 116, 129, 139, 210, 220. Robinson MS., 10, 243, 250, 256, 261. This is shown in the application of corporal punishment and of additions of time, and in the disposition to claim negro and Indian servants as slaves. In 1640 the addition of time for a negro runaway servant was, in a case brought before the General Court, servitude " for the time of his natural life here or elsewhere." Hening, II., 118, 288, 481; III., 277; IV., 168, 171, 174, 202; Va. Gazettes, 1737; Tucker's Blackstone, Appd., 55-63. Though slavery assumed a comparatively mild form in Virginia, much of the criminal law relating to slaves was of a very discriminating and harsh character, as was also the procedure. Cf. acts of 1723, 1748, 1764, 1772; Minor, Institutes, I., 161 et sq. Until 1772 no restriction was put on the outlawry of a slave, he might be killed in resisting arrest, and until 1788 the murder or manslaughter of a slave by his master might go unpunished, the presumption being that he would not wantonly destroy his own property.
[179] Va. MS. B. R. O., 302; Jones, Present State, 36
[180] Beverley, 219; Jones, Present State, 37; Hening, II., 170; Fitzhugh, MS. Letters, Jan. 30, 1686-87; Force, III., L. and R., 12.
[181] Carpenters, joiners, sawyers, bricklayers, blacksmiths, engravers, weavers, shoemakers, tailors, saddlers, bakers, teachers, surgeons and other craftsmen were imported. Va. Gazettes, 1736 sq
[182] Col. Reo. Va. Laws, 1610, 21, 28; Winder MSS., I., 245 (1667); Hening, III., 462, 463; IV., 425
[183] IMd., I., 143, 144, 157; II., 260; III., 459; IV., 133; XIL, 681; Jones, 92, 94; Stat. at Large Va., III., 124. Before 1667 baptism had in many cases been refused to slaves and their offspring, since doubts existed as to its effect on their status. It was then settled that baptism did not free the slave
[184] Robinson MS., 8
[185] Force, III., L. and R., 14; IMd., Virginia's Cure, 7, 10; Bul-
lock, 52 sq. Instances are related of their appearing at social gatherings in their masters' houses on equal footing with the family and their guests
[186] Hening, I., 146, 552; II., 170; III., 86, 252.
[187] Virginia Court Records

---

[188] Beverley, 232, 233; Wirt, Life of Henry, 34. Va. MSS. B. R. O., Vol. II., pt. I., 291. The importance of the introduction of these persons into Virginia society has been probably exaggerated. Gov. Nicholson, writing to the Lords of Trade, Dec. 2, 1701, says: " Fit and proper persons to serve"
[189] Hening, II., 168, 280; III., 86, 87, 453, 454; Rob. MS., 256.
[190] Fyffe, Mod. Europe, I., 21, 24, 26
[191] Taswell-Langmead, Constitutional History of Eng., 316, note; Cunningham, 40-42, 184, note, 192, 198-200, 362, 387, 388
[192] Cunningham, 192, 193, 196; Beverley, 220; Jones, 92. Oldmixon, 290: " If hard work and hard living," he says, " are signs of slavery, the day laborers in England are much greater slaves." Middlesex Co. Rec., II., 22, 100, 101, 120, 130, 138; III., 23, 117, 318; Ibid., S. P. Rolls, Oct. 8, 1655; IW., 6 Chas. I., p. 34; 18 Chas. I., 117; 13 Chas. II., 318; Aug. 27, 1652, p. 209; 4 Chas. I., 23.
[193] Middlesex Co. Rec., II., 22, 100, 101, 120, 130, 138; III., 23, 117, 318
[194] Ace. Rec., 80; Hening, II., 35, 53. In 1661 the Assembly confirmed an order of the General Court forbidding a man and his wife " to keep any maid servant for the term of three years."
[195] Force, I., L. and R., 4; Hening, I., 435; II., 117, 118, 129, 488; Beverley, 219, 220, 222; cf. Bullock, Jones, Virginia's Cure, Leah and Rachel, pp. 11, 12, 15-17. John Hammond in 1659 warns servants against mariners, shipmasters and others who imported them merely for gain, and advises them to covenant for liberty, to choose their own master and a fortnight's time after their arrival in which to do so, " for ye cannot imagine," he says, " but there are as well bad services as good but I shall shew ye if any happen into the hands of such crooked dispositions how to order them and ease yourselves when I come to treat of the justice of the country which by this they may prevent." From this traffic in servants by middlemen it is evident that much deception and fraud might be practiced upon the unwitting, both before and after reaching Virginia. They were deceived in making their contracts by such general stipulations as for an allotment of land " according to the custom of the country," which was represented to them as being 50 acres, when no allotment to the servant was customary at all until after 1690. False indentures seem to have been made also, either through corruption in the registry office or by forgery, as a number of blank indentures, properly signed and sealed, were brought to the notice of the Assembly in 1680, and all judgment of their validity, when alleged, was lodged in the discretion of the justices. The practice of selling men on shipboard to the highest bidder, or of consigning them to merchants at Jamestown or other ports for sale, might, of course, result very unhappily for servants, and during the voyage to Virginia they often suffered great hardships for want of clothes, bedding and diet. These were mild, however, compared to the " horrors of the middle passage" in the days of slavery.

[196] Hening, II., 280, 388; III., 447; IV., 133; MS. Rec. Genl. Ct, 159, 162, 166, 173, 204, 218, 238; Robinson MS., 2, 8, 256, 265; Gen. Ct., 154, 156, 158, 161; MS. Rec. Va. Co., III., 233, 292; Ace. Rec., 2; Essex Rec., 132; Henrico Rec., 85; Force, III., L. and R., 16. Verbal agreements were sometimes alleged, and where proven, or where the servant could not produce his indenture, they might be enforced. An indenture, however, was an effectual bar to any such agreement.
[197] Hening, II., 167; III., 453; MS. Rec. Genl. Ct., 8. The number of false pleas brought into court by servants to get a reduction of their time, and the offenses of which they appear to have been guilty, show that the master was more likely to be imposed on than the servant. Genl. Ct, 8, 12, 15, 44, 47, 158, 188, 1675, Oct. 2; Ace. Rec., 85; Henrico Rec., 41; Robinson MS., 27
[198] Except in the early period and in 1777, the servant was free from the obligation of military service, and, as in the case of slaves, the law did not allow the sale of spirituous liquors to them. Hening, III., 400; VI., 74; VII., 93, 101; IX., 32, 81, 271, 275, 592; Sparks' Washington, Vol. II., 168, 169.
[199] Beverley, 220 sq
[200] Wirt, Life of Patrick Henry, 33, 36; Id., British Spy, 192- 194; Anbury, Travels through the interior parts of America, London, 1789, 371-376
[201] Col. William Preston, of Smithville, Va., bought at Williamsburg, about 1776, a gentleman named Palfrenan, as a teacher for his family; he was a poet and a scholar, a correspondent and a friend of the celebrated Miss Carter, the poetess, and also of Dr. Saml. Johnson. This man educated many of the Prestons and Breckenridges in Virginia and Arkansas. The distinguished Wm. C. Preston of S. C. was one of his pupils. Richmond Standard, June 9, 1880, Letter of Mrs. Floyd; Va. Hist. Mag., Oct., 1894, p. 236, Will of Col. John Carter (1669).
[202] Neill, Va. Car. 279, 290; Force, III., Virginia's Cure, 16; Howe, 207. Peter Francisco, a Revolutionary soldier celebrated for his personal strength, had been an indented servant for seven years. " He was a companionable man and an ever welcome visitor in the first families in this region of the state," says a contemporary living in Buckingham County. Cf. " A Declaration," etc., 4, 57; York Rec., 1633-34; Rob. MS., 52; Col. MS., 17
[203] Rob. MS., June 3, 1640; Wm. Byrd's Letters, June 9, 1691; Bullock, 52 sq. Bullock advises English fathers to send their daughters to Virginia rather than their sons, and promises that they " will receive instead of give portions for them." " Maid servants," he says, " of good honest stock may choose their husbands out of the better sort of people. Have sent over many but never could keep one at my plantation three months except a poor filly wench made fit to foille to set of beauty and yet a proper young fellow served twelve months for her." He tells men-servants how they may prosper by their service, " and then," he says, " if he looks to God, he may see himself fit to wed a good man's daughter." Bullock was a Yorkshireman and had had seven years' experience in Virginia when he wrote in 1649. Cf. McDonald, II., 68. Large importations of

craftsmen had been made by the planters without satisfying their needs, and men were especially encouraged to remain in the employ of their former masters or to serve the community in their trade. Many servants received in addition to their transportation and support, wages equal to those paid the best servants in England. Though the colony was chiefly agricultural in character and dependent on England for many of the ordinary articles of manufacture well into the eighteenth century, it is a great mistake to suppose that no manufacturing or attempts to build up trade appeared in Virginia. The fact that attempts were not largely successful was due not to domestic causes alone, but to the policy of the English Board of Trade, whose interest it was to keep Virginia agricultural for the benefit resulting to English commerce. The repeated efforts of the Assemblies to develop manufactures and to crush out the slave trade were defeated in England rather than in Virginia. In the late years of the seventeenth century and early years of the eighteenth, the difficulty of obtaining goods from England and the low price of tobacco gave the planters excuse for establishing considerable manufactories on their plantations; cotton, woolen and linen goods were made, and shoemaking and tanning were undertaken on a somewhat large scale. These industries grew to such an extent that great fear was aroused among English merchants of the loss of a very profitable part of their trade. The letters of the Lords of Trade are full of questions in regard to this new departure, and of recommendations and instructions to discourage it as much as possible. In 1707 as many as four counties on the south side of James river were given over to the production and manufacture of such goods, and a considerable trade had sprung up with New England and the islands. The Lords recommended the Queen the next year, from fear of a great loss to her revenues, to appoint a fleet and a convoy to sail from England every year with all such commodities as the planters needed, to prevent their applying their labor to any other product than tobacco. Exports of corn, pork and " great cattle " were made from Virginia to New England as early as 1639. Rob. MS., 180.

[204] Ace. Rec., 36, 37, 42; Va. MS. B. R. O., V., pt 2, pp. 302, 317, Beverley, 225; Hening, I., 208, 301; II., 172, 472, 503; III., 16, 30, 50, 53, 75, 81, 108, 121, 187, 197, 386, Nov. 11, 1708, Nov. 29, 1728; Robinson MS., 180; Bullock, 62 sq.;

[205] Va. MSS. B. R. O., 318; Ibid., II., pt. I., 81 (1698); Henrico Rec,, 36; Hening, I., 161, 209; Rob. MS., 57, 61. In 1626 much of the common land that had belonged to the London Co. was leased to the large number of tenants and servants, then freed, in such quantity and for such a number of years as seemed necessary, at the yearly rent of one pound of tobacco per acre. Cf. McD. MS., I., 295

[206] Hening, IX., 226; Va. MS. B. R. O., May 31, 1721, Spottswood to Lords of Trade; Spottswood's Letters, II., 227. The abolition of the system of entails, which had been stricter in Virginia since 1705 than even that of England, was a

further step in this process after 1776 in eastern Virginia also. Spottswood, writing in 1717, says that frontiersmen were generally of the servant class.

[207] In Virginia and Maryland the existence of such a staple as tobacco, which could only be produced profitably on a large scale and constantly required large quantities of new land, made such a development certain from the first. Tobacco was introduced into Virginia in 1616 and almost immediately became the staple product. The ready adoption of the system in the New England colonies, where such conditions did not exist, however, shows its industrial efficiency

[208] It is a significant fact that the first negroes were brought to Virginia in 1619, the same year in which the principles of indented servitude may be said to have been fully developed, and yet forty years later there were but three hundred negroes in the colony. From 1664 to 1671 several shiploads of negroes were brought in, and there were two thousand slaves and six thousand servants in Virginia. By 1683 the number of servants was nearly doubled, according to Culpepper, while the negroes numbered only three thousand. (Hening, II., 515; Culpepper's report, Doyle, 383.) From this time servitude gave way before slavery, forced on the colonies by the large importation of negroes by the Royal African Co. under its exclusive charter. It was the policy also of the King and the Duke of York, who stood at the head of the African Co., to hasten the adoption of slavery by enactments cutting off the supply of indented servants. In 1698 the African trade was thrown open to separate traders, and an active competition at once sprang up between them and the African Co., the separate traders making large importations and underselling the Company. Though a law of 1660 gave practical encouragement to the importation of negroes by the Dutch, the colonists had become sufficiently aware of the dangers of slavery in 1699 to lay a discriminating duty upon them for three years, and upon alien servants in favor of the Welsh and English born. The act was continued in 1701, allowing a rebate of three-fourths the duty where the negroes were transported out of the Dominion within six weeks. The duty was continued by the acts of 1704 and 1705 where the duty was laid simply upon " negroes or other slaves." The excuse of revenue was alleged, and brief limitations given to the acts in order to secure their confirmation in England, but the slave traders readily saw that the design was to lay prohibitive duties, and they secured the withholding of the King's assent to as many as thirty-three different acts passed by the Virginia Assembly to discourage the slave trade. (Hening, I., 540; III., 193, 213, 225, 229, 233; Tucker's Blackstone, I., Appd., 51; Minor, Inst, I., 164). The importation of negroes, however, could not be checked, and the chief advantage Virginia reaped from these acts was a large revenue for her public works. In 1705 the number of 1800 negroes was brought in, and in 1708 there were 12,000 negro tithables compared with 18,000 white, while the revenue from white servants was too inconsiderable to deserve notice. (Va. MS. B. R. O., Nov. 27, 1708,

---

Jennings to Lds. of Trade.) Intended insurrections of negroes in 1710, 1722, 1730, bear witness to their alarming increase, and by the middle of the century the blacks were almost as numerous as the whites. Va. MSS. B. R. O., V., pt 2, p. 352; II., pt I., 211; 1708, Nov. 21; 1710, June 10; 1712, July 26; 1722, Dec. 22; Burke, 210; Gal. Va, State Papers, I, 129, 130.

[209] Ford's Washington, II., 408, note

[210] Fitzhugh, Letters, Jan. 30, 1686-87, 1686, Aug. 15, 1690; Wm. Byrd's Letters, Feb. 25, 1683, June 21, 1864, Mar. 29, 1685, 1686, May, June, Nov.

[211] Kalm, Travels, I., 29, 388, 390. They were frequently in good circumstances, and sold themselves to learn the language or methods of agriculture.

[212] Gambrals Colonial Life of Maryland, 165, and Neill's Founders, 77, quoted in Brackett, Negro in Md.; Eddis, Letters, 63, 66, 67.

[213] Plymouth Col. Laws, VIII., pt. IH., 34, 35, 47, 58, 61, 65, 81, 140, 195

[214] Hurd, I., 254 sq.; Bancroft, I., 322; Conn. Rev. S., 40; Hening, I., 300, 334, 403, 411, 475; II., 82, 280, 356, 380; Col. Rec. Va, Assemb., 1619. Hurd, I., pp. 228-311, gives a valuable abstract of all laws relating to bondage hi the colonies

[215] Eddis, 63; Hurd, I., 271 sq., 309, 310; Pa. Laws, 1700-1, 13 sq., 230, 552

[216] Hurd, I., 271 sq

[217] Gea, c. 11; 6 Geo. III., c. 32; 8 Geo. III., c. 15; 19 Geo. III., c. 14; Prendergast, 52, 53, 163, note; Carlyle's Cromwell, II., 457; Neill, Va, Vet., 102, 103. As the Stuarts systematically encouraged the deportation of troublesome persons and petty criminals to the American colonies, so Oliver Cromwell in preparing for his settlement of Ireland did not hesitate to transport large numbers of the dispossessed Irish as slaves to the West Indies, or as servants to the English plantations in America, nor to sell the survivors of the Drogheda massacre as slaves to Barbadoes.

[218] penal statutes of the Georges continued to send the felons of Scotland and England to the American colonies. (Of. DeFoe, "Moll Flanders" (1686) and "Captain Jack.") Large numbers of servants were brought into Maryland and Pennsylvania from Germany, Switzerland and Holland. They were generally known as " Redemptioners," from redeeming their persons from the power of the shipmaster who transported them, usually by a voluntary sale into servitude. The system continued in active operation in Maryland well up to the year 1819. Cf. Laws, Feb. 16, 1818.

[219] Franklin, Works (Bigelow ed.), IV., 108, 254. Jefferson, Works (Ford ed.), H., 11, 52, 53

42830753R00172

Made in the USA
Middletown, DE
22 April 2017